Georgiana McCrae wa in 1804. She was educated by French nuns at a London convent and showed an aptitude for languages, music and particularly painting. On leaving school she lived in Scotland for seven years and attempted to make a living as a portrait painter. She married Andrew McCrae, a lawyer, in 1830 and they migrated to Australia several years later, living in various parts of Victoria. Georgiana was closely associated with many of the leading political and cultural figures in the colony. She died in 1890.

IMPRINT CLASSICS

GEORGIANA'S JOURNAL

GEORGIANA McCRAE

Edited by
HUGH McCRAE
Grandson of the Diarist

Angus&Robertson
An imprint of HarperCollins*Publishers*

AN ANGUS & ROBERTSON BOOK
An imprint of HarperCollinsPublishers

First published in Australia in 1934 by
Angus & Robertson Ltd
Second edition published in 1966
Reprinted in 1966
This Imprint Classics edition published in 1992 by
CollinsAngus&Robertson Publishers Pty Limited (ACN 009 913 517)
A division of HarperCollinsPublishers (Australia) Pty Limited
25-31 Ryde Road, Pymble NSW 2073, Australia

HarperCollinsPublishers (New Zealand) Limited
31 View Road, Glenfield, Auckland 10, New Zealand

HarperCollinsPublishe·s Limited
77-85 Fulham Palace Road, London W6 8JB, United Kingdom

Copyright © in this edition Collins/Angus&Robertson 1992

National Library of Australia
Cataloguing-in-Publication data:

McCrae, Georgiana, 1804–1890
    Georgiana's Journal.

    2nd ed.

    ISBN 0207 17564 0

    1. McCrae, Georgiana, 1804–1890 – Diaries. 2. Melbourne (Vic.) –
    Social life and customs – 1834–1900. I. McCrae, Hugh, 1876–1958
    II. Title

994.5103092

Cover details: Georgiana Huntly McCrae 1804–1890
            Self-portrait c. 1825
            Watercolour on ivory, 5 x 3.2 cm, in gilt brass oval frame 9 x 8 cm
            Gift of Mr Ian Scott and Mr Anthony Scott 1987
            Courtesy of the State Library of Victoria, Melbourne
Printed in Australia by Griffin Press

5 4 3 2 1
96 95 94 93 92

To
Helen McCrae

Acknowledgment

THE editor wishes to thank Miss Helen McCrae, Mrs Walter Outhwaite, Mrs Carey Handfield, Mrs William Mant, and Mrs E. A. Bligh, granddaughters of the diarist, also Mrs Norman Lethbridge Cowper, great granddaughter, for generously supplying material for illustrations to this book; and to make due acknowledgment to Colonel Pestell (who contributed the pen-drawing of old St James's); and especially to the trustees of the Mitchell Library for having given permission to reproduce several pictures of early Melbourne from the William Dixson Gallery.

A further debt of gratitude is due to Mr William Bede Dalley for his ever-ready advice and kindly assistance in reading the proofs.

Foreword to the Second Edition

GEORGIANA'S JOURNAL, edited by my father, Hugh McCrae, was first published in 1934 and has long been out of print. The present edition will be welcomed by all who are interested in the early days of Melbourne and the men and women of that time.

It is in format a smaller volume, and therefore easier to handle. It is also, I think, easier to read because my father's notes are printed in italics and so are more easily distinguished from the diary entries. The reduction in size has made it necessary to leave out a number of illustrations that appeared in the earlier edition. Those I have kept are mostly by Georgiana's own hand, miniatures of members of her own family and sketches of the houses she lived in and of the countryside. Also included are photographs and drawings not to be found in public collections, which show the life and topography of Melbourne one hundred and twenty years ago. There are a few additions, notably Georgiana's fine miniature of herself at the age of twenty-one.

Some small errors have been corrected. Otherwise the present edition is the same as the first.

The journal consists mainly of entries in her diary made by Georgiana day by day as events took place; occasionally she made additions which were nearly contemporaneous with the entries; but the whole was written out again in her old age and she then added notes on the changes she had seen taking place around her since she had made the original entries. Wherever possible these notes have been shown as "Supplements", and the contemporaneous additions have been indicated by placing the year in which they were made at the beginning of the paragraph.

Mayfield on the Yarra, the first house designed and built by Georgiana and Andrew, was pulled down some time ago.

Since the journal was first published the small village round the house at Arthur's Seat has been named McCrae. The house still stands and in 1961 was bought by my cousin George Gordon McCrae, Georgiana's great grandson. He has restored it as nearly as possible to its original appearance and furnished it much as it was when Georgiana lived in it. Her little piano is there, and china, silver and pieces of furniture that she used, as well as portraits, sketches and other things of interest which have come down through the generations of the family.

HUNTLY COWPER

Wivenhoe,
Wahroonga,
November 1965.

Foreword to the First Edition

THIS diary tells the Australian story as it has never been told before and can never be told again.

The entries start a century ago in London. The McCraes are packing for Melbourne, which then has "but three brick houses in it". In a few years Melbourne is a capital. England fastens on the tag, "Our colonial possessions". The Victorian era has begun.

The calm of the long reign was so profound that the episodes in the Crimea and the Transvaal were regarded as wars. The Franco-Prussian affair ruffled nobody because it concerned foreigners and was therefore immaterial. Parliament was a Field of the Cloth of Gold. Yet its costumes and pageantry cost little because its members served for glory. It interfered so little that all save criminals went about their business as they listed. Of its twin towers Gladstone is forgotten and Disraeli remembered, if at all, because of the Canal shares. Of its glittering miscellany of functionaries the immanent figure of the Queen alone survives. And rightly so.

The Queen's achievement was the institution of the Victorian Household. Its gloom drove the adventurous to found an Empire and kept the rest respectable. Among its shrewdest annalists were Isabella Beeton, George du Maurier, and Georgiana McCrae.

The affinity between the three is singular. They were artists to their finger-tips. Each knew that art is the elimination of super-fluities: each had the eye of a lynx for the significant.

Mrs McCrae, like du Maurier, commanded two mediums. He was an artist in words: she was an artist in line. She had been the favourite pupil of John Varley, the "Patriarch" of English water-colour, who still shares suzerainty in this realm with Bonington and Cotman. Varley in his turn had mastery of words—as witness his imaging of Venice: "a city about to put to sea".

To make this document possible all sorts of impossible things had to happen. That all should have dovetailed is a miracle of letters.

In the first place it is fantastic that a woman of Georgiana's grace should have been part of the muddle of shacks and humpies that was Melbourne. Being there it was vital that she should be a chronicler of genius. To fulfil the scheme she had to be so lonely that only in a diary could she find a confidant. To save the diary from the dustheap it was vital that she should transmit her genius to her son George Gordon and to her grandson Hugh. For a George Gordon McCrae was requisite to detect its value, and a Hugh McCrae was requisite to sift it.

The sifting was a task to make the stoutest quail. The McCraes were cherishers of relics. Their sideboards, trunks, cupboards and chests of drawers were reliquaries tended and kept with a devotion that was medieval. So when it came to sorting, there were other diaries, letters and photographs, plans by architects and naval architects, bills, rare books, inventories, Varley drawings, receipts, pastels, recipes, miniatures, engravings, drawings both complete and in the *croquis* stage by various members of the family and other persons, a pastiche of trifles such as visiting cards and invitations, boxes stuffed with vestigia; and, lastly, a lock of Adam Lindsay Gordon's hair. Such tokens were there, not in dozens or in hundreds, but in thousands upon thousands. Many of them had been waiting a hundred years for Hugh McCrae to touch them with life.

W. B. DALLEY

Sydney,
15th October 1934.

Illustrations

Andrew Murison McCrae	xxii
Westbrook, Scotland	8
William Gordon McCrae and his wife and daughters	9
William Gordon McCrae ("Little Willie")	24
Alexander McCrae ("Little Alexander")	24
The barque *Argyle*	25
The wrecked *Piccolo Jachimo*	25
The sloop *Jemima*	40
The course of the *Argyle*	40
Dr Farquhar McCrae's house in Bourke Street, Melbourne	41
Old St James's Church, Melbourne	56
Melbourne from The Falls	57
Melbourne in the Forties	57
Melbourne in 1851	72
An early map of Melbourne	72
View from Flagstaff Hill, 1841	73
Flagstaff Hill before the days of telegraph	73
Bedford House	88
The old Government House, William Street, Melbourne	88
Water-cart of 1841	89
The Chalet, La Trobe's cottage at Jolimont	89
Superintendent La Trobe	104
Captain Foster Fyans	104
Robert Hoddle	105
Joseph Hawdon	105
The brig-yacht *Wanderer*	120
Mayfield, on the Yarra, 1843	121
The first Melbourne land-sale	136
Hobson's Ferry	136
Prince's Bridge, Melbourne	137
Men in stocks	137

ILLUSTRATIONS

Victorian gold-licence 1854   137
North Melbourne, looking west, 1854   152
A view of Queen Street, Melbourne, 1853   152
The great flood of 1852   153
Tichingorook station, 1844   153
The Minister's house, 1843   153
The McCraes' house at Arthur's Seat   168, 169, 184
The Heads from below the Arthur's Seat house, 1846   184
Watercolour by Georgiana of the Arthur's Seat house, 1849   185
The huts at Arthur's Seat   185
Mr McLure's hut   200
The school hut or "University of Arthur's Seat"   200
Eliza, Ben-Benjie, Sally and George, Arthur's Seat aboriginals   201
The Squatter's Rest, 1844   216
"Up at sunrise . . ."   216
Little George McCrae's picture of a corroboree   216
Luncheon time at the Melbourne Club, 1863   217
Melbourne Club members, 1863   232
Andrew Murison McCrae   233
Georgiana in her later years   233
George Gordon McCrae in 1922   248
Hugh Raymond McCrae   249
The *Governor Arthur* meets the *Argyle*   254

Introduction

GEORGIANA HUNTLY McCRAE, *née* Gordon, keeper of this diary, was born in London at the beginning of last century. Coming to the Port Phillip district of New South Wales in 1841, six years after the foundation of Melbourne, she missed the christening party; but became well acquainted with most of the godfathers and godmothers later on. Her husband, Andrew Murison McCrae, a lawyer, preceded her in 1839; as he, in turn, was preceded by his brother, Dr Farquhar McCrae, who, incidentally, was the first to use chloroform in surgical practice at the settlement. Thus, the family began its Australianization, if not abreast of the original pioneering group, scarcely a step behind.

A skilled artist, especially in portraiture, and a cultivated woman, Georgiana seems to have been the chronicler opportunely born. She spent forty-nine out of her eighty-seven years in Victoria, meeting many people and witnessing events of public importance— grist to her mill, and now, by flux of time, increased in value and interest. This volume contains social history hardly realized anywhere else; consequently, it needs no stretch of imagination to call it unique.

Paragraphs chosen from her English note-book tell about the girlhood of the diarist and explain what sort of men and women they were who took upon themselves responsible roles as character-makers. The first entry, dated 28th July 1809, describes Georgiana being carried on board the *Sykes* transport, "alongside Ramsgate pier". "After dinner," she says, "the captain filled my pockets, worn sporran-wise, with almonds and raisins; then we all went on deck, and I was lifted on to the top of a water-puncheon to enable me to see ships of the fleet going out under command of Lord Chatham to Walcheren." She pictures the flota, "like a forest moving", and tells of the effect made upon her by the sight of yards manned and the sound of cheering, "so loud and so lengthened out, that I felt goose-flesh all over. . . ." Before embarkation, the soldiers said farewell to their wives in the guardroom; "and there the poor women were kept *locked up* till the ships had cleared the harbour".

Later on, Georgiana became a *journalière*, or day-boarder, at a suburban convent-school dedicated to St Aloysius, kept by "some noble French ladies who had a shilling per diem allowed by the English government for their support". La Supérieure, Madame la Comtesse D'Escouilles, although ugly, was pleasant to speak to. In her boudoir she used to make "soldiers' trowsers at $\frac{1}{2}$d the pair for Trotter the army outfitter"; while her maid, Célimène, invented a mouth-wash sweetened with honey, which she dispensed at *dix-huit sous*.

The head of the convent-school, Abbé Carron, preached English sermons once a month, in a voice gentle and sweet; yet his pronunciation was peculiar, viz.: "Our Holy Mozzer ze Chossche commands" and so forth.

One day several girls arrived at their class-rooms wearing blue sashes inscribed "Burdett for ever!" This was to celebrate Burdett's release from the Tower. Outside the establishment were many cottages occupied by emigrants—light-hearted, irrepressible people, almost contented in exile. Some of these still survive in Georgiana's descriptions; for instance, M. and Madame Dumolard and their *p'tit Jean Boule*, a baby in arms; the Chauvet family, consisting of mother and two sons, the elder of whom was *maître de langues* as well as professional flautist; the other, an effeminate hunchback, very handsome, and devoted to his *Maman*; Doctor Marchadé (a shilling a visit), in a long surtout, like a medicine-cupboard, stuffed with *fioles* in the pockets. He was breathless, "even before he had begun to climb our stairs", then, at the top . . . " *'Moiselle, 'tendez un p'tit mo-ment que je res-pi-re.* . . ." The poor man carried everywhere the miniature of his wife—a naughty cat who preferred Italy, with *un ami*, to domesticity in the English climate. "We had also, for our neighbour, Madame Mosse, daughter of another doctor called Rouveyre, who brought the unfortunate Louis Seize into the world." This woman's husband, an Englishman employed by Russian merchants, always had in his cottage samples of millet seeds, hemp, tallow, caviare, and reindeer tongues. They kept open house and, during their *petits soupers*, sang at the table glees, catches, or solos, without accompaniments.

Presently, Georgiana's guardians, uneasy regarding the influence of her Romanist friends, had her translated to Claybrook House, Fulham—an old Manor, opposite Munster House where then resided the Margravine of Anspach. The ages of the pupils at Claybrook ranged from twelve to sixteen years. Besides going through the usual course of studies, these children were taught by Oscar Byrne and his son to dance the *menuet de la cour*, the hornpipe, etc. "In practising the low curtsey, we used to stand in a sort of contrivance called *The Stocks*; an exercise that made the knees ache. But a worse quarter of an hour was spent in hanging from a rope equipped with a leather attachment which passed round the back of the head. Often our feet rose four or five inches clear of the floor. . . . This extension of the spine was supposed to improve one's carriage."

Georgiana's pocket-money amounted to "tuppence" weekly; so that during a tour through Brook Green Fair she had to borrow before she could acquire an imitation guinea. "On the face of the coin appeared the King's Head; on the reverse, these words: *25th October: the Day on which His Majesty began his Happy Reign.*" This was Jubilee Year 1811.

Soon the little girl became ill, and for a while wasn't allowed to go to school; but, in the meantime, a visiting master taught her writing and arithmetic; both weak subjects. "My Capital C. was not considered symmetrical; so that I was set to copy 'Charge, Chester! Charge!' till my fingers ached along the pen." A sad fate overtook this young man: he cashed a banknote, not knowing it to be spurious, and was sent to Botany Bay.

One afternoon Georgiana, entering a shop, found a Frenchman unable to say the English word for the thing he wanted. "He had a profile like the medallion of Washington . . . I offered to be his interpreter." The stranger proved grateful and, entering into conversation, said he was an artist out of work who earned a temporary living by the manufacture of jumping-jacks and carton

xvii

boxes for toy stalls. Georgiana took him to her guardians, who employed him to teach her drawing *at a shilling a lesson*. A thorough-going master, he showed his pupil how to burn her own charcoal sticks; procured the wing of a Pintado for brushing off outlines, and made two sets of carton boxes to contain *porte-crayon*, charcoal, and chalks; also, an extra one, in which to keep mussel-shells (her ink and colour saucers). Moreover, he cut pens out of crow-quills, and occasionally had her walk a minuet with him. "*Tenez-vous droite, ma fille!*" Sometimes he came to tea, *en grande tenue*, with black satin knee-breeches and silk stockings. "Since he was unable to play on any musical instrument, he taught me, instead, to sing a German hunting-song, *Führet hin!*" This man, who had been an officer in the Dutch service and A.D.C. to the Stadtholder, called himself Louis Mauleon. Becoming a prisoner of war, he was carried into England, where the authorities committed him to Mill Prison, near "Portsmoot"; but after two years allowed him to go to London on parole. Eventually, Mauleon gained complete freedom and, before he departed for Mauritius, went to visit Georgiana on 13th August 1813. "The dear old man kissed my hands and bade me adieu, promising to write and to send me some coconuts." The next news is "Mauleon drowned."

Soon afterwards, her favourite aunt died. "The coffin, covered with rue, rosemary, and lavender, was brought across the church-yard under a shower of rain. I followed, in a black hood and scarf, many sizes too big but previously pinned up so as to allow me enough freedom to walk without embarrassment."

When Georgiana had got quite well, she was placed at the New Road Boarding School, kept by Mrs Dunbar, a Frenchwoman born at Quebec. "We all spoke French, except during recreation and after lessons were over for the day." Illuminations to celebrate Vittoria are mentioned: cut-out paper emblems representing laurel-wreaths, and so forth; London streets lighted with whale-oil; candles at every window. We hear of the Thames being frozen over for six weeks: "Coals, two guineas the bushel; bread, at a famine price; and all out-of-door work suspended."

After the winter vacation our heroine left school, so that she became free to attend a drawing-class on Mondays, Wednesdays, and Fridays, from 10 a.m. to 3 p.m. Tuesdays and Thursdays were set aside for music lessons, imparted by the daughter of Thomas Holcroft, author of *The Road to Ruin*. Through Miss Holcroft, Georgiana got to know John Varley, who, besides being a great *paysagiste*, was admitted to the councils of the stars. "It was amusing to hear Mr Varley calculate the positions of the planets and afterwards count up the evils that might ensue." Lisping pronouncedly, he asked Georgiana: "Pray, when wath you born?" She told him the fifteenth of March 1804; whereupon he exclaimed, in a perplexed way, "Bleth my thoul! ... Venuth and Jupiter! ... I never would have believed a Venuth could be of tho dark a complecthion, or have thutch blue eyeth!" "He cautioned me to beware of saturnine men, and fair women." Varley's sister was the wife of Mulready, who had etched a portrait of him on copper—"This I often contemplated with particular delight."

Georgiana became Varley's pupil, doing her work well and seldom missing a day. "Whenever I arrived at Conduit Street too early I studied Lavater's *Physiognomy*, or practised how to strain and mount drawing-paper."

On 7th July 1814 the young artist accompanied a party to the Proclamation of Peace at St Paul's Cathedral. From early morning until past 2 p.m. she starved in a balcony, "without biscuits or sultanas", looking down upon a mob that shouted tremendously. When the City Herald advanced before the statue of Queen Anne to blow his trumpet, the people exulted beyond belief, and, "on account of our position outside a window, we heard the noises most severely". One day after this, when the Emperor of Russia and the rest of the Allied Sovereigns had come to London, "I was taken by Doctor Grestock to the porch of the Duke of York's house, in the stableyard, St James's. The young Prince of Orange brushed past me, and, presently, we saw him again; this time, kneeling on a tabouret, while the Duke fastened some order about his neck. The Prince was tall and slim, with an abundant crop of fair hair; his jacket was short, and he wore yellow Moroccoa Hessin boots. Then, towards evening, we came across Blücher, seated at an open casement, smoking a pipe with a buff-coloured bowl."

"On the first of August, we went to Hyde Park to gaze at the pagoda, and ships on the Serpentine; but the crowd at Gloucester Gate carried me off my feet, and only through Providence I managed to escape. Meanwhile, in order to get a better perspective, people were climbing trees in the Park; a sight which, notwithstanding my recent danger, made me eager to do the same. As we watched, a soldier fell from a high-up branch on to the neck of a nice-looking countrywoman in a chintz dress; killing her outright."

In the evening, there were illuminations. "Above Ackermann's, in the Strand, we admired a transparency of Napoleon building towers of cards, while Wellington puffed them down." A still more impressive spectacle awaited Georgiana at the corner of Parliament Street, where there was a representation of Prince of Wales's feathers, "done in gas for the first time". Carlton House, Pall Mall, had been dotted with multitudinous lights; "but the smell of smoke from so many of them was very unpleasant".

Here follows Georgiana's description of the landlady of her newest apartments . . . only just taken. . . . Widow of a Capitaine de la Marine, *nommé* du Bosc; and daughter of a coffee-planter in Guadeloupe. Her brother, M. le Cardinale, was Chancelier du Collège Electorale à St Brieux. "Madame, herself, elegant; yellow-complexioned, with mournful eyes; her hands very French; that is to say, the fingers thick nearest the palm of the hand and tapering rapidly to their tips." The du Bosc household was frequently visited by M. l'Abbé Huteau, an acquaintance of Madame's and a dweller in England since 1793. This man became the young girl's next tutor, instructing her thrice a week in composition, history, geography, and the use of the globes. He noticed Georgiana's sweet voice and brought Mr Taylor of Covent Garden Theatre to hear her sing. Mr Taylor said "she needed very little study in order to develop a fine mezzo-soprano of two octaves in compass"; but there the idea seemed to end. Madame wished for Georgiana's conversion to Roman Catholicism, but M. l'Abbé would not connive at it; so the poor lady desisted, only sometimes remarking,

"Ah, ma chère Georginée, vous êtes trop bonne pour ne pas mourir catholique!"

After Georgiana had completed her set of lessons with Varley, she became a student under Glover and, later on, under M. D. Serres. These artists taught her to sketch rapidly in indigo and India ink. Next in order of teachers came "Old Hayter", a most amiable man who had written a book on *The Art of Miniature Painting*. "While he criticized my work he asked questions which I answered, sometimes too energetically, down his ear-trumpet. . . . One day he invited my mother and myself to meet his son Jack, 'an ugly dog, but a clever fellow; and Miss is just the wife I should like him to have'. Nothing could have been more injudicious, and the result was the breaking-up of our pleasant acquaintance with him. Years later, I met one of Hayter's nieces in Melbourne; she was then a widow, her husband, Captain Ferguson, having been harbour master at Williamstown. This member of the Hayter family died in Western Australia, December 1885."

Here the requirements of space prevent the inclusion of further extracts from a note-book rich with interest, and it is under a feeling of genuine obligation that I record my thanks to the owner (one of Georgiana's granddaughters), Mrs Walter Outhwaite.

HUGH MCCRAE

ANDREW MURISON McCRAE

From a miniature by Georgiana

This diary has its beginning before Separation, at a time when Port Phillip was looked upon as the fag-end of New South Wales.

Only three years earlier, the town (subsequently to become known as Melbourne) consisted of no more than "two brick buildings, three weatherboard shanties, and eight turf huts".

1838

She was going to a strange country; "supposed to have been a comet dropped in the sea". —Samuel Butler

Augusta Place, Clapham Road, September 1838

It is irrevocably decided that we are to sail for Sydney per *Royal Saxon* from Gravesend November 13. Mrs Robertson's brother, Dr Johnson, and his two boys are to be our fellow passengers, and, as they are residing at Gravesend, Mr McCrae will take lodgings there for two months before we sail, so that I may have the doctor to attend to me in my confinement and be spared the land journey afterwards.

SEPTEMBER

September 5th Went to Cavendish Square to say good-bye to the Morisons, and, strange to say, not one of the family at home. So I walked back to Augusta Place.

6th Sent Jane [*Shanks*] and the boys, with the greatest part of my luggage and all their own, to the lodgings engaged at Gravesend. This to enable me to complete packing the chests of drawers for our cabin, to follow at the end of the week.

7th Awoke at 4 a.m., aroused Sybella, got a cup of tea, but found myself worse instead of the better for it. Sent Sybella for Simpson and despatched him for a spring-cart and a "fly", to take my easy chair and other luggage, and drive me to Billingsgate in time for the first trip of the Gravesend steamboat.

Perry born at 9 p.m.

Mr McCrae congratulated me on my speedy despatch of the packing! Vexed to find Dr Johnson not returned from Scotland,

and had, perforce, to accept the services of another practitioner, who proved neither skilful nor attentive. Finally, just before the reappearance of Dr Johnson, I took ague, which left me so weak he said it would be at the risk of the child's life, and perhaps my own, should I go to sea.

[*With children, a responsible venture. During and before 1840, a passage from England to Australia which lasted only four months was considered a fair thing, and provided a captain had a conscience, he could bring his vessel home again within the limits of a year. Conditions, judged by modern ways of travel, were hard in the extreme.*]

So it was decided that I must wait till the New Year before venturing on the voyage, and this made it requisite that the chests of drawers should be unpacked and all my things taken out of them. Jane and the boys have returned.

NOVEMBER

November 5th Guy Fawkes Day. A seafaring man, with a mask over his face, appeared at our first-floor window. Balancing on stilts, this fellow roared so that George roared back again, and, although I was afraid myself, I went towards the intruder, who lost hold of the sill and crashed into the street. Then George cried louder than ever, and I put him to bed.

Extract of letter from Melbourne 1840:

This town, which 18 months ago had but three brick houses in it, has now a population of 300 souls, with suitable dwellings. There are five places of worship for the various denominations of Christians, and a court of justice. Two schools, two banks, a club consisting of 60 members. A fire and marine insurance office, six clergymen, 12 medical men, and five lawyers. The country for 180 miles round Melbourne is under cultivation, or used as pasturage by the settlers, and stations already extend along the line of road to Sydney.

Amount of wool exported during

1837	amounted to		60,233	lb.	weight
1838	,,	,,	213,233	,,	,,
1839	,,	,,	806,877	,,	,,

and this year's clip is expected to exceed the former one. There are two newspapers under capable conductors; and a daily increasing population. Crops are abundant, and the seasons fine. The price of land has gone up amazingly. There is a great demand for sofas, tables, sideboards, and for furniture and stores of all kinds.

Sunday 11th Fyvie came down in a post-chaise from London to stand sponsor for Farquhar Peregrine, born September 7.

17th Mr McCrae, Dr Johnson and his boys sailed.

[*For Sydney, New South Wales, per "Royal Saxon"; skipper, "Bobby" Towns, of Townsville. Mr McCrae eventually settled in Melbourne*].

[*In December, Georgiana removed to "Priory Place", Wandsworth Road, and on Christmas Day dined at Cavendish Square with her Uncle Sandy (Sir Alexander Morison, Bart.) and her Aunt Mary; William Gordon, laird of Fyvie Castle, also being present. In February 1839 she became so ill her life was despaired of, and it wasn't until June that she began to recover.*]

1839

SUPPLEMENT

In March 1839 Dr Farquhar McCrae, his wife (Agnes Morison) and child, Mrs McCrae, Miss Thomas, Aunt Margaret, and servant sailed from Leith per *Midlothian* for Port Phillip and Sydney. On arriving at Port Phillip the doctor determined to stay there; he invested £5000 when he went to practise his profession in Sydney; after a few years, however, he was enabled to redeem his property from his bank. He died in 1851, and, when his youngest child came of age and the various properties were sold, the amount realized £52,000, exclusive of the rental of the house owing all the foregone years.

*   *   *

[*On 8th April 1839 the diarist received a letter from Mr McCrae, in Rio Janeiro, "telling of their progress so far. All well."*

She bade good-bye to Fyvie, who was wholly against the Australian venture and said so. From Fyvie, Georgiana went to Nasmyth, Byron's dentist, to let him see her teeth. "Instead of one, two were found that would have to be taken out, to prevent future suffering at sea. After the tooth from the lower jaw had been drawn I fainted, and Nasmyth gave me a glass of sherry and comforted me by assuring me that my teeth were 'never intended to be removed', yet he took out the upper one as soon as I was sufficiently recovered to bear the wrench."

Returning to Priory Place, she gradually got better.

On 4th July her eldest boy, George, put on his first pair of "trowsers", and a Mr Lane (not hitherto mentioned) gave him sixpence to hansel his pocket with.

Soon, another letter reached her from Mr McCrae, with news of his arrival at Sydney on Easter Sunday, 31st March 1839.]

October 20th (21st Sunday after Trinity) The Rev. Mr Macartney [*subsequently Dean of Melbourne*] preached in the morning, and Mr Clissold in the evening.

On *Christmas Eve*, Fyvie (a cousin of my father's) came out in a post-chaise and pair—his favourite mode of travelling—crammed full of Christmas gifts from Fyvie Castle for distribution among his kinsfolk and friends. For us, he brought two large cakes, one of "diet-bread", and the other of plum-cake especially for the boys, also a fine fat goose. As Mrs Clissold had invited me to dine with her on Christmas Day, I had the goose roasted for the boys' and the servants' early dinner, and carved for them and had a slice for my luncheon [*in agreement with the Gordon tradition—*

> *A goose for a Gordon,*
> *A haggis for a Hay,*
> *Dirt for a Dalrymple,*
> *Puddings for Lord Reagh.*]

On the morrow, it being Christmas Day, 1839, Georgiana writes:

Mrs Clissold came to tell me that their friend and neighbour, the ex-Lord Mayor of London (to whom Mr Clissold had been chaplain during his mayoralty), would take no denial from them and requested that I, too, would join their family dinner-party.

Mr Farebrother, hospitality personified. In the evening, the young ladies got up a set of carpet-quadrilles, and their aunt played for them—I had to make up a set with Mr Clissold for my cavalier. King William the Fourth had offered a knighthood to the mayor, but he declined the honour, saying he did not wish to be made a great goose of, and all his youngsters to be only little goslings.

On New Year's Eve I went to Mr Cummins's to stay till after New Year's Day.

SUPPLEMENT

Alderman Farebrother was a waxchandler, who also had bleaching grounds at Stockwell. He was a fine-looking man—much respected and esteemed for his plain commonsense. Being a widower, his sister-in-law, Miss Broadhurst, presided over his household, consisting of three handsome daughters and a son.

1840

JULY

AT last Her Grace arrived in London and I wrote to let her know that I had met Mrs Shaw at my new friends', the Cumminses. This brought a reply saying she would be glad to see my friend Mr Cummins, and to confer with him concerning the desirability of my going to join my husband in New South Wales. He went, and was charmed by the bland behaviour and pious conversation of the great lady. On being asked what he considered ample for our voyage, etc., he told Her Grace "it couldn't be managed for *less* than £500"; and this sum was afterwards placed in his hands for my behoof. He took my passage, insured my goods, and had George and myself to stay with them during the fortnight that our houseful of furniture, etc., was being packed.

SEPTEMBER

[Georgiana's contract with the shipping company]

Stockwell, September 18th, 1840

"Mr Cummins and Mr Marshall agree that Mrs McCrae and her four children are to occupy the larboard stern cabins below in the ship *Argyle* for Port Phillip as Chief Cabin Passengers, with two female servants as intermediates, one to sleep in her cabin, if she shall so decide, for £200—and the Bounty paper to be furnished for the servants, to enable Mr Marshall to receive the bounty for them in the colony."

[During 1840–41 passengers on emigrant ships were ranked: cabin, intermediate, and steerage, the last-named being roughly provided for.

As regards the cabin-folk and intermediates, sleeping accommodation, deck-space, and so forth, were about equal, so that the only difference seems to have been a social one. Georgiana messed with the captain, enjoying a good dinner plus a pint of wine; whereas Jane Shanks messed among other Janes and Johns plus Hysonskin tea instead of claret. Fresh meat and soft bread were supplied "until one day after passing the Downs". The menu for the rest of the journey included "prime new Irish East-India pork and preserved meat". Besides food, there was the consideration of dress, and, in a circular given away at the shipping office, appeared the following paragraph: "A sufficient stock of clothing for a four months' voyage should be procured, since it is not possible to wash linen during the voyage."

Although Georgiana could read Hebrew and Latin, she failed at Greek, and, to her, arithmetic was Greek in another form. Hence, the imperial subscription, pridefully attached, to an infantile table, finally learnt]—

How to find the cubic capacity of a box or other figure:

Multiply the length by the width in inches, then multiply the product by the depth, the result is the exact number of cubic inches. Next divide the whole amount by 1728 (for there are 1728 inches in a cubic foot) and the result is the number of cubic feet in the package.

OCTOBER

Gravesend, October 1st, 1840.

Inventory of Packages per "Argyle" from London Landed at Melbourne March 1841

No. 1. Case containing bedsteads.
„ 2. Dining-table and bedding.
„ 3. Sofa and pillow.
„ 4. Case of chairs.
„ 5. Cellarette, brushes, etc.
„ 6. Side-table and smaller ones.
„ 7. Pictures.
No. 8. Chest-of-drawers full of clothing.
„ 9. Cabinet-drawers, pictures.
„ 10. Books and dressing-table.
„ 11. Pedestal. Tartan and plaiding.
„ 12. Baby-linen. Box of books.
„ 13. Book shelves. Kitchen-ware.

No. 14. Copying press.

" 15. Two easy-chairs. Pillows.

" 16. Glassware.

" 17. Hogshead of chinaware.

" 18. Chest of earthenware.

" 19. Bedroom chairs, carpets.

" 20. Four-post bedstead.

" 21. Fender, pots, kettles, etc.

" 22. Small case, folio books.

" 23. Hardware.

" 24. Bath tub.

" 25. Tinned case of dresses.

" 26. Saddle, habit, etc.

" 27. Bed and table linen.

" 28. Jane Shanks's chest.

" 29. Books, work-box, etc.

" 30. Jane Sutherland's chest.

" 31. Black trunk (M) clothing.

" 32. Tin box of dresses (cabin).

" 33. Leather bonnet-box.

" 34. Hair trunk. A.M. clothing.

" 35. Bonnet-box (cabin).

" 36. Jane's box (in her cabin).

" 37. Jane's trunk (do.).

" 38. Letters, papers, pencils, etc.

" 39. Trunk, G. M. C. Children's clothes.

" 40. Chest-of-drawers (do.), these placed side by side in my cabin to form a bed for Willie and Sandy.

" 41. Chest-of-drawers. Clothing.

" 42. Box of Elgin oatmeal (cabin).

" 43. Books and toys (cabin).

" 44. Preserved fruits, and jams, do.

" 45. Soap and candles (Jane's cabin).

No. 46. Shoes, boots, etc.

" 47. Nine square bottles of water from the pump in the Tower of London.

" 48. Box with rope handles containing my box of plate.

" 49. Flat bath and hand shower.

" 50. Table for my cabin, with folding leaf and borders.

" 51. Children's chairs.

" 52. Portable folding-chair; this useful walking-staff was broken to bits on our voyage from Arthur's Seat to Melbourne 1851.

" 53. Roll of oilcloth.

" 54. Two mahogany chairs.

" 55. Clothes-bag (cabin).

" 56.   do.   do.

" 57. Books (cabin).

" 58. "Aunt Martha's Bag."

" 59. Cabin lamp.

" 60. Case of maps. Not tinned. Destroyed by sea-water during a gale.

" 61. Basket containing bottles of drugs.

" 62. Large carpet bag ⎫
" 63. Smaller do.   ⎬ cabin.

" 64. Jane's do. (in her cabin).

" 65. My writing-desk.

" 66. My dressing-case, damaged by sea-water.

" 67. Medicine-chest.

" 68. Tin case of medicines.

" 69. Work-basket.

" 70. Hamper.

8

WESTBROOK

The McCraes' home in Scotland, where Dr Farquhar McCrae and Agnes McCrae were born

WILLIAM GORDON McCRAE
of Westbrook, Scotland

MARGARET MORISON
Wife of William Gordon McCrae

AND THEIR DAUGHTERS

THOMAS ANNE McCRAE
Mrs Ward Cole

MARGARET McCRAE
Mrs David Thomas

From miniature portraits by Georgiana

These packages cost nearly £50 for freight at 42s. per ton bulk—and the twelve packages brought from Hobson's Bay by the lighter cost 10s. per ton extra, though the distance to Melbourne is only ten miles.

[*Having studied Georgiana's inventory, extensive as it seems, we are surprised that Samuel Butler should have said "It is quite unnecessary to carry out anything from the mother country in the shape of furniture; such articles can be procured at as cheap a rate in the colony as in England."*]

October 18th Sent our packages and furniture by Fox this morning, for shipment on board the *Argyle*.

19th My bill from Fox for packing (two cases and barrels, and the dray) £30; which I paid.

23rd The H. W. Fennings, and Mrs F.'s brother, Mr Weymouth, and other neighbours of the Cumminses came in for a musical evening—and *colonial talk*. Mr Weymouth sang Campbell's (?), a most lugubrious chilling composition.

24th The most trying day of all.

25th About 10 a.m., having parted with our dear friend, Mrs Cummins, George and I called at Mr Cook's in South Lambeth, for Willie and Alexander, then at Mr Fenning's for Jane Shanks and Farquhar.

Thus, surrounded by my children, and accompanied by Harry and Richard Cummins, I arrived at Gravesend, where Mrs and Miss Sutherland anxiously waited our arrival.

We talked about the *Argyle* while we looked at her looming up opposite Tilbury fort, and discussed the country that was soon to become my home, but the boatmen were anxious to be off, so we took leave of everybody and went on board.

The wind blew hard, and, when we reached the ship and I saw how tall the sides were, I felt anxious for Farquhar, but Mr Quarry, who ascended first, took the child with him, other passengers assisting Willie and George. With some difficulty I followed, and was saved from falling on the deck by kind Dr Ronald, who exclaimed while he steadied me: "Eh, Mrs McCrae! Weel! Weel! Were ye oot in yon squ-a-a-al?" I fancied myself on the "plain stanes" of the guid town of Aberdeen; where, to say the truth, I would rather have been than on an emigrant ship bound for the

9

Antipodes. The captain had not yet come aboard, so the doctor brought me to the cuddy, where we found Mr Hamilton, of the Steam Navigation Company, Edinburgh, with his nephew, Charles Hamilton Masling, who was going to settle in Port Phillip. Mr Hamilton didn't stay long, and, as soon as he had departed, his nephew retired to his cabin—the starboard stern one—next to ours, below.

After a while I copied his example, feeling the way to my dark and gloomy den.

I was glad when tea-time came, with its cheerful noise of plates and pleasant effect of light. Later, during the evening, the rain stopped, and I heard across the water snatches of music from a barrel-organ out of tune and time: *"Les Grâces"*, an air not at all suited to my present situation. Then a gust of wind came and the music ceased. Returning to our cabin, I found everything damp, comfortless, and strange . . . with a persistent odour of paint.

DRAMATIS PERSONAE OF THE VOYAGE
taken from
unsigned scraps in the Ship's Paper, headed
ARGYLE 1840
generally considered to be the combined efforts of
WILLIAM CAMPBELL and GEORGIANA McCRAE.

WILLIAM CAMPBELL, of Dunmore: Major of the Argyle and Bute Artillery Militia, twenty-four years of age, a proficient swordsman and composer of pottering verse. Boasts of his "Cousin Mary" having married Prince Polignac.

[*A prominent French monarchist, and son of August Jules Armand Marie, head of the last Bourbon ministry. Macaulay speaks of the father's "frantic wickedness".*]

JAMES IRVINE, "Auld Drum": a clannish young beau, whose one song, "I love to rove", is first favourite with cuddy audiences on musical-supper nights.

WILLIAM ANDERSON: nephew of "Mangalore" Anderson, first occupant of the Goulburn country, below Seymour.

You're the man can bait a good salmon,
And pull like a native of Bucky;
Or lose a few bob at Backgammon,
And swear that you're deuced unlucky.

DR NEWMAN: "a feelosopher"—muzzy and prosy. Fond of his glass.

FREDERICK HINTON: a lawyer—"in garments grotesque". He laments the loss of his friends, also the lack of good claret and champagne.

CAPTAIN RANKINE, "Ninepence": who has come to sea dresst for the Park. Coat and trowsers from Nugent, a neckerchief *voyante*, and double-milled doeskin boots. His musical snuff-box coveted by Mrs Sconce.

JEPHSON QUARRY: an attorney—"Hurrah for Ould Oireland!" The broth of a bhoy, very pugnacious, not prepossessing to look at. A pale-faced man. Wrapped in a sheet, he would make a capital spook.

[*In a separate division, Georgiana has placed the Bunbury family, viz.*]:

MARS (Captain B.); VENUS (Mrs B.); CUPID (Baby Harry). Again CAPITANO, SIGNORA, and PICCOLO Harry. Harry called PICCOLO, because, being born at Malta, and speaking Italian, he had become the special pet of the captain of the wrecked *Jachimo Piccolo*.

Once more, CAPTAIN BUNBURY: inclined to be dogmatic, but generally right in his point.

MR SCONCE: introspective, a careful and precise speaker.

MRS SCONCE: *So playful and artless she seems,*
                    That you almost would think pretty Betty
                    Drew naught from her quiver but beams . . .

MRS SCONCE (repeated):
                    Robin's Jenny-Wren of a wife:
                    A daughter to me; delighting my life.

FRANCISCO: mate of the *Jachimo Piccolo*, beloved of Nina, and Isola d'Ossola, Gulf of Venice.

The REV. MCKNIGHT, of Edinburgh: member of a well-known Deeside family.

THE BOSUN: "Aye, aye, sir!" Quite Greekish was he. . . .

THE HORSE: undisturbed by the bawling of the hands and their wild "Hoorays!"

THE COW-MINDER:

                    Tam Thampson, the bonny cow's chief Adie Kong,
                    With a mouth like his mistress, and a voice like a gong,
                    When calling the weemin to "bouilli," "so bong!"

STEERAGE FOLK:

> Such groups you see clustered together
> Of these merry emigrant wretches,
> With clothes made to let in the weather:
> O, for Cruickshank, to take a few sketches!
> There's no end of striking and biting;
> There's no end of bawling and squalling;
> Love-making, scolding, and fighting;
> Cly-faking————and eke caterwauling.

[*The McCrae children have been immortalized in another part of the paper*]:

> "Big G.": his small brothers three;
> "Young Brickbat", "Van Dunk",
> And "Little Farkee",
> So timorous; so valorous;
> In giving, so free.

[*This last one, the baby of the family, has many tributes offered to him under a constantly changing name.*]

"Young Fawkquier"—"Little Admiral"—"so saucy and joyous, the pet of the fold." "Gravesend his birthplace, near Tilbury in Kent."

[*These sobriquets of the brothers are accounted for, by Georgiana, in the following note*]:

"Big G.", for George, is self-explanatory.

"Young Brickbat" was the name given to Willie by Charles Hamilton McKnight.

"Van Dunk", also godfathered by C. H. McKnight, typified Sandy, a boy, as broad as he was long.

"Fawkquier", for Farquhar: Captain Gatenby's pronunciation of the Admiral's name. The Admiral was Agnes McCrae's uncle by marriage.

[*When the children had grown up, "Big G." became deputy registrar general of patents at Melbourne, also winning recognition as one of the leading poets of his day. "Brickbat" and "Van Dunk" remained "goufba's o' Fortune" and were never more than ordinarily successful in the world, whereas with "Little Farkee" it was otherwise, for, accepting a stool in a counting-house, he rose to be inspector for the Bank of Australasia in Queensland and New South Wales.*]

OCTOBER 1840

For a better understanding of this diary, it seems reasonable to include separate genealogical tables relative to the people concerned, beginning with—

I

The European-born McCraes of the first Australian generation, viz., children of William Gordon McCrae, and of his wife, Margaret, née Morison.

ALEXANDER	Captain in the 84th Regiment.
ANDREW MURISON	Writer to the Signet; and husband of GEORGIANA
AGNES, AND JOHN MURISON	Both dead before the inception of this diary, and, therefore, not included.
FARQUHAR, M.D.,	Surgeon in the Fifth Dragoon Guards; the Inniskillings.
THOMAS ANNE	Married to George Ward Cole—Lieutenant R.N.
MARGARET FORBES	Married to Dr D. J. Thomas.

II

The Second Generation: Children of Andrew Murison and Georgiana McCrae (omitting Elizabeth Gordon, who died in her childhood, before the family migrated) some European-born; some Australian-born:

GEORGE GORDON	Born at "Anchorfield," Leith, in Scotland, May 29, 1833.
WILLIAM GORDON	Born at Edinburgh, Scotland, March 1, 1835.
ALEXANDER GORDON	Born at Edinburgh, Scotland, November 31, 1836.
FARQUHAR PEREGRINE GORDON	Born at Gravesend, County of Kent, September 7, 1838.
LUCIA GEORGIANA GORDON	Born at Melbourne, Port Phillip District, December 29, 1841.
MARGARET MARTHA	Born at "Mayfield," Port Phillip District, June 25, 1844.
FRANCES OCTAVIA GORDON	Born at Arthur's Seat, Port Phillip District, June 20, 1847.
AGNES GORDON	Born at Arthur's Seat, Port Phillip District, March 27, 1851. Died at Melbourne, January 6, 1855.

13

Returning to the diary]:

Our bosun, John Flatt (Samson Redivivus), was very handsome, except for his nose, which had been staved in by a blow from a stuns'l-boom. His voice showed a fine barytone, and Captain Gatenby would sometimes have him in to sing to us in the cuddy, but he was at his best telling stories of the time when he had served aboard Lord Yarborough's yacht, cruising among the Isles of Greece. Tam Thampson, shoemaker by trade, had charge of the "Bastille", fed the cow, "mucked out" the byre, and did the milking. He also served rations to the emigrants.

Sunday, 26th While the church bells at Gravesend were ringing for morning service, we moved towards the Nore, where we lay-to, the ship tossing uneasily all through the day and night.

27th The wind being unfavourable, we still drifted with the tide. During my perambulations, I noticed that our quarterdeck had been encumbered with two wooden sheds, one occupied by the Durham cow and calf, the other by a bay stallion.

For his protection, each side-wall of the stallion's shed had a horse's skin nailed over it, the skin being padded underneath like a sofa-back. A dog called "Wag" was lodged in a kennel, snugly weatherproof, among bundles of fodder, trusses of hay, etc. Further on, the jollyboat, hanging from davits, was filled with spars and spare booms, and, underneath its keel, a space had been kept for chicken coops and a pig's parlour. The wind freshening, I went below and found the children more or less ill. The maids, Jane and Jenny, quite *hors de combat.* . . .

The night rough, and myself added to the sick-list.

[If she had been despairful enough, now was the time for Georgiana to try her chemist-friend's specifics against the mal de mer: *"The creosot, No. 2, may be taken on a knob of sugar. The prussic acid is more certain. . . . It should be kept in a jar of cold water in the dark. . . . With sincere prayers for your welfare. Very faithfully, Thos. H. Silvester." The original note, as well as its medical direction, has been preserved, and proves only semi-acquaintance by being addressed to—*
> *Mrs McCready,*
>> *J. Cummins, Esq.,*
>>> *"The Oval", Brixton.]*

The gale increased to such a pitch that we lost our "Best Bower" anchor. In the meantime, Dr Ronald and young Dr Traill (straw-coloured gloves, and a withered nosegay) went their rounds among the emigrants. Just before midnight Ronald came along to our cabin.

"I've been roond to the intermediates," said he, "puir leddies! They've a' been deid-sick this while, sae I had a guid pan o' gruel made for them, and pit it in a bucket wi' a flavour of brandy to comfort their hearts!"

Kitchen physic and cheering words beyond praise.

28th Off Deal. The captain signalled for a new anchor, and, after some considerable time, we observed a boat making towards us with great difficulty. There was a heavy sea running, and it was a good while before we were able to distinguish clearly the men at the oars, or the shape of the anchor (probably seventeen, or eighteen hundredweight). However, they eventually delivered their charge, and the anchorsmith, a native of Sunnuck, who came with them, declared: "She's the best anchor in the world!" So they received £50 in cash, besides grog all round, after which some of their company hawked boiled crabs, and I bought two for the children. When they had returned to their boat, I watched them row back to the shore, now high up on a wave, now sinking into the trough beyond. The night covered them and everything faded away.

30th Anchored off Plymouth, after having encountered a stiff gale. Captain and Mrs Bunbury, their child and nurse, and two men-servants, came on board, also Mr and Mrs Sconce, attended by their servants.

Late in the afternoon, to our dismay, no less than 150 emigrants (in addition to as many already embarked), swarmed up our sides, a drab and ugly crowd, who had been waiting several days, in-sufficiently provided for; this in spite of the fact that Marshall had assured Captain Bunbury, and other cuddy passengers, that al-though the ship would carry Bounty emigrants, they would be so few as to be hardly worth mentioning.

[*It should be remembered that this voyage was to end in 1841, a record year for the importation of emigrants, forty-four ships having in that time* carried eight thousand people to Hobson's Bay. On the journey out, un-assisted passengers stayed separated from the so-called Bounty emigrants, a wise arrangement, if there were basis to Dr Thomson's conclusion that "this drab and ugly crowd" ranked "inferior to our aborigines". The remark struck at the Bounty system, under which the local government issued orders on the land revenue department at the rate of £15 for each adult imported.]

Day after day, the wind against us, the ladies keeping to their cabins. Captain Treadwell (the ship's husband) and Dr Ronald gone ashore, Dr Traill having already left to rejoin the *Susan*.

NOVEMBER

November 11th Hoisted anchor. Sailed out of harbour. "Chops" of the channel. Farquhar ill. [*These pizzicato sentences illustrate the difficulty of writing during a storm.*]

14th Terrific gale, lasting forty-eight hours. The sea white to the horizon. Every roll of the ship filled me with horror.

Captain Gatenby said it was the worst sea he had known. We were still within soundings; Eddystone light struggling through the gloom.

17th Spars and booms washed out of jollyboat and thrown on to the deck. We, below, supposed our mainmast had gone by the board. All deadlights put in and caulked round. Emigrants marched up to cuddy to give them breathing room, some of the women praying, others dumb from despair. After these had returned to their quarters, Captain Gatenby astonished me by saying: "If ever we are compelled to take to the boats, only cuddy-passengers will be allowed to embark. *The emigrants must stay behind.*"

Blown out of our course.

18th The wind dropped as we entered the Bay of Biscay, riding across dark-coloured waves dappled with foam.

19th From the cross-trees, Dr Dawson, R.N., made out a vessel in distress; he at once called to Captain Gatenby, who went to join him aloft, but immediately came down again. Through a sub-sequent interchange of messages, we learnt that the ship was the *Jachimo Piccolo*, from Trieste to Dublin, with a cargo of grain in bulk. Seventeen days out from Algeciras: she had lost her main-mast on the fourteenth; her foremast on the seventeenth; then, after her caboose had been washed overboard, she became water-logged. Her captain offered Gatenby salvage, but Gatenby refused to take the *Piccolo* in tow, because there was the chance that she might suddenly drag us down. Urged on by the passengers' offer of a pound a-piece, four sailors manned a boat and set out towards the wreck. Meanwhile, through Captain Gatenby's cabin-window at the stern I watched their cockle-shell make its way, until, rising on a huge billow, the oarsmen seemed to rest. The fellow at the tiller signed to those who were on board to jump; five did so and had to swim for it, but six others waited to be taken off on a second trip. At last all were safely transferred to the *Argyle*. The crew, soused with sea-water, looked wretched and starved, their appearance seeming worse through contrast with a stout Hebrew merchant who travelled with them. This merchant was accom-panied by his nephew, a boy about twelve years old. Against the undulating sea, with a box of ship's papers suspended from his neck, the stranger Capitano impressed us very much. He was an elderly man, so dignified he might have been the reincarnation of some ancient Doge.

Francisco Ragusa, the first mate, young and impetuous, not satisfied with having saved his life, was furiously angry on account of the loss of his gold watch. For several days he remained in this state, then, forgetting his watch, he remembered his betrothed and wrote songs to her, some of which I copied—when he didn't give me the originals.

Neither the Capitano nor any of his people had any English, but, with Captain Bunbury (who talked Italian) for our interpreter, we got to understand each other very well.

20th When I woke, Jane told me the *Piccolo* had sunk during the night. [*"During the night" is opposed to my father's recollection, and, since he is precise in statement, and careful of recording facts, his version has been added here. "It was broad daylight, and, being a small boy, I had been lashed to the mizzen-mast, in order to watch the wreck safely. The wind blew great guns and a tremendous sea was on. Gradually, her forefoot rose out of the water, then perhaps half her keel, and down she went, uncomfortably close to us, stern foremost.*"] With great regret I remembered her beautiful lines and glittering figurehead. Purposely avoided seeing the Capitano all day.

22nd Our first Sunday at sea. Captain Bunbury and his brother-in-law M. R. B. conducted the service. The singing so bad it had to be given up.

[*Our earliest pioneers sang with unexpected effect, as witness the story of aboriginals attending the first open-air service at the Port Phillip settlement; how they stood curiously by, until a sudden burst of hymnody caused them to throw down their chattels and run.*]

26th Sighted Madeira—like a cloud in the offing. The *Argyle* becalmed. Captain Gatenby said he couldn't land the shipwrecked crew at Funchal for less than forty pounds; also, Madeira being an open roadstead, he was averse to entering the harbour.

DECEMBER

December 6th Cast anchor in the Bay of Porto Prayo, Cape Verde Islands, opposite to where, not long since, the *Red Rover* had been wrecked. The passengers subscribed a sum of money towards getting new clothes for the Capitano and his men, who immediately went ashore to hear Mass, in recognition of their escape. Meanwhile, the consul secured for them passages to Lisbon by a frigate due to sail on the next day.

The Capitano boarding the *Argyle*, roughly clad and dripping from the sea, had appeared a figure of romance; very different from the man who now came to say good-bye. It seemed a shame, and I was afraid we might offend by some unguarded look, or smile, when he kissed our hands, rigged out in a full stand of Brougham and Shepherd's plaiding, topped off with a low-crowned white straw hat which Captain Gatenby had given him. Francisco was not altered so much, although we missed the sombrero.

Land-birds flew about the rigging, and boats full of coconuts, bananas, oranges, and baskets of eggs, rubbing against the sides of the ship were so thickly clustered together it seemed possible to have walked across them, dry-shod, to the shore. The strong

sunshine affected my eyes, but there was no escape from it while
daylight remained.

Towards nightfall the harbour-master arrived to dine with us,
and Mrs Sconce and I dressed for dinner for the first time since we
had come to sea. Besides the harbour-master, we entertained the
captain of the *Grampus*, Boston, U.S.A., a clever but over-talkative
man, whose conversation was not improved by a lisp. Captain
Gatenby told us of the American consul's invitation to a public
reception this evening, given in honour of his bride whom he
married last night. Because the invitation came too late, we were
unable to go.

It was my fixed habit to hear the boys say their lessons every day
in the cuddy until noon, when biscuits, cheese, and Bass's ale
would be placed on the table for the captain and passengers. In the
evenings I usually accompanied Mr and Mrs Sconce to the Bunburys' cabin for the purpose of studying Cobbett's *French Grammar*,
as it was supposed that Madame La Trobe could not speak English.
At other times we played whist, or looked at some capital landscapes
painted by Captain Bunbury with his left hand, he having parted
with his right one, so he said, "to feed the Turks, at Navarino".

[*Richard Hanmer Bunbury was post-captain in the Royal Navy, and,
incidentally,* brother-in-law to Robert Knox Sconce recorded in this
diary. Bunbury became port and harbour-master at William's Town;
he also owned a station at Mount William in the Grampians. My father
was present when he died, at Murray's Prince of Wales Hotel, Flinders
Lane East, in Melbourne.*]

7th Mr McKnight, Mr and Mrs Sconce, Captain Gatenby, Mr
Campbell, Mr James Irvine, my boys, Jane Shanks, and I went on
shore for a holiday. Captain Gatenby spoilt his socks by slipping
into the surf while he handed Mrs Sconce from the boat to the
beach.

First we went to the consulate to pay our respects to the consul's
bride, also, to apologize for our absence from the reception on
Sunday night. The consul said he regretted we had lost the opportunity of seeing all the "rank, fashion, and beauty" of the island,
but we did not tell him the principal reason for staying away,

namely, the captain's refusal to allow any of the *Argyle's* passengers to spend an evening ashore, on account of "pirates and thieves"! It appears that, not long since, a wealthy traveller had been slashed to pieces in a cookshop and stripped of everything he possessed. During the afternoon somebody proposed an excursion to the orange-groves, but, though there were donkeys for hire in the square, not one had a saddle for a girl. However, the boys were soon accommodated, and, for a single hour of this deadly jog-trot, I had to pay half a dollar each.

On our return to the consulate, a long two-story wooden building, we entered at the ground floor, traversing a cellar and suite of store-rooms, thence, by a high-stepping staircase, out on to a veranda, thence again, through French windows, to the *salle à manger* itself. When we sat down the time was a quarter to four. The consul's Portuguese wife, the daughter of a salt-mine proprietor from the island of Sal, being unable to converse either in English or French, her husband (Mr Geyer) had to speak for both.

At each corner of the dining-table appeared a small antique silver candlestick, supporting a slender wax taper within a glass shade.

All the plates were piled in a heap, face downwards, with a corresponding heap of knives, forks, spoons, etc., beside the host and hostess, who sat at the head of the table, ready to hand these accessories when the proper moment arrived. After the soup we were given poultry and a spare rib of pork. Then sweets to follow, and different kinds of wine. At the conclusion of the meal, we two womenfolk followed madame to her own room, the servants and children staying behind to finish off the repast.

Observed madame's bed-hangings: white muslin, caught up by bows of saffron-coloured ribbon. Pillow-slips and bed-bases trimmed with Spanish lace. Madame opened her *armoire* to let us see her bridal dress; she also showed us some fine open-work stockings, hand-wrought, from the island of Maca, one dollar the pair! This we made out by the ever-ready polyglot of pantomime, aided by a few Spanish words thrown in. When we were about to take our leave a servant entered carrying a flask of *eau d'anisette* in one hand, and a salver spread with candied fruit in the other, whereupon madame clapped her hands, as a signal for the boys to be brought in. A few sips of *anisette* all round, a few kind words between us, and our visit had come to an end.

Meanwhile our escort was beginning to be restive, especially Captain Gatenby, who had a horror of any delay.

On our return to the ship I went through the contents of my pockets and came across the following receipted bill which shows a strange mixture of purchases, as well as of language:

MADAME MCCRAE
dans la navire, "Argyle".

3 monkey (really 3 porous water-bottles) ..					3 shillings
100 du pain ..	..	..	..	..	3 dollars et demi
400 de l'oranges ..	..	..	..	..	8 shillings
6 yard de coton bleu ..		..	..	..	12 shillings
2 chapeaux ..	..	..	..	..	4 shillings
			(Pour apporter		3 shillings)
3 baskets ..	..	..	..	..	4/6

MADAME PORTOGUERA
Chargé d'affaires

11th We sailed from Porto Prayo.

12th As I returned from breakfast I saw Captain Bunbury holding his cabin-door ajar. He beckoned me in and told me he would be obliged if I would stay beside his wife while he went for the doctor, because Aguilar, the nurse, had taken little Harry on deck, to be out of the way. The doctor arrived, and, within half an hour, a fine boy was handed to me. For the first time in my life I was present at a birth, but being accustomed to infants, I did all that was needful.

19th Crossed the line in Lon. 28° West.

23rd Ran for west, within 300 miles of Pernambuco.

29th In the latitude of Rio Janeiro.

31st Terrific orgies among the emigrants!

1841

JANUARY

January 14th   Captain Bunbury twenty-seven today.

15th   Rounding the Cape of Good Hope. A heavy sea following the ship.

16th   Rose about 4 a.m. to see the sun rise; a grand, but unpaintable, picture.

17th   Still "rounding the Cape". Ship unsteady.

FEBRUARY

February 21st   Ran down to Latitude 40°. Kept pretty straight on our course until. . . .

22nd   When we sighted Cape Bridgewater. Coasting along, saw smoke from supposed native fires, or "clearing" near Portland Bay.

23rd   Going slowly, then contrary breezes.

24th   Driven back on our course.

25th   Regained our meridian of the 23rd.

26th   Off Cape Otway. A very rough night, but the wind off shore.

27th   As we were trying to enter the heads of Port Phillip, we encountered a fierce gale from the north-west. Sky as black as ink. At last we got into smoother water, and anchored off Swan Pond. On the cliff opposite, saw the foundation walls of a lighthouse. All the buoys adrift, and no pilot within hail. Captain Bunbury remarked what a fine natural position the heads afford for defence, supposing a fort on Point Nepean and a corresponding one on Point Lonsdale, and a chain sunk across the entrance to the bay. Captain Gatenby consulting the chart of the bay and sailing directions, but unwilling to risk the ship and passengers by attempting to go on without a pilot.

Sunday, 28th A clear morning. Wind still north, and fresh. On walking through the cuddy to look at the shore, I surprised Captain Gatenby and Captain Bunbury *tête-à-tête*. As I entered, the former had just said: "The insurances will hold good", and would have added more had he not become aware of my presence. I immediately told him how much I had heard, whereupon he asked me to treat this "as a matter, in confidence, between ourselves", and then continued: "The anchor is dragging, and I fear we shall go stern foremost on Point Nepean. We shall be able to get ashore, but the shock of the ship striking may take you off your feet, so you'd better feign headache and go to your bed, and get the boys to lie down till the wind lulls." I did as directed, and lay in suspense for a long time, my tin box at hand [*the box containing her miniatures*], ready for carrying off. As Mr Cummins had insured my passage and goods for £800 I was less anxious than I might have been. Suddenly, the wind shifted from north to south-west, and we were blown inward. At sun-down the wind fell, and we went on deck to enjoy the fresh air. The mate of a vessel on our larboard bow visited us, and told us that his ship the *Harvest Home* had been weatherbound for several days. He spoke with a Yankee accent and apologized for his captain being too "grog-sick" to accept Gatenby's invitation.

MARCH

March, Monday, 1st Port Phillip.

["*An immense place; large enough to contain every British ship that swims, measuring forty miles by about thirty-five miles; and containing not far short of a million acres of water.*"—SAMUEL BUTLER

"*1841 opened with a population of between 5000 and 6000 in Melbourne; protected by ten constables and a chief, twenty-five soldiers for guard and escort duty; and two hundred and fifty ticket-of-leave men—thirty as a street gang; and the rest assigned servants. Three pilots, to superintend the navigation of the Bay.*"—THE VICTORIAN HISTORICAL MAGAZINE]

At 8 a.m., after the anchor had been walked-up to the bows, Tobin, the pilot, came aboard; a man like John Flatt, dresst in a frock-coat and chimney-pot hat. He went straight to the poop, where nobody else was to remain, except Gatenby and a seaman called Adams, but, later on, the captain took George up too, and allowed him to help Adams hold the chart while Tobin steered. Thus George had his share in bringing the *Argyle* into port!

About 2 p.m. we anchored in Hobson's Bay off William's Town: a collection of houses, shingled and clap-boarded, and one large stone building.

[*In '41, a mud bar at the mouth of the Yarra blocked out any vessel drawing over seven feet of water, consequently, for overseas ships, William's Town represented the nearest approach to Melbourne, and here they discharged both passengers and cargo. Seen from the "Argyle", its buildings not well assembled, this place appeared smaller than it was. Robert Dundas Murray criticized "a propensity that disposes houses all over the colony to keep far apart", and declared William's Town no exception to the rule; nevertheless, after he had been ashore, he found it a thriving station, remarkable for "the magnitude and solidity of its warehouses". Then, as if to rout, utterly, our over-occupied diarist, he concludes with this sentence: "In the present year, it ranks third among towns of the province." So alas, for Georgiana's estimate of "a collection of houses, shingled and clap-boarded", which, despite the make-weight of "a large stone building", seems to compose an error of fact. In 1837 William's Town received its name from Governor Bourke, who, on account of its position, believed it must become the capital of the south. Having thus honoured his sovereign, he remembered the inland settlement, which he dubbed Melbourne, after the English prime minister; to mark it second, or next to the King. R. H. Horne used William's Town's pioneer designation, The Fishing Village, which village, twenty years later, had grown into what the Rev. Frederick Jobson called "a dingy, boat-building Blackwall sort of a suburb. . . ." A many-titled place. If, at different intervals of time, the reader, or the writer, had been able to visit Koort Boork, (She-oak), The Fishing Village, Point Gellibrand, and William's Town, he must have trodden, always, the same ground.*]

We lay alongside the *Eagle*, Captain Buckley; and the *York*

WILLIAM GORDON McCRAE
"Little Willie" of the diary
From a pencil portrait by Georgiana

ALEXANDER McCRAE
"Little Alexander" of the diary
From a pencil portrait by Georgiana

THE BARQUE *ARGYLE*
From a pen-drawing by
George Gordon McCrae

"*Piccolo Iachimo*"
Lat. 48°. N.   19th Nov. 1840 -

THE WRECKED *PICCOLO JACHIMO*
From a pen-drawing by Georgiana

(seven other ships being in the bay). Captain Gatenby gave us dessert and champagne to celebrate our arrival in Australia, with appropriate toasts. Willie completed his sixth year.

2nd All kinds of people came on board, chiefly for the purpose of hiring servants; but our emigrants aren't yet at liberty to engage.

[*Aleck Hunter, writing in 1841, says:* "*Three emigrant ships have arrived in the last fortnight; and men are to be had for £25; women, from £12 to £15.*"]

3rd Our cow and calf sold for £100.

4th Jane Shanks (the maid), the boys, and I went aboard the *Governor Arthur*, a scrubbishy [?] grinding little steamer without any cabin. Half-way up the river the rain began to fall, whereupon I extended the folds of my plaid so as to take in the children and keep them out of the wet. The boat landed us opposite the Yarra Hotel, Flinders Street and we had to wade through mud and clay, up the hill to Dr McCrae's in Great Bourke Street West. My good London boots, *abimés*!

[*The Yarra Hotel was kept by Augustus Frederick Adolphus Greeves, "one of the ablest men of a bygone generation", for as well as being a hotel-keeper, he was a skilful surgeon, editor of the "Gazette", a fine public speaker, and, according to Garryowen, "the best Mayor that ever filled the Civic chair in Melbourne". He entered history when he fathered the shrewd move which secured the return of Earl Grey as a member for the New South Wales Legislature, 1848.*]

5th I went off in a boat from near Cole's Wharf to the ship to pack up the remainder of our cabin-gear, and stayed on board to wait for the morning's steamer.

6th Sent off our heavy luggage by the lighter, then returned to Melbourne in the *Governor Arthur* with Jenny.

7th Attended service in the wooden church against which are the walls of the stone edifice of St James's in course of erection. In the afternoon we all attended and I stood proxy godmother for little Francis Argyle Bunbury. The clergyman, Mr A. C. Thomson, seeing the group of children gathered round the crockery basin doing duty as a "font", supposed they were all waiting to be

25

baptized, a natural conclusion since it's a common event for five, or more, in a family born in the bush to be baptized on their first visit to a church. The group consisted of George, eight years; Willie, six years; Sandy, five years; Farquhar, three years; and Harry Bunbury, two years; (A goodly subject for a photograph.)*

[*Adam Compton Thomson was an old Indian Army chaplain; successor to "Stammering Grylls", the first Anglican minister in the settlement.*]

8th Went to see our new home, "Argyle Cottage", in Little Lonsdale Street West, consisting of one tolerably large room, with four closets, *called* bedrooms, opening out of it. The walls of wood, about half an inch thick, and the ceiling of the same. The building raised on stumps to about two feet from the ground, and three wooden steps, like those of a bathing-machine, lead up into a French window, which is the front door of the dwelling. At a little distance from the back door is a kitchen hut, *à rez-de-chaussée*. And for this accommodation the rent required by Mr Simpson is £100 per year!

[*After her home in England it seems a pitiful habitation. Nevertheless, there were many people of good family at Port Phillip just as badly off. Moreover, the position of the house was excellent, since it abutted on the west end of the town, viz., that area bounded by Spencer, William, Flinders, and Great Bourke streets.*

Earlier housing problems are touched upon by Captain King (1837): "We called upon the ladies of the place and found them enduring great discomfort, some living in mud hovels, some in tents, and others just entering their new abodes of wattle and daub."]

After helping Jane to arrange as much as we could I returned to dine at Dr McCrae's, and met there the Rev. A. C. Thomson, Captain Fyans, and Mr Lloyd Jones.

9th Perambulated the town with Agnes, that is to say, we went up the north side of Collins Street, without any sign of a pavement; only a rough road, with crooked gutters—the shops, built of wood, and raised on stumps.

*Added later by Georgiana.

SUPPLEMENT

The *shop* furthest east was a draper's, Donaldson and Budge, and the nearest *house* (further east) Crook, the undertaker's. Four weatherboard cottages, with verandas, stood where is now the Melbourne Club, and Bedford House, a two-story brick hotel, stood opposite.

★   ★   ★

[*Mr Meek, mentioned later on in this diary, was first honorary secretary of the Melbourne Club. Under his ministration all went merry as a marriage-bell, until one evening when Mr Thomas pulled Mr Cobb's nose. The news coming to bold Mr Meek, that gentleman insisted on Mr Cobb being allowed to pull Mr Thomas's nose by way of requital. But Mr Cobb was afraid.*

"Another recognized resort was George Smith's old 'Lamb Inn' where I saw my first dead man: a bushranger, stretched out on the billiard-table, with a bullet through his head."—George Gordon McCrae.

"— — the unpaved streets of Melbourne, famed for gutters that meander from side to side; purposely neglected; in order to instruct the population in leaping during the day, and to furnish broken limbs by night for the advancement of medical science."—"A Summer in Port Phillip", by the Hon. R. D. Murray.

One night, in 1858, a man and his horse were drowned in Elizabeth Street, under "the miserable dark lanterns that disgraced the metropolis". At about the same time, a horse and dray were carried down Swanston Street, past where Young and Jackson's now stands, into the river. These happenings afforded a chance to some sardonic joker, who wrote to the mayor, John Thomas Smith, suggesting he should set up life-buoys "the whole length of the post office coast". During summer, instead of floods, the inhabitants suffered dust-storms, full of specks and straws, so that it became difficult to breathe. The sky like London fog; the atmosphere that of a lighted oven.]

10th Agnes and the children came to spend the day with us at "Argyle Cottage".

11th Removed our things from Dr McCrae's, and took up our abode at "Argyle", then went to the Union Bank to verify my signature before Mr William Highett [*first manager: beginning service in '38. He died wealthy, and, according to Finn, although the money was unwilled, "it found plenty of legal owners"*]. Dined at Dr McCrae's.

12th Jane and I busy all day, unpacking and arranging our cabin-gear.

13th Agnes and the children went to the Doctor's station at Dandenong. Our packages by the lighter were brought up.

14th A fine warm day. At church in the morning.

15th Thermometer 84°. Completed my thirty-seventh year. Busy all day unpacking.

16th The *Argyle* sails for Sydney tomorrow. Captain Gatenby came to say good-bye: sorry he missed the little pilot.

17th Unpacking, arranging.

18th Called at "Jolimont Cottage"; everything peaceful inside, but the rooms dark, on account of the trellised veranda. While I waited for Madame [*Mrs La Trobe, wife of the Superintendent of the district of Port Phillip*], I smelt flowers in the garden, and listened to a clock on the shelf. *Madame très aimable pour moi . . . et très myope.*

[*The following is another description of the same room, on a wet day, jotted down by the diarist's son:* "I noticed a map pasted between pictures against the wall, and, underneath it, on a desk, manuscripts, with saucers of seeds. There were, also, butterflies in glass cases, dimmed by humidity, at different parts of the room, the whole creating a meditative atmosphere, saddened by the perpetual tack-hammer sound of a drip from the roof."]

20th Went for a ride to try my new saddle. Saw our allotment on the Yarra—nine acres and a half—with a river frontage, the ground thickly covered with boulders of which the house is to be built. Mem.: the direct course to the allotment from the top of Great Bourke Street East—twenty-one degrees north of east.

SUPPLEMENT

At this time there were no houses on the south side of Little Lonsdale Street, only a wattle-and-daub shack, built and inhabited by one, Minifie, a carpenter, and his wife. This building didn't encroach on our view across the flat to Cole's Wharf. In La Trobe Street West (behind "Argyle Cottage"), were two brick houses, numbers 144 and 146, the former occupied by Captain McLachlan and his family; opposite these houses were the Flagstaff and Observatory Hill, with graves of some of the earlier settlers. The burial-place was surrounded by a fence, six feet high, painted black—but the wild bush had penetrated inside. On the hill were she-oaks (so named on account of their likeness to American beefwood trees, called *sheacs*) which echoed the *ramage* of parrots and everywhere about the grass appeared strange flowers, some of which were yellow, while others were white, or turquoise, tinged with green.

★   ★   ★

[*In 1841 Georgiana, trudging from Spencer Street to Russell Street (then a name only), covered five blocks before she came to Swanston Street, and in that space measured, east to west, all the town there was. Her most difficult passage would be across Elizabeth Street, once a tributary to the Yarra, and, during bad weather, unfordable, except high up along the ridge of Lonsdale Street. Another thoroughfare, baulked at one end by thick forest, had become crooked through recoil, losing its likeness to a road, so much, as to necessitate the use of a board inscribed—*

THIS IS GREAT BOURKE STREET EAST

On the north, the occupied part of the settlement began to thin away towards Lonsdale Street, and, six blocks south, wilted again to Flinders Street. Here a few houses stayed, fastened to the first firm ground emergent from the river; beyond them, all was bog, a number of planks set end to end showing the way to the punt on the Yarra.]

[*1841*]
Mrs Thomson, the clergyman's wife, is a niece of Spengler, curator of the Museum of Stockholm; her extra names are Adelaide Zélee— or, as she expresses it: "My letters are Alpha and Omega." She possesses two chalk drawings by Vandyck: "A Lady of the Howard Family", and "A Cavalier", both being preliminary sketches for portraitures in oil. Mrs Thomson teaches, and has initiated a Dorcas Society. I have presented to her my set of *Colonial School Lessons*, also my Abacus, and clock-face with cardboard hands.

SUPPLEMENT

Where now stands Hawthorn Bridge and the Punt Hotel, was formerly a road leading to Palmer's Punt, for crossing the Yarra eastward. The nearest house to "Mayfield", southward, was that of Mr Westgarth, in what is now "Menteith Place", Erwin Street. At this time, "Northumberland House"—now a ruin in Flinders Street (between Stephen and Russell streets)—was a cottage of some pretensions. [*Stephen Street is now Exhibition Street.*] I was told that, in earlier days, the whole population of the settlement, about fifteen persons, had assembled there to drink tea. At the time of my arrival it was occupied by P. W. Welsh and it was there I made my *début*, at a dinner given in honour of P. W. W.'s sister, after her recent marriage with Mr George Smythe [*Mrs Captain Lonsdale's brother, known among the early settlers as "Long Smythe", on account of his height*].

[*A top-sawyer in finance until his crash in '43, "Paddy" Welsh was the unprincipled principal director of the Port Phillip Bank. Anthony Beale mentions P. W. W.'s Flinders Street dwelling, but calls it "Yarra Yarra Cottage", not "Northumberland House". Beale matches "Paddy" against Dickens's "Arthur Gride". "I could see but little in Mr Welsh to make me believe he was any other than a grasping selfish creature." The old devil charged Anthony 2½ per cent for cashing a Launceston £5 note. Welsh was trustee of Batman's estate.*]

After dinner, Mr Meek drove some of us home in his trap: a fearful experience—the horse sent at top-speed through the worst country in the world. At one minute we were completely off the ground, at the next, suddenly down again—gutters, three or four feet deep, and, everywhere, jagged tree-stumps interspersed with boulders!

[*Describing Port Phillip, a couple of years earlier, Edmund Finn gives a list of "six shoemakers, two saddlers, three bakers, four butchers, three tailors—and oh—happy land, Australia Felix in reality! only one blessed limb of the law, bearing the unprofessional name of* MEEK". *William Meek, first attorney in the settlement, was a gentleman who lived above the mildness of his name. He braved Judge Willis, and, driving at mid-*

night across canyons in Collins Street, woke, not only echoes, but all the goats and blackfellows that hung about the place. Dr Thomas said Meek showed his beaver hat, with a hole over the band, the hole being made by the passage of a bullet fired by Barry Cotter, wide of Mr Arden, in 1838.

N.B.—Meek and Sams (Sheriff of Launceston) were seconds in a duel between Cotter and Arden].

Moonlight nights gave occasion for tea-drinking, and evening parties to which (since no *trottoir* existed) ladies walked in their husband's Wellingtons over their dress-shoes. During "Dark Moon" a lantern used to be carried in advance by a servant, or one of the gentlemen. Even so late as 1850, Bishop Perry's literary butler used to precede his master, on his return from St Peter's to Jolimont (after Sunday evening service), with a lantern-and-candle.

[*1841*]
Potatoes at this time cannot be had for less than 6d. per lb.; carrots, turnips, onions, etc., are brought across from Van Diemen's Land [*called after Anthony Van Diemen, Governor-General of the Dutch East Indies, but changed to Tasmania in '55 and '56*] and cabbages, grown here, cost 9d. for a very small one. Bream is the only fish I have yet seen. A fisherman comes around occasionally with a basket of these which he takes in the salt-water river.

Water is conveyed from the Yarra in a large barrel mounted on a dray. These loads cost from seven to fifteen shillings, barely enough for a week's supply.

[*Yarra Yarra: "Flowing Flowing". Among the natives, things of a rippling character were indicated by the use of the word "Yarra" in its various modifications. The tide rolling up on the beach became "Yarrain", the beard, "Yarragondook". A modern Australian cricketer, bowling a deceptive ball, could be explained in aboriginal parlance by the following sentence: "Mine tinkit that p'feller Grimmett gibbit a 'Yarragoogly', boss!" Some authorities say "Yarra" is the blackfellow word for river, in which case it carries no distinction, paralleling the way of a child who names a horse, "horse". During the pre-Yan-Yean era, water-cart*]

31

owners grew rich, carriers alone earning their £2 and £3 a week. As a boy, my father enjoyed shaft-rides to a station on the river called "The Pumps", so that in after years he was able to entertain us with descriptions of horses dragging casks upon wheels along wooden platforms, of clanking pistons, and of conversations which had to be shouted on account of noisy machines. Pump-proprietors charged 5s. weekly for the use of their instruments, and most proprietors had at least six customers each per day. This water-station was situated on the northern bank of the Yarra, close against the junction of Elizabeth and Flinders streets, where a natural reef, which had been added to by Lonsdale, formed a dam, and the stream preserved its clarity, unspoiled by tides from the bay. When the time came for a change to the pipe system, pump-gentlemen organized against the Yan-Yean, but were only able to cumber the way. Horne was a strong protagonist for the innovation, while Dr Wilkie ranged on the opposite side.

At a public meeting, held at the "Lamb Inn", 25th May 1840, and presided over by the Rev. James Clow, a resolution was moved by Mr A. M. McCrae, seconded by Mr W. Meek: "That, for the purposes of affording a better and cheaper supply of water to this town, a joint stock company be formed, intituled 'The Melbourne Water Works Company'; the capital whereof shall consist of £20,000, to be raised in 2000 shares of £10 each." A provisional committee was nominated, but nothing practical resulted, and the business fizzled out.]

Fortune-du-pot dinners, which were then the vogue, tried my patience and ingenuity. Mutton and beef were to be had at moderate prices, but vegetables and fruit were costly, having to be imported from Launceston. Poultry was exceedingly scarce, and at exorbitant prices. My ever-ready help was Mrs Howe, our baker's wife. Mrs Howe had been a housekeeper in Yorkshire, and, ordinarily, she used to particularize in beef-steak puddings; but when her "big boy" shot a spur-winged plover on the swamp, she would be "brought to table of a game-pie" (Captain Fyans's phrase)—according to Mr McCrae's wish. (The beef-steak puddings cost 5s. each, the pies 7s.) Tarts were out of the question, but, as Ellen always had capital soup ready, we managed pretty well. How she managed to cook at the clumsy fire-hole in the kitchen-hut was a mystery!

[*Note. The Howes lived at a place in Queen Street, next to the Wesleyan Chapel; today, the Bank of Australasia occupies the site of the chapel.*]

[*1841*]
Sold my staircase-carpeting brass rods and eyes to the Port Phillip Club for £9—just what they cost in London. They offer me £26 for my dining-table, and Mr McCrae thinks the Singapore one might do us in the meantime. But I'm resolved not to give up my five-leaved table. Thomas and Stribling were engaged at the current wage to build the house. Thomas, a married man, with three children. Stribling, single, a carpenter.

[*Mr McCrae was vice-president of the P.P.C., which seems to have been a humdrum institution although it was lodged in the most comfortable quarters in Melbourne: once, the home of John Hodgson, candidate for the first Victorian Legislative Council and member of the Goldfields Commission in '55. The building, in Flinders Street, still survives, under the name of the Port Phillip Club Hotel. Horne speaks of Port Phillip Club members in a strain of sarcasm: "Impersonators of the tradition of fine old English gentlemen, buttoned up in black, and blue, and drab; drinking their decanter of port on the hottest days with abnormal dignity. This small party has been broken up: the natural youth of the colonies is struggling for development——" and so forth. Another association, of later date, announced in its prospectus the comforts of an English club. "The plan is as liberal as can be wished: intelligence and gentlemanly bearing being the only test."*]

Thermometer readings were posted up three times daily at Flagstaff Hill, and, on Sundays, it became a habit with the better sort of people to go there in parties, where they could study the lists of ships that had come in, or perhaps, stretcht on the sward, recognize the vessels themselves at anchor in the bay.

* * *

APRIL

April 6th   The *Eagle* sailed with our letters for England.
   8th   Rain falling in torrents.

9th Willie laid up with fever, also Jenny. Dr McCrae attending them during the day.

MAY

May 3rd Rode out to fix the site for our house at Carroncarrondall.

5th Not well. Fainted at tea time.

9th Dr McCrae to dinner. I fainted in the evening.

11th Busy drawing the plan and elevation of our house.

15th Mr Montgomery to dinner.

16th Mr Elliot Heriot to dinner. During his visit a gale came on with deluging rain which rendered the flat impassable on foot, so that I had to improvise a bed for our guest in the sitting-room.

22nd A *triste* visit from Agnes McCrae. "All is not gold that glisters." Mr Highett and Mr Ephraim Howe to dinner.

23rd Tremendous showers of rain. Elizabeth Locke, Mrs Sconce's servant, baptized by the Rev. James Forbes.

30th A shock of earthquake, while we were in church, made the Rev. Mr Thomson pause in the prayers. The sensation was like when the chain cable runs down and the ship gives a jump. Mr McCrae and Dr McCrae felt the shock while they were walking at Dandenong at the same hour.

JUNE

June 3rd The *Duchess of Sutherland* arrived. Captain McCrae landed in the evening and visited us.

4th Dr McCrae, Agnes, Thomas Anne [*Agnes, the doctor's wife; Thomas Anne, the doctor's sister*], and I went on board the ship to pay our return-calls to Mrs McCrae. Mrs Thomas, not approving of Mrs M. (tho' of good yeoman ancestry) stayed away. We brought back with us the Captain's children, Maggie, George, and Aleck.

[*Dr McCrae was the son, and Thomas Anne was the daughter, of William Gordon McCrae, of Westbrook, near Edinburgh, Scotland. The doctor, who had been surgeon in the 5th Dragoon Guards, the Inniskillings, arrived in Australia by the "Midlothian" (Captain Morrison): the first ship to come direct to Melbourne.*]

5th Dined at Dr McCrae's, with Captain McCrae and Elliot Heriot.

8th Little Maggie went home to her mama.

10th Mr McCrae boarded the *Freshfield*, and hired Ellen Hume as cook, on the recommendation of the ship's doctor. Ellen is from Donegal, and lived in Glasgow with a Mrs Campbell.

11th Mrs Sconce gave birth to a daughter.

12th Dinner at Dr McCrae's, and musical evening.

24th Mr McCrae engaged Robert Lowry, also passenger on the *Freshfield*, as our house-servant.

27th Mr Deane sent us a native turkey, and invited himself to dine with us. In the evening, another present—a kangaroo tail—arrived from Captain Reid.

28th Mr John Reeve, from Gippsland, came to early dinner. As he is interested in art, I had great pleasure in showing him my prints and paintings.

[*Just about the time that the Port Albert Company was being established, John Reeve arrived from England, and, probably backed by Wentworth, became a landholder to the extent of five or six thousand acres of riverside property in Gippsland. Since his special survey existed at a fair distance from the Alberton settlement, Reeve profited nothing in the sale of land conducted 26th July 1843, and was satisfied with letting small farms, at Taradale, "near Port Albert". (Résumé of portion of an article by A. W. Greig, Esq.)*]

30th Went to town. Met Captain and Mrs Bunbury, and she returned with me to taste the kangaroo soup. We both agreed that, *to our taste*, ox-tail is a superior article. Mr Montgomery, Lauchlan Mackinnon, and the Rev. James Clow to dinner.

JULY

July 1st Took the boys down early to Dr Thomas's to spend the day, as Jane and Ellen wish to carry out a thorough cleaning and re-arrangement of the furniture.

2nd Mr and Mrs George Smythe to dinner.

5th Mr Wentworth, from Vaucluse; P. W. Welsh and Mrs Meek to dinner.

[*William Charles Wentworth: a friend of the "emancipists", and the destroyer of military absolutism. Still in his prime at forty-eight.*]

8th A lovely morning. Walked to Newtown [*now Collingwood*] and had luncheon with Mrs Sconce, and, afterwards, called on Mrs Woolley, Mrs G. Smythe, and Mrs McLachlan.

9th Pouring rain: a day of rest and needlework. Willie and Farquhar have severe colds.

Sunday, 11th Captain and Mrs Bunbury came to luncheon. In the afternoon we all went to church to meet the Sconces; I stood proxy for Miss Limond as godmother to Madeline Sconce.

12th Robert Lowry left with a load of timber, from Mr Kemmis, for Thomas and Stribling to put up huts for themselves, and a stable for the horses.

13th Unpacked the boys' schoolbooks.

14th Mr Jacob Hagon came to say good-bye as he is going back to Adelaide.

15th Mr Samuel Raymond, Mr Quarry, and Dr McCrae to dinner.

[*Samuel Raymond, one of the two deputy sheriffs of the province, arrived from Sydney with Judge Willis. He was a barrister, whose* bienséance *seemed remarkable beside the roughness of his superior on the bench. His father was James Raymond, Post Master General of New South Wales. George Gordon McCrae married this Raymond's niece, Augusta Helen Brown.*]

17th A damp, misty day. Dr Thomas, Mr Dunbar, Mr Barber, and Mr Bland to dinner. The *Royal Saxon* arrived from Cork with emigrants. The *England*, from Liverpool, and two other vessels came in today.

18th Advanced Lowry £1 to buy a pair of boots.

19th The new dray, six working-bullocks, and their driver, Henry Blackford, arrived. Mr Woolley's servant remained to witness the agreement "for three months, at the rate of £52 per annum".

[*Mr Woolley might be brother to that splendid scholar, Dr Woolley of the Sydney University.*]

20th Mrs Bunbury sent back the chairs and other things I lent her, as they are removing to "Stanney" on the Darebin Creek.

21st Ice, a quarter of an inch thick, on all the puddles. Walked to Dr Myer's, and called on Mrs Forbes.

22nd A black frost, which became intense at night. Thermometer down to 35°.

23rd Frank Cobham came to breakfast, just down from the Sydney-side. It's five years since I last saw him and he has grown quite manly. The boys went to bid the Bunburys good-bye. The pole of our new dray and the shafters' yokes broke in getting through the swamp.

[*The roads were terrible. In the main street of Kilmore, a bullock sank out of sight, and, subsequently, it is said, a trooper swimming his mare through the mud staked her on the animal's horns so severely she had to be shot. A friend of Georgiana's wrote of similar adventures: "The draymen were now occupied in marking trees to guide them to the spot next summer, when they might be able to dig out the dray"; following which he describes a box of books and clothes being opened "after a month embedded in mud, and three days under the water of a creek".*]

24th Jeanie McCrae three years old today. The boys spent the day at Dr McCrae's with her. In the afternoon, we rode out to "Mayfield", and to Mr Manton's, where "Lotus", my mare, in backing just after I had mounted, disarranged the sheeps' shank bordering of the flower-bed.

[*Frederick Manton (of Manton and Company): owner of the "Vesta", maid-of-all-work steamer on the Yarra. This iron vessel towed wind-jammers up or down the river, giving George McCrae the pleasant occupation of counting masts across the trees, so that he might say to his mamma, "'Tis a barque", or "a square-rigged ship", whatever she happened to be. Besides her everyday "grind", the Manton boat had*] *special moments, such as carrying people to the races, and wearing flags like flowers, while the passengers danced to Tickel and Milstead's band.*]

Mr Highett, Mr McLaren, Mr Gore, and J. B. Were came to dinner. [*Jonathan Binns Were: a merchant and honorary magistrate; he was once, spitefully, committed for contempt of court by John Walpole Willis, the first resident judge for the district of Port Phillip.*] A fearfully stormy night with deluging rain.

25th Dr Myer and Mr Ephraim Howe to see us. Mr Ballingall to dinner. Mr McLure sent an excuse, he being too ill to leave his room.

26th A cold rainy day. Minifie's hut looking most miserable amidst the dubs.

27th Mrs Thomas and Thomas Anne came to see me and to tell me of a remarkable dream and its fulfilment. At breakfast she told David she had dreamt that two Scots cousins of his had arrived. After the doctor had gone out, a Mr Lawlor called and announced himself as a Scots cousin—husband of Ann Thomas, of Edinburgh; so, of course, Mrs Thomas saw him, and learnt that they have been four months on their way thus far towards New Zealand to their purchased land, and Mrs Lawlor was confined only a fortnight since.

28th George struck his forehead and fell back from the violence of the shock.

29th Met Mr and Mrs Lawlor at Dr Thomas's, also Mrs Meek and her two little boys, just arrived from England per *Stratheden*; Mr Goldsmith, Trewallan, Mr Jamieson [*who, in 1839, travelled overland from Port Phillip to Sydney, reversing the process which usually obtained*], Mr Mollison [*an overlander, more famous than Jamieson, who travelled with numerous flocks and herds, and brought upwards of fifty servants to take charge of them: an extremely wealthy man, regardful of appearances*], and Dr McCrae to dinner.

30th Rode out to Mr Hodgson's at "Studley". Returning, was caught in a heavy storm of thunder and lightning, and wind and rain, which continued all night long.

[*On 11th September 1851 John Hodgson stood for the first Victorian Legislative Council, but lost to Westgarth, O'Shanassy, and Johnston, who pulled as indicated; however, on the enlargement of the council two years later, he secured a seat.*]

31st A fine, calm, springlike morning. Dr Thomson, from Geelong, came to dine with us, also Dr and Mrs Thomas.

[*Dr Alexander Thomson shipped the first cattle for Port Phillip in 1835. The doctor himself, accompanied by his family, arrived in March 1836. He was the* soi-disant *catechist of the Batman régime, and we imagine him* en plein air *belted and buckled, making doxological noises, three beats ahead of a choir reluctant to sing.*]

AUGUST

August 1st Dr Nicholson will allow Mr McCrae to include the reserve for a road to a future bridge within the fencing of our acres. Learnt that Harry, the bullock-driver, had betted £3 on the fight that came off today during the time of morning service! [*A Sunday prize-fight became an ordinary affair, so that those not interested in the "Book" found solace in the "Ring".*]

2nd Mr McLure, the boys' tutor (that is to be), came to dine with us. He appears to be fond of young children and has a pleasant way with them. In the evening, an exciting scene took place between Parson Thomson, Sandy Hunter [*of Devil's River*], young Patterson, and young Kennedy—the parson armed with a long pole, and the youths with palings driving intruders out of the cabbage-garden.

3rd Mr Lawlor came to have a long talk with me.

4th Dr McCrae completes his thirty-fifth year.

5th Incessant rain. Grievous for the emigrants camped in miserable thin tents exposed to the south-west wind, while the flats are dotted all over with pools of water. Yesterday, a woman drowned herself in the river, from sheer despair.

6th Went to the bank for my half-year's pay; quite knocked up on my return from wading through the mud; and my boots—*abîmés*.

7th Wrote letters for England. Mr and Mrs Browne and Mr Lawlor to dinner. Charmed with Mr B.'s description of the Sandwich Islands.

8th Mr Goldsmith [*of Maiden Hills*] and Mr Browne to dinner.

[*Octavius Browne: head of a well-known counting-house, within which, on 12th March 1851, twenty of the principal merchants assembled and passed a resolution recommending the establishment of a Melbourne chamber of commerce.—Garryowen.*]

9th Captain Bunbury and Dr Myer to luncheon.

10th Mr Wentworth called to say good-bye as he was leaving for Sydney. Mr Highett and his brother John came to dinner.

11th Mr Horsman to dinner. Willie not well. The *Adelaide* sailed with our letters.

12th A fine frosty morning. The foundation walls of our house at "Mayfield" duly laid.

13th Busy making suits of tartan for the boys.

14th The boys suffering from the effects of their damp room. Mr Vignolles, Mr Rawson, and Mr O. Browne to dinner.

[*This Vignolles was a mischievous scapegrace who lived in officers' quarters at the west end of Bourke Street. Just at present, he would be feeling disgruntled, on account of having lost a libel action against Johnnie Wood.*]

15th Dr Myer brought news that Baby Bunbury is very ill, at Darebin, from teething.

16th Dr Thomas came to see the boys.

[*David John Thomas, M.R.C.S., L.S.A., a Welshman, arrived at Melbourne in 1839. He married Thomas Anne McCrae's sister*, and thus became uncle to George Gordon McCrae. Dr Thomas was kind and hearty. Money being no object to him, it would accidentally fall into his pocket and roll out again. He helped the poor and set unadvertized examples for the rich, letting his light so shine across the forties that stories of his goodness are perpetuated yet.*

Dr G. T. Howard, writing in the "Medical Journal of Australia", 17th March 1934, says of him: "During the intermediate period Thomas was the undoubted leader of the profession. . . . In 1840, at the age of twenty-eight, with his colleagues Wilkie, Myer, and Mullane, he established a stop-gap general hospital in Bourke Street West, which

---

* Margaret Forbes McCrae.

THE SLOOP *JEMIMA*, FOR ARTHUR'S SEAT FROM MELBOURNE
From a pen-drawing by George Gordon McCrae

THE COURSE OF THE *ARGYLE* AS
FAR AS MADEIRA AND THE
CONTINUATION OF HER VOYAGE
TO PORT PHILLIP
From maps drawn by Georgiana

DR FARQUHAR McCRAE'S HOUSE IN BOURKE STREET, MELBOURNE, AS IT APPEARED IN JULY 1905

"The first roof under which we slept in Australia, 1 March 1841."

carried on until the opening of the Melbourne Hospital in 1848. In August 1847 he administered ether (the first to do so in Victoria), and then amputated an arm under dramatic circumstances. He was also one of the first to administer chloroform." He was surgeon to the Melbourne Hospital at the date of its commencement, and, except for a break of six years dating from 1853, he kept this position until his death. The six years mentioned were spent in Europe during which time he acquired "the extra qualifications of F.R.C.S. (England), and M.D. (St Andrews). In 1865, he became president of the Medical Society of Victoria, and, after a very full and useful life, died suddenly in 1871."

"Robin" Russell's account of Dr Thomas's arrival at Port Phillip reads like the scenario for a cinematograph play. He said Thomas was overturned coming ashore from the "Louisa Campbell", and that he swam to save his life. Soaked to the skin, there was nothing the doctor could do except wander about the scrub looking for the cottage by the Yarra where Russell used to live. At last, when he reached R.R.'s gate—in the pitchdark night—a dog seized him by the breeches, but he escaped into the surveyor's skiff, and, after shooting the Falls, continued down the river till he boated oars opposite Fawkner's hotel. Thomas himself told this story, stuttering delightfully, as he always did.]

17th Pouring rain. Completed the tartan suits.

20th Walked to Spence's to buy bargains of drapery brought from his old shop at Edinburgh. The footpaths were terrible, and the road, all the way, like a bullock-yard.

21st Poor Baby Bunbury past recovery.

No Date. One day I perceived Major St John riding across the flat towards "Argyle Cottage" with what, at first sight, appeared to be a large green parrot held hawkwise on his wrist. On his arrival at the gate, the major flourished a fine full-grown Cos lettuce in his hand, exclaiming: "One of the first of the kind raised in Port Phillip!"— the lettuce, not inferior to a prime Covent Garden specimen, bound round the middle with a band of grass. A most acceptable present, recalling the green stuff we had been accustomed to have in profusion at Stockwell.

[*Major St John was a town magistrate who sold justice to the highest bidder, so, no doubt, the full-grown Cos lettuce represented a fine—let*

41

E

off—for someone drunk and disorderly. An insolent blusterer in court, the major has been ironically explained by his contemporary, Garryowen, when he said of him, "The probability is that, though his virtues were few, his vices were not numberless." Yet in '42 he rode alone through the middle of a hostile mob with stones and cudgels going. "A man aimed a tremendous blow at the magistrate, whereupon the latter took the fellow near the butt end of the ear with the hammer of his riding-whip and floored him. The pluck and promptitude of the act, and a few conciliatory words, caused the assemblage to quietly disperse."—Facts and quotations from "The Chronicles of Early Melbourne". Major St John, accused of bribery and corruption by Fawkner, gave up his position of Commissioner of Crown Lands for the County of Bourke, thus anticipating his departure from the colony in the ship "Stag" for England, from whence he never returned. The following are the words used by Fawkner in his indictment of St John: "He takes bribes from all conditions of men—from the half-dozen eggs, or the pound of butter, up to a cow or a calf, horses, grog, wines, champagne, brandy, and gin."]

24th The boys and I went to the burying-ground, to meet the Bunburys who came in their spring-cart with dear little Frankie's coffin. After the burial, the Bunburys drove up to "Stanney", and the Rev. Mr Thomson accompanied us home and stayed to early dinner. Dr McCrae and Agnes came in the evening. Mrs Myer gave birth to a son—her first child.

25th Mrs and Miss Macarthur, Mrs Thomas, James Grahame [*Isaac Selby describes James Grahame as "The merchant politician . . . greater than Bismarck"*] and Thomas Anne took me for a long walk in the bush. [*Mrs and Miss Macarthur, wife and daughter of Mr D. C. Macarthur, who, a year ago, minus three days, had opened a branch of the Bank of Australasia in a cottage at Little Collins Street.*]

26th Hot wind. The boys and I walked to town.

27th Mr McLeod and Thomas Anne to dinner. At night, squalls of wind and rain.

28th Dr McCrae looking ghastly. Thermometer 48°, while yesterday it was up to 65°. A package of vine cuttings arrived from Mr Wentworth, for planting at "Mayfield".

31st Thermometer 54°. Mr and Mrs Lawlor came to say good-bye, as they resume their voyage tomorrow.

SEPTEMBER

September 3rd Major Webb and his son to lunch; Captain Webster, Mrs Campbell, George Weir and Mr Goldsmith to dine with us.

4th Our dog "Pepper" went off (chain, collar, etc.) to hunt ducks and "soldier". Late at evening he came back, shot in the chest and head.

7th Farquhar's third birthday. Jenny McCrae came to dine with him, and Aunt Agnes gave him a beautiful copy of *Paul and Virginia*, in English, with illustrations.

8th Took the boys to see Mr George Arden's dromedaries.

[*Close to Batman's Hill, where the Spencer Street railway station now is. George Arden edited, with Tom Strode, the "Port Phillip Gazette". If it had been possible, these two would have annihilated Fawkner, as well as any other trespasser from Van Diemen's Land.*]

9th With the boys to Jolimont to sit awhile with Mrs La Trobe who gave us cakes, and claret and water. Then called at Captain Lonsdale's, and, afterwards, crossed in the punt with two black-fellows and a gin, to Sandy's great terror. Didn't find Mrs Le Souef, but Mr Le Souef [*of the Custom House, son of William Le Souef, assistant Protector of Aboriginals*] ferried us across to Flinders Street in his own boat.

[*Thereby saving the diarist her return fare, although punt-rates must have come down by that time from their original tariff of 4s. 6d. per passenger. The natives on the outward journey were exempt from payment, and on a par with Melbourne councillors, who, by virtue of an act tabled in '45, were privileged to cross the river free of toll. The Hon. R. D. Murray wrote: "Melbourne is without a bridge, and is probably destined to remain so until a governor is drowned in being ferried over." Horne compares the ferryman's charge of 4s. 6d. with the sum of three cents per mile paid by him when travelling in a barge the whole length of the Erie Canal.*]

11th Mr Bebb Morris, G. D. Mercer [*who, with some others,*]

helped towards the foundation of Jillong★ *(native word for "Cliff country"),
before government was impressed, and at a later period became manager
of the ill-fated Port Phillip Bank]*, Mr Kitsen, Mr Kersopp, and
Norman McLeod to dinner. [*Kersopp was captain of the yacht "Midge",
and, in '47, commander of the "Juno", first steam-boat to ply between
Adelaide and Melbourne. Besides this, Kersopp was one of the founders
of the Gippsland Company, which eventually became known as the Port
Alberton Company.—A. W. Grieg.*] During a heavy squall the boys'
room window was blown in, while the rain poured into the servants'
room. The parrot's cage upset, but Ellen rescued the bird from
drowning, and nailed a packing-case lid across the boys' window
for the night.

14th   Busy cutting out and making chair-covers.

15th   Mr McVittie and Frank Cobham to dinner.

18th   Still very boisterous weather.

19th   Heavy storm of thunder and lightning and rain, with a
gale of wind that made the house quiver and creak, the glasses on
the shelf ringing with every detonation—then hailstones clattering
across the roof to the terror of the children. About 4 a.m. the storm
abated.

20th   Mr Octavius Browne and Hunter Ross to dinner. [*James
Hunter Ross, Jephson Quarry's partner, an attorney, whose bark was
worse than his bite. Nevertheless, he once "called out" James Croke,
leader of the Port Phillip Bar, and would have fought, too, if Dr Black
hadn't intervened.*] Another night of fearful wind from south-west.
Sleep out of question.

23rd   Blowing strong from north. Thermometer 64°. The sky
livid. The yard of the flagstaff was unshipped today. [*The flagstaff,
on Flagstaff Hill.*]

25th   Captain Lewis, harbour-master, Neil Black, and Captain
McLachlan [*of Smeaton*] to dinner.

26th   The bullocks let into the garden at "Mayfield", and many
cauliflowers and strawberries destroyed. Harry suspected of having
done this to spite Osmond the gardener. [*The same Harry who
"betted £3 on the fight on Sunday". Perhaps Osmond was the tale-
bearer.*]

★ Geelong.

30th Mr O. Browne gave me a sitting for his portrait to send home. He is a brother of Habelot Knight Browne (*Phiz*) the artist who illustrated Dickens's works.

OCTOBER

October 1st Thunder and rain until past 5 p.m.

2nd Mr Jones Agnew Smith, John McLeod, and Mr O. Browne to dinner.

4th Martha Cummins twenty-five today. Second sitting from Mr O. Browne.

5th Mr O. Browne to breakfast. Afterwards, a most satisfactory three hours' sitting.

7th Mr Browne rode with us to "Mayfield"; the workmen were raising the rooftree—the chimneys, within four feet of their full height. Didn't return till past seven. Mr McCrae pressed Mr B. to take "pot luck" with us; and very bad luck it was. Mr Browne began, like a farmer, drinking his soup with great *éclaboussement*, until he tasted it burnt, when he sent it away. Being half famished, I made my own share palatable with wine.

8th Busy writing letters for Sydney.

9th Lovely morning. Saw the smoke from the steamer at Cole's Wharf, and the boys mounted towels on tall sticks by way of farewell signals to their friend "Okitawia Paraone" (Octavius Browne) . . . New Zealanders' pronunciation.

10th Unpacked George's trowsers—the ones I had made in London; found them already two inches too short.

11th Arranging bills and inventories. Thomas Anne came to tell me that Captain Cole had offered to marry her; she seemed undecided, and was eager for advice. Harry upset our dray and broke it. Mr McLure returned the books he had borrowed, and stayed to dine with us.

[*The Honourable George Ward Cole, Commander R.N., F.R.G.S., and member of the Executive and Legislative Council: served through the Napoleonic Wars, and was wounded at New Orleans. In 1840 he arrived at Hobson's Bay in his own schooner, the "Waterlily", and, two years later, married Thomas Anne, daughter of William Gordon McCrae, of*

Westbrook, near Edinburgh, Scotland. Cole helped to found the Port Phillip Steam Navigation Company, and, interesting himself in politics, combined with Fawkner "to nullify the Port Phillip elections to the Sydney Legislative Council". He represented the first McCulloch ministry in the new council, although without office, from 1863-8.

The Chief Justice, Mr George Higinbotham, wrote of him as follows: "To one who had the privilege of intimate acquaintance with him during nearly the whole of the last twenty years of his life, no politician in recent Australian history appears to present a record of purer and more sincere patriotism, or of more unselfish and benevolent political action than Captain George Ward Cole."—Extract from Isaac Selby's "The Memorial History of Melbourne".

"Captain Cole, having decided to set up as a shipping agent and bonded-store keeper, bought the site on the north bank of the Yarra, between King and Spencer streets, afterwards known as Cole's Wharf. This quay contained a dock 45 feet by 110 feet deep; and, included in the wharfage area, was the buildings known as Cole's Bond; and others, as offices; also a gate leading into the wharf from the east.

"Here, the captain employed, as his first tally-clerk, Mr H. C. E. Childers; later on Chancellor of the Exchequer! The land occupied by the wharf, which had a frontage of 150 feet, with a depth of 350 feet, was purchased by the government in 1868 for £18,910; and, eventually, the old dock lost its identity in the wider area of Queen's Wharf."—ARGUS, 1905.]

14th Visited the Sconces. Robin to be ordained by Bishop Broughton. [*The only Bishop of Australia: consecrated 14th February 1836.*] He was eligible for a fellowship at the time of his marriage; but "fellows" must be bachelors! I feel sad at losing Lizzie.

16th Thermometer 82°. A delightful day. At dinner-time the famous "overlander", Mr Murchison, came in. A sitting from Mr Sconce: to be a present for his sister-in-law, Miss Repton.

19th Mr Sconce talked much of Sir George Gipps and his expected visit.

[*With only superficial knowledge, G. G. McCrae, the diarist's son, writes of Gipps as being "every inch a governor", while Captain Fyans, well acquainted, says "an unkindly mannered man . . . known in Spain as 'Dirty Gipps'."*

"*It is exceedingly hard that you should be cramped by the jealousy or bad feeling of Sir George Gipps in any scheme which, without implicating him, might have tended so much to the advantage of the colony. The great evil is being governed by a power at so great a distance acted upon by selfish and ignorant advice. The wonder is that the colonies prosper in spite of the Home Country."—John Richardson, 21 Fludyer Street, London, 4th August 1844, in a letter written to Andrew Murison McCrae, Port Phillip.*]

20th Another delicious day. I feel all alive!

21st Thermometer 84°. Sent Jenny Sutherland to learn dress-making from Mrs Osmond, the gardener's wife.

22nd The first *Quarterly Assembly Ball* to take place this evening. ["*The seed-bed of gentility." This Assembly Ball, run by first-class people trying to keep second-class out, precipitated a war which spread to the newspaper press. However, in the end, society sorted itself and settled down. Three years afterwards, from Van Diemen's Land, a similar cry went up for the opposite reason, viz., that Sir Eardley Wilmot was inviting well-born persons to meet the commonalty on terms that knew no difference in his house. See entry for 30th January 1844.*] Walked to the Rev. James Forbes, thence to Dr Myer's, but could not continue to Mrs Sconce's on account of the headache.

23rd After breakfast, Willie said he heard "guns making a noise!" and I knew at once that the Governor-in-Chief, Sir George Gipps, had arrived from Sydney. [*Sir George Gipps: successor to Sir Richard Bourke. He gave his casting vote for the separation of Port Phillip from Sydney.*] He crossed the river on the punt [*built from the timbers of an old ship*] and, at twelve o'clock, made his public entry into Melbourne. The sound of cheering became very loud, so that I wished to be there, but the pains in my head made it impossible.

[*To make up for Georgiana's absence, we append her son's description of Gipps's entry into Melbourne. "A straggling procession. . . . Grandest of all, not even omitting the majors and captains who rode on His Ex-cellency's staff, was the Father of Sandridge, and of Sandridge Pier, progenitor of post offices, and carrier-general of Her Majesty's mails, Mr W. Frank Evelyn Liardet. This gentleman, attired in a white cavalry uniform, and mounted on a smart little grey, shone like a glittering star. Gipps himself went, surrounded by a bodyguard of native mounted police in green and red, with spurs buckled to their bare feet. The buffoons of the company were three: one drinking out of a black bottle, another beating a pair of cymbals, and, last of all, a half-tipsy fellow with a pair of working-bullocks in bows and yokes, the heavy chain trailing behind."]*

24th Absent from church, morning and evening.

25th A letter and a parcel from Sydney, with toys for the boys and, for myself, a quaigh made from an oaken beam out of Queen Mary's room at Holyrood.

27th The Cobhams landed from the *Lysander*, but cannot get their luggage for a day or two, so Mrs Thomas fitted a dress of hers for Mamie. I gave Lizzie my Chellé dress, and my wedding-shoes, to enable her to go to the ball in honour of the Governor, at the Criterion, this evening. Went to the ball, but not to dance. Put on my best black satin dress, and a bit of ivy in my hair, so that I felt myself *comme il faut*.

Quite a clan gathering. Dr McCrae, with Agnes; Dr Thomas, with Margaret; Captain Cole, and Thomas Anne; Lizzie and Mamie Cobham; Captain, and Mrs Bunbury; Mr and Mrs Sconce, and ourselves. Robin tripping it featly for the last time, as, after ordination, it's not orthodox to dance. [*Robin (Robert Sconce Knox): a college chum of Napier's at Oxford, afterwards ordained by Bishop Broughton, and had the living of Penrith, New South Wales. Subsequently he joined the Church of Rome and studied for the bar. He died of scarlet fever, leaving his wife and three children.*] During the evening I was introduced to Mr Redmond Barry [*Not yet the judge, who, in '55, acquitted the Ballarat rebels. First Chancellor of Melbourne University. Prior to the present date, he had formed one of the sub-committee of three appointed by the Separation Association, the two others being A. M. McCrae and J. B. Were.*], Dr and Mrs J. F. Palmer [*The Doctor: later on, Sir James Frederick Palmer, Mayor of Melbourne, and Speaker of the first Victorian Legislative Council. Henry Gyles Turner allows him to have had "a portly presence and dignified demeanour", but not much else. Perhaps the dignified deamour was a lateral inheritance from his grand-uncle, Sir Joshua Reynolds.*], the Hon. Mr and Mrs Murray, Aberdone, Mr and Mrs James Smith, and all the *élite.* [*Mr James Smith, Batman's appointed catechist, drew the breath of life so sibilantly that Port Phillipians said he "Jemmy-whistled" through the prayers. He was perplexed always, and if ever he arrived at a moment's decision, he rescinded it and began the thing over again. When the Rev. W. Waterfield reached the settlement in 1838, "Jemmy Whistle" handed over the church service to his care. Williams, the auctioneer, in his "Patriot" advertisement, 17th February 1840, speaks of "Mr Smith's fine sloping garden in Collins Street, the admiration of all strangers arriving from the seaward; and the view from that gentleman's veranda is not to be surpassed in Melbourne." Edmund Finn less respectfully reports: "Mr James Smith was berthed cosily, like an old hen, on the south side of Collins Street West."*] The Bunburys, Sconces, and ourselves formed a snug little supper-party, as on board the *Argyle.* The supper was served in a temporary wooden room at the back of the Criterion. We were near enough to hear Sir George Gipps's speech . . . with its *finale* "Advance Australia!"

[*During the course of this banquet, Mr La Trobe made use of that impolitic expression which has been held against him ever since. Bowing to the Governor, he remarked: "I shall have much pleasure in playing second fiddle to any tune you choose." Not long afterwards, Fawkner dealt with La Trobe, scathingly, in the Council. He said: "The whole tissue of the Superintendent's misrule of the province has been one texture. It has one aim: to please the 'First Fiddle'——never regarding the people who pay the fiddlers." La Trobe had the* politesse *of a flatterer, differing from his secretary, Edward Bell, who was a ruthlessly truthful young man. In order to bring home this trait in the Superintendent's character, besides the fiddle story, there is that revelational one Fyans used to tell: of how the narrator and La Trobe, being at breakfast one morning, heard footsteps outside; whereupon La Trobe exclaimed: "Here comes that infernal old rip!" and continued straight on as the visitor entered, "How are you, doctor? Sit down and partake of something; we are glad to see you," emphasizing the whole with a hearty shake of the hand. By the instances just given, we may appraise the exquisite balance of Washington Irving's*

49

opinion when he describes the future governor as being "an Englishman by birth, but descended of foreign stock . . . who had all the buoyancy and 'accommodating' spirit of a native of the Continent." See entry of 3rd July 1843.]

28th The Cobhams came to see the boys. Heard the guns, announcing the departure of the Governor per *Sea-Horse* [*pioneer boat of Ben Boyd's line of steamers, running between Sydney and Port Phillip*].

30th Sitting from Mr Sconce. Likeness considered most successful.

31st A clan-gathering at church.

NOVEMBER

November 1st A fine clear day. Completed my small needlework.

2nd Hot wind—then thunder with rain. At noon thermometer 85°, and all night at 72°. The closeness of the house and the heat of its wooden walls quite stifling.

3rd Thermometer 75°. Lizzie Cobham and Thomas Anne; also Mr Heriot, and his new-arrived brother, Ancrum Heriot; and young Baillie Polkemmet to dinner.

4th Final sitting from Mr Sconce, as Mrs Sconce won't allow me to put another touch to the picture, which she considers "perfect", and, as I have painted it *con amore*, I feel pretty well satisfied.

10th Mrs Sophia Were, Rev. Yelverton Wilson, C. H. Mc-Knight, Mrs Lyon Campbell [*Bullarook and Campbellfield*], and Mr A. L. Thompson to see me.

12th Captain Pearson, Dr Stewart, George Were, and Mr Dunsford to dinner.

15th Hot wind. Thermometer 85°. Busy writing home. The horse in Pickett's water-cart bolted past the house, with the hose down behind . . . and the water dashing out in the middle of the street. [*No doubt the fault of the driver . . . a frequenter of the "Highland-man Hotel". See entry of 3rd December of this year.*]

17th Went early to Mr Sconce's; met Mr La Trobe there. Mr McCrae exchanged my pony "Lotus" for Mr Highett's "Don

Quixote", formerly belonging to Mrs Yeo, in Van Diemen's Land, where she used to follow the hounds on "Don Q."—a descendant of "Eclipse", and like the painting of him. [*Just by way of a wet blanket, Caveat Emptor, Gent., in his book of "The Horse", says it was reported that the celebrated "Eclipse" was a roarer.*] The Sconces must leave for Sydney tomorrow.

19th The "Bizzwizzes" (cicadae) making a deafening noise in the gum-trees. George brought two into the house to add to the racket. Went, *en masse*, on board the *Aphrasia*, to bid good-bye to Robin and Lizzie Sconce.

20th Thermometer, at noon, 78°. Jane Shanks and Farquhar spent the day at Newtown.

23rd Captain Fyans and Mr Clark, nephew of Talbot de Mala-hide, to dinner. In the evening, Mrs Thomas, Lizzie, and Thomas Anne to tea: the captain unaware of a rival in the field. [*Was Fyans an aspirant for the hand of Thomas Anne?*]

24th James Grahame and Mrs Alfred Langhorne to dinner. [*According to Westgarth, Mrs Alfred Langhorne was "one of the most beautiful young women in early Melbourne". Her husband was Lonsdale's nephew.*] Mrs L., under pretence that her hair was ruffled, came to my room, where she occupied the looking-glass for ten minutes at least, more *pour s'admirer* than for anything else I could see! [*A double meaning: Mrs Langhorne had cut off Mrs McCrae's share of the mirror.*]

26th After an early dinner, Mr McCrae started off with Tom Clark on a shooting expedition.

27th The boys accompanied me to Aunt Maggie's. Heard from her of Thomas Anne's deadly quarrel with Dr McCrae.

Sunday, 28th Neither Dr McCrae, nor Agnes, at church.

30th Thomas Anne came to spend the day, and told me her griefs. . . . Sandy five years old today.

Mr McCrae dined at the club. Thermometer 74° with hot wind. Heard distant rolling thunder, or noise underground.

DECEMBER

December 1st First anniversary of Margaret's marriage with Dr Thomas. Mr John Mundy (from Hobart) to tea.

2nd Lizzie Cobham came to stay with us. Mr McCrae brought Mark Nicholson, a cousin of Dr Cobham's [*and future M.L.C.*] to dinner. I noticed that Mark and Lizzie met as if they had often seen each other elsewhere; wagered Mr McCrae a pair of white gloves that it would be a match, but he pooh-poohed the idea. [*Nicholson occupied Garvoc, in the western district, Panmure, and Cudgee, stretching out so far as Craigieburn. Then, about '49, he bought Wangoom from Manning brothers.*]

3rd Sandy crying for a glass of water, and not a drop to be had . . . Mr McCrae tells me he saw the driver of the [*water*] cart outside Jemmy Connell's, at twelve o'clock, and then, again, between two and three. [*Jemmy Connell's: Highlandman Hotel.*] Thomas Anne disposed to take my advice, i.e. to accept Captain Cole's offer.

4th Thermometer 75°. Thomas and Stribling admit their inability to have the house ready before two or three weeks to come.

6th A letter from Miss Quarry, per *Brankenmoore*, recommending the bearer, Miss Julia Gavan, to our good offices and protection; she and her sister wish to be employed as governesses.

7th Wrote to Miss Julia Gavan, inviting her to come to us until she can find a suitable situation. Mrs Montgomery has engaged Miss Anne; and Miss Emily is engaged by the Thomases at Heidelberg.

9th Lizzie, the boys, and I spent an hour in Mr Carfrae's shop inspecting the fine books brought by him from Edinburgh. Saw Mr Fawkner traipse into the street.

[*If Fawkner was not the founder of Melbourne, he was, at least, the father of our Press. His first paper, the "Melbourne Advertiser" (a manuscript production), came out once a week. The issue was limited to twelve one-shilling copies, each copy being contributed to solely by himself, and written with his own hand. A thirteenth number, for free reading in the tap-room of his hotel, was kept on a shelf, in a window, where the light was good.*]

10th Farquhar suffering from an eruption on his face . . . Dr Thomas tells me it is called, in colonial talk, "Dibble-dibble"—a kind of confluent pock—much uglier, and more offensive, even than smallpox. Cloths wetted with diluted chloride of lime must be kept constantly on the child's face to prevent the pock from spreading.

11th Thomas Anne has accepted Captain Cole's offer. Thermometer 80°. She and all the clan go tonight to Mr D. C. Macarthur's ball. Heard of the death of a son of Gordon of Cairnbuly. Had I known the poor fellow came from Sydney among utter strangers his father's son should have had proper attention. Captain Smith of the *Brankenmoore* came early with Miss Julia Gavan. Thermometer 80°, and, in the evening, it rose to 95° with not a breath of air stirring.

13th I engaged the two front rooms at Landall's for one month, at £1 per week, for Jane and the children to sleep there. In the evening, removed my own particular luggage and slept at Landall's.

[*Although the diarist writes this name Landall, my father's manuscript shows it everywhere spelt Landells. If the latter form is correct, the man concerned might be the same who started out second in command of Burke's exploring expedition. To justify the assumption I have only knowledge that this particular Landells was travel-mad, and constantly talked to my little-boy father about Marco Polo and Bruce.*]

14th Captain Cole called *en qualité de beaufrère futur.*

15th Thermometer 103°. By advice of Captain McLachlan, who lived in Sicily with his regiment, I rolled myself in a blanket and lay outside my bed, to keep cool, until 4 p.m., when a furious storm of wind and rain cooled the air most rapidly.

16th A fine fresh morning. Thermometer 72°. Sponged the boys with vinegar and water. Farquhar's face better.

17th Captain Cole sent invitations to everybody to attend his picnic at Brighton Beach on Tuesday next. . . . The match now openly talked of in town.

18th, 19th——

20th Looking out things for Thomas Anne's *trousseau*, since the captain begs her to name an early day for their wedding.

21st Dr and Mrs Myer arrived in their carriage to take me to the picnic, but, on account of the wild-appearing sky, I elected to stay at home, and it was well I did, because at three o'clock a southerly gale sprang up, which continued until five, with such hurricane force that the gentlemen of the party had to hold on to the tent with all their might to keep the canvas from being blown away. Returning at dusk, there were upsets and bruises, even broken limbs . . . yet the Myers and our people escaped unhurt.

22nd Cutting out work, with Miss Gavan to help me, for our new house, but *je ne suis pas en train aujourd'hui!*

23rd Lizzie Cobham and I went to Mrs Thomas on purpose to consult with her about the wedding arrangements. . . . In the evening, Captain Cole: deafer than usual, and, *en conséquence*, most irascible. [*Cole broke the drum of his left ear through being stationed too close to an active 13-inch mortar, at the Baltimore fight (American War, 1814).*]

25th Christmas Day: Captain Smith came early for Miss Julia Gavan, and Lizzie Cobham went to keep her engagement at Dr McCrae's.

26th Frank Cobham returned from the bush, and I engaged Eliza Impey in Jenny Sutherland's stead.

27th Mr Archibald Cunninghame, of Caddell, to dinner. [*Archibald Cunninghame: "the horse-haired, sabled, talking automaton of the Supreme Court. . . . His style, prolix, dry and tedious; his voice, harsh."—Garryowen.*] In the evening I wrote to Mr Crawley a list of commissions for his friend to execute for the bride; at night, tired and breathless.

28th Robert Lowry brought in a load of firewood from the allotment, and took out some of our packing-cases, and the rabbit-hutch. Thermometer 64°. Lizzie Cobham off to Dr McCrae's picnic at the Moonee Ponds. Thomas Anne and Mr John Mundy came to our early dinner. Captain Cole, to tea, and whether for the sake of prolonging his stay beside his lady-love, or from actual thirst, he took no less than *nine* of our small teacups full of tea. While pouring out the seventh cup I could hardly conceal the effects of a twinge of pain, but the captain and Thomas Anne didn't make a move till 10 p.m. The moment they were gone, I hurried off to my room at Landall's, and sent Jane for Dr Myer (his house at the end of Great Bourke Street East—Gardner's Cottages).

Soon after eleven, Jane and the doctor arrived. At 3 a.m. I gave birth to a fine girl. [*Her first Australian baby: "and it thrave weel, for it sookit weel."*] The doctor, on his way home, tapped at the window of Mr McCrae's bedroom, and told him what had happened while he had been asleep.

29th Thermometer 85°. My kind neighbour, Mrs McLachlan, came over and took away the boys to spend the day with her family. At night the thermometer fell to 60°.

30th The boys all day with Mrs McLachlan.

31st Again the boys go to play with the McLachlan children.

1842

JANUARY

January 1st The Cobhams came to see me. Also Mrs Thomas and Thomas Anne.

2nd——

3rd Hot wind. Thermometer 103°. Change of wind to south-west and temperature fell to 65°. Was seized with a shivering fit and had a fire put in.

7th Rose early and went to our own cottage to spend the forenoon. Jane left behind with the children.

8th Mr McLure and Mr Harper to dine with Mr McCrae. I went in to make their tea.

Sunday, 9th Lizzie Cobham, the boys, and I strolled out to the allotment and didn't get back till 7 p.m.

10th A fine, warm day. A long visit from Captain Cole.

11th Thermometer 76°. Captain Smith, of the *Brankenmoore*, brought a saddle-horse for Julia Gavan to ride to Brighton, but she had scarcely trotted twenty yards from the house when the animal shied and threw her on to a heap of bricks, hurting her hip-joint severely.

[*Present-day Captain Smiths whisk Julias to Brighton, either in their own cars, or in hired taxis; failing these, they use a swiftly-running tram or train. In Georgiana's time there were no public conveyances, so that those who could afford horses rode* à cheval; *and some, who couldn't, stole them: a fact borne out by twelve columns advertising these depredations, in a single copy of the "Argus" (1853). Samuel Butler, speaking of Sydney, without prejudice, says: "The number of horses now kept there is greater than in any other city of the same size in the world."*]

Dr Thomas tells me Miss Gavan may have to lay up for three

OLD ST JAMES'S CHURCH, MELBOURNE, IN THE FORTIES
From a pen-drawing by W. Pestell

MELBOURNE FROM THE FALLS
(THE TOWN'S ORIGINAL WATER-SUPPLY), 1837
From the original in the William Dixson Gallery, Sydney

MELBOURNE IN THE FORTIES
Showing, close to the right, Skene Craig's Collins Street vineyard
From an old woodcut

weeks. Thomas Anne and Mr McCrae went to Newtown to dine with the Thomas Saunders Webbs. [*Thomas Saunders Webb: our first post-master.*]

12th Walked with Thomas Anne to Captain Cole's house. The Rev. P. B. Geohegan, Gheegen (*comment s'écrit ce mot?*) Geoghegan, Hugh Walker, and Mr Bland came to dine with us.

[*The Rev. Patrick Bonaventure Geoghegan: a man beloved and admired by all denominations. On the arrival of Charles Perry, Anglican Bishop of Melbourne, Geoghegan paid that prelate a courtesy call, but he might as well have visited a Goth or a Vandal, since the door was shut in his face. Contrariwise, William à Beckett (future Chief Justice, and always a Church of England man) became P.B.G.'s friend: a relationship particularly stressed by his torpid muse in "A Protestant's Farewell". Geoghegan laid the foundation-stone of St Francis's, the first Roman Catholic house of worship in Melbourne, on 4th October 1841.*]

13th Miss Emily Gavan came to see her sister. Captain Cole sent for me. Storm-stayed by thunder and lightning till half-past nine.

20th Dr Myer told me that Mrs Thomas gave birth to a boy—still-born—last night.

21st Miss Emily Gavan came to sit beside Julia and remained to dine with us.

22nd Mrs Thomas still in danger.

23rd Dr Myer called here on his way to see Mrs Thomas.

24th Thermometer 101°. Mrs Thomas better, but exceedingly weak.

25th P. B. Geoghegan and Mr McLure to dinner. Thunder and lightning. Kitchen chimney took fire. [*Like a chapter from one of Lever's novels. Father Geoghegan sang "Cruiskeen Lawn" to Mr McLure's accompaniment on the flute.*]

26th Mrs Thomas better. My baby very poorly.

27th Packed crockery and chinaware, ready for sending out to "Mayfield".

28th Sent away three drayloads of packed cases.

30th Lucia Georgiana baptized in the wooden church of St

James, by Rev. A. C. Thomson. The temporary font—a bowl belonging to Mrs Thomas's best tea-set.

31st Busy packing. In the evening Mr McCrae smoked no less than ten cheroots with young Charles Le Souef, and, in future, he promises to pay me one pound for every cigar he smokes. Thomas Anne asked if I could be ready to have her wedding breakfast for the 1st of March. A chilly evening.

FEBRUARY

February 1st Woke suffering from neuralgic pains . . . despatched the rest of our luggage to "Mayfield", and went early to bed. Julia Gavan (much better) left us to spend a few days at Captain Roach's where she will be well attended to. [*At the original sale of Melbourne allotments, 1st June 1837, Roach bought that block which constitutes the northern corner of Little Flinders Street and Swanston Street, for £28!*]

SUPPLEMENT

The "Mayfield" site, "Carran-Carranulk", so called by the natives after the *Carran*, or prickly myrtle, consists of nine and a half acres of land badly encumbered with boulders, requiring much labour to raise them out of the soil. The allotment is bounded on the north by the Yarra, on the west by Nicholson's Paddock, on the east by a fence enclosing the space reserved for a road to a future bridge across the river, and on the south by a track leading to the bend of the stream, eastwards.

In the "reserve" the boys kept a kitchen-garden where they grew quantities of pumpkins, etc. Here, too, the women servants carried on their laundry arrangements.

From the dormer-windows of "Mayfield", looking south, nothing was to be seen but the tops of gum-trees all the way to Richmond Hill.

In 1842, about seven acres were sown with barley, which yielded a fair crop—and in the following year, with oats, which yielded well.

Our opposite neighbours, though on the same side of the **Yarra,** were the Edward Currs, from Circular Head, Van Diemen's Land. Their property called "St Helier's". [*Edward Curr: A Roman Catholic of high character and extraordinary ability, once secretary to the Van Diemen's Land Agricultural Company—a company owning the whole of northern Tasmania—on which account, Curr himself became known as "the Nawab of the North". Curr crossed to Port Phillip, and contested, without success, the seat for Melbourne in the Sydney Council, although he was eventually returned, when he fathered the Separation movement, and was chosen President of the League. It has been said that the dates of Curr's death and of the arrival of the news that Victoria had been granted Home Rule were coincidental; but Georgiana, writing from La Trobe's house, proves the story not to be true. The news came on 11th November 1850. Curr died on 15th November 1850.*] Then there were the Orrs at "Abbotsford" [*John Orr, of Turnbull and Orr. In the Town Council, he appeared like a maiden among lions.*] and the Hodgsons at "Studley".*

★ ★ ★

2nd Dr Thomas advises me to keep my bed. The house empty, and almost stripped of its furniture. Eliza Impey gone out to stay at "Mayfield".

3rd Still in bed. Miss Emily Gavan has promised to stop here and to assist with the preparations for Thomas Anne's wedding.

4th At 2 p.m. started in Kirk's phaeton for "Mayfield". On the way, lost my little old white Indian shawl from round poor baby. Lizzie Cobham, Miss E. Gavan, Ellen Hume, Jane Shanks and the boys, with Robert Lowry, followed in our dray, arriving about 5 p.m.

The road an everlasting chain of bog-holes, with figures of eight and many deviations on account of fallen trees and other obstacles; only the first mile from town is in repair, and I feel positive it was at the ditch where the smooth piece ends that my shawl has been lost. . . .

[*Another description of the same event, given by George McCrae, a dray-passenger: "Coming in from the forest, to an accompaniment of whip-smacking, axle-grumbling, bell-tinkling, and objurations, we found ourselves under a huge spreading red gum, at the northern end of the new house. . . . It was quite a mansion after the wooden cottage in town."*]

Thomas and Stribling had arranged sprays of native myrtle over the front door, and came to welcome us. The house is only partly completed. The largest room is roofed, but neither plastered nor floored. In the meantime, it is used as a storeroom, the kitchen-hut being too small, and not weatherproof. The window-frames to the house are screened with unbleached cotton, waiting the arrival of glass for them.

[*This unplasteredness, unceiledness, and floorlessness, formed a characteristic of the time. Samuel Butler, referring to houses belonging to gentle-folk, says: "There is not the least finish about the buildings: most of them unceiled and unplastered: while they contain elegant and tasteful articles of furniture."*]

5th   Better today. Unpacked trunks.

6th   Hot wind. Most welcome! Thermometer 70°. Didn't rise till noon. Dr Sullivan to dinner.

7th   Hot wind, thunder, lightning, and rain. Stormy all night, and sleep impossible.

8th   Miss Emily Gavan, keys in hand, baby on arm, going hither and thither getting everything ship-shape.

9th   Still busy with the house. "Miss Emily" most efficient, and cheerfulness personified.

13th   Boisterous day. Yet a "day of rest" for all of us.

14th   Prepared the little room off the lobby for Mr McLure. [*John McLure, A.M. of Glasgow, and Edinburgh.*] Until his engagement with the Scots School is completed, Mr M. will only be able to teach the boys before breakfast. In the evening he came to dinner and took up his quarters. [*The Scots was a State-aided school, the prospectus of which began thus: "Masters—Messrs Robert Campbell and John McLure. Teacher of Sacred Music—Mr William Tydeman."*]

15th   Mr George Airey to dinner, and remained for the night.

19th   The boys down with the mumps.

20th   Miss Gavan completed the sewing and fitting of the carpet

I had used in my English home. Later on, she and I nailed it down on the dining-room floor.

23rd Mr McCrae with Miss Emily to dine on board the *Branken-moore*.

25th The *Sea-Horse* in from Sydney last evening, so we have arranged to be ready for the bridal on Thursday next.

26th Mrs Campbell, and Mr Raymond, the sheriff, to early dinner, sorry to learn that Dr Thomas has had to file his schedule.

28th Captain Cole came out to see Thomas Anne. He tells me Agnes gave birth to a boy . . . baptized John Morison . . . who died twelve hours after birth.

MARCH

March 1st Willie completes his seventh year. Thermometer 90°. Unpacked glass and china. Mr and Mrs Eyre Williams to early dinner. [*Mr Williams, a future famous judge.*]

2nd Thomas Anne helped Miss Emily and me to lay the table for tomorrow's festivity. It was nearly midnight before we got to our beds.

3rd Rose at 5 a.m. Captain Cole, Mr and Mrs D. C. Macarthur, and the Rev. James Forbes with his black book for the registration arrived early, and by 9 a.m. the marriage had been celebrated and recorded. Then, when we were about to sit down to breakfast, I learnt that my *pièce de résistance*, a cold roasted haunch of mutton, had been taken by one of the dogs from the storeroom and been so mangled that it wasn't presentable. Happily, the things we had ordered from town were sufficient for our guests, viz.: Mr James Simpson [*Georgiana meets her first Australian landlord. Mr Simpson was a member of the Port Phillip Association; he arrived from Van Diemen's Land on the "Caledonia" (April 1836) with Batman, who had him appointed public arbitrator. In the distribution of country among members of the Association, James Simpson took Block 14, which included plains beyond the Werribee to the foot of Station Peak. Simpson, Gelli-brand, and Swanston, were delegated to go to Sydney to lay the case for the Association before the Executive there. Garryowen, who knew Simpson, describes him as "the best liked man in the Province".*], Mr

C. H. Ebden [*an original representative of Port Phillip district in the Sydney Council. After Separation, he became auditor-general of the new colony. See entry of 23rd May 1843*], Mr and Mrs Montgomery, Dr Sandford, George Canty, Luke Ward Cole, Dr and Mrs Thomas, James Grahame, Frank, Lizzie and Mamie Cobham, Mr McLure and the two Misses Gavan. At 3 p.m. the happy pair left for "St Ninians", under a shower of rice and salt. The Montgomerys, on their way to Brighton, managed an upset of their borrowed vehicle, entailing the cost of repairs.

4th Busy all day setting things to rights.

5th The *Eagle*, Captain Buckley, arrived, bringing Dr Thomas's two sisters, Mary Anne and Sarah, whom he had sent for before his affairs became entangled by the bad times.

6th Lizzie Cobham and I walked to Campbellfield to call on our neighbour, Mrs Lyon Campbell.

8th Mrs Eyre Williams came in Kirk's phaeton, and I took her to call on Mrs La Trobe, Mrs Lonsdale, Mrs Myer, and left cards for Mrs Kemmis. Home again by 4 p.m.

9th Sent in a load of melons by the dray.

10th Rev. James Forbes, Rev. Mr Gunn, Rev. Mr Mowbray and Mr Turnbull to dinner.

11th Rev. A. C. and Mrs Thomson drove out to see us. The Rev. rather annoyed at not having been invited with his wife to the wedding-feast.

12th Lizzie and I walked across the flat to Mrs Bell's. Mr Mollison came to dinner and remained all night.

13th Mr Mollison and Mr McCrae left after breakfast to spend the day at Chelsworth with the Wills. [*The Murrumbidgee Wills.*] Mrs Beker dangerously ill.

17th Lizzie and I walked to Newtown, to see Mrs Eyre Williams and enquire for Mrs Beker. [*Mrs Ludwig Becker (here misspelled), wife of the Government Meteorologist.*]

19th Dr McCrae returned from Sydney very ill. Captain Reid came out and stayed all night.

20th Lizzie, George, Willie, Captain Reid, Mr McLure and I walked to the Scots Kirk for morning service. Flora and James McLachlan returned with us. Leslie Foster and his brother came—

uninvited—stayed late, and stayed for coffee. [*Nephew of the last Lord Fitzgerald, upon whose death he took the name of the testator, in compliance with a clause of the will, but, in the history of Victoria, he remains John Leslie Foster, the man who passed the act bringing independence to the colony, with a distinct constitution and a Legislative Council of its own. Foster was a pastoralist also, and he owned a large station on the east side of the Pyrenees. He died aged seventy-four. Facts gathered from the "Australian Encyclopaedia".*] Mrs Beker died. She was a sister of Septimus Martin.

21st Mr and Mrs Alfred Langhorne, and Mr Highett to dinner. [*Alfred Langhorne: overseer of Captain Lonsdale's run, which had its head station near the bridge over the creek, where the township of Dandenong (Big Hill) is at present situated. In 1839 Dr McCrae took over this station, as well as the adjoining one, "Eumemmering". Dr McCrae retained the Dandenong holding for years, but "Eumemmering" was early transferred to Leslie Foster before mentioned.*] Mr Highett leaves for Sydney tomorrow to sail then for England per *Alfred*.

27th Lizzie Cobham returned from "La Rose", and *par conséquent* Mr George Airey came to see us. [*The Aireys lived on a property which they had selected and "originally occupied" near Mount Gellibrand.*]

28th Captain McLachlan [*owner of a squatting station on the Avoca River*] and his son Ronald to dinner.

29th All of us suffering from headache and feverishness.

30th Dr Myer tells me I have intermittent fever.

31st All of us better, excepting little Farquhar.

APRIL

April 1st Heavy rain and wintry sky. This morning, because Lizzie had given Mr McLure the purse she had netted for him (his old one being useless), Mr McCrae took it into his head that this token is a proof that poor Lizzie wishes to delude his tutor into the toils of matrimony. "This would deprive us of his services, as he might easily establish a school." Nothing could be further from the girl's

* 1927.

mind. I had given Lizzie the purse-silk, and out of good nature she had worked it for the security of Mr McLure's silver.

After breakfast, Lizzie was told to get all her traps ready to be sent in by the dray, tomorrow, as she had better go out to her mother and uncle at "La Rose". Lizzie was dumbfounded . . . and I could not tell her why.

2nd   Captain Cole came out. I sent Mrs Cole's luggage and poor L's trousseau by the dray; Lizzie, herself, rode in it as far as the top of Great Bourke Street. With her I have lost my right-hand helper and companion, while she, by her own wish, would rather stay here than out at "La Rose".

5th   Farquhar not at all well. Heavy rain and a gale of wind at night.

6th   A tempestuous morning. Mr McLure's tramp across the gullies and swamps not enviable, and "rough on the boots" as Ellen remarks when she "pays" them with grease to keep out the water.

7th   Farquhar ill with dysentery.

11th   Cold and rainy. Baby very cross, and no Lizzie to carry her about and amuse her. Sandy ill with dysentery.

13th   Dr Thomas came. Willie fell this morning while he was playing with my bunch of watch-trinkets, and broke my small black-water marble heart, made for me in 1826 by Jamie Robertson, as a keepsake of Gordon Castle. *Tout passe, tout casse, tout lasse. . . .*

SUPPLEMENT

Jamie Robertson was a handy man at G. C., so clever that he was even said to have put new "cleeks" to the housekeeper's "fixturous teeth"; his chief business was the care of the Duke's turning-lathe. Jamie's eldest lass married a "merchant" in Torres.

*   *   *

15th   Dr Thomas brought the medicine he had left at the Club yesterday for Mr McCrae to bring out for the boys. Farquhar a little better.

16th   Willie ill. Dr Thomas and his brother Charles to dinner.

18th   A fearful gale from the south-west.

19th   A fine morning. Mr Howe from the Murrumbidgee and Mr Princock came.

23rd   Mr La Trobe, Mr and Mrs James Smith, and Mrs Henri Bell came to enquire for the children. Mr Clark and Mr John Mundy to dinner. [*Mundy: a relative of Sir Charles FitzRoy.*]

25th   Farquhar out of bed, but very weak.

27th   Suffering from violent palpitating of the heart. Dr Thomas prescribed for me.

MAY

May 1st   Willie went in the dray to town to see Mrs Thomas.

7th   Captain Lewis, Mrs Freeman, Mr and Mrs D. A. C. G. E. Erskine, and Mrs Meek paid us a forenoon visit.

8th   Willie returned from Melbourne mounted on "Don" led by Mr McCrae.

9th   Mrs Osmond came to stay for a week to help me with the boys' winter suits.

14th   Sandy put on his first pair of trowsers.

15th   Mr and Mrs Eyre Williams and Mr Baker came to see us. Mr B. about to sell off, even his law books, and return at once to England. (Mr Baker, a barrister, son of Sir Frederick Baker, Chief Magistrate of Bow Street, London.)★ At this time Mr Eyre Williams was intending to become a "squatter", but Mr McCrae advised him to buy all Mr Baker's books, and to practise his profession. Mr Eyre Williams at once decided to do so. (Mrs Baker's father, the Rev. Martin of Bexley, Kent, kept a boys' school which was attended by James Robertson between 1838 and 1840.)★

21st   Captain Buckley came to say good-bye as he leaves for Sydney tomorrow.

25th   Cleared out storeroom for plasterers to begin their work of transformation of it into our dining-room.

28th   My Brown's Patent Cooking Stove and a box of books arrived from London. Heard of George Canty's death.

★ Added later by Georgiana.

29th George nine years old today. Claud Farie [*of Warrnambool; at one time, owner of Merang station; at another, Sheriff of Melbourne*], Mr Black, Archibald Cunninghame and Mr Powlett came out in the evening.

30th "Ningalubbel" and "Sally" very troublesome. . . . Arthur Bridgeman, two Miss Currs, Julius and Marmaduke, came to keep George's birthday.

31st The plasterers started work.

JUNE

June 1st Planted some special bulbs sent me by Mr Curr.

3rd Sent to Jolimont for the cuttings of creepers, geraniums, and roses promised by Mr La Trobe.

6th Captain Webster [*of Mount Shadwell*] came to dinner, and stayed the night.

7th Mrs Curr came across to see me.

16th Mr Urquhart came to dinner. [*William Swan Urquhart: government surveyor; under Hoddle's direction, he surveyed the Mount Alexander and Bendigo goldfields.*] Mr Atkinson and J. P. Mollison came in the afternoon.

17th Mrs Bunbury and Harry arrived to stay with us.

18th George, Willie, and Sandy went in the dray with Jane on a visit to their Aunt Cole at Brighton. Mr McLure having terminated his engagements with the Scots School, brought out his luggage.

19th Walked with Mrs Bunbury to Campbellfield.

20th Mr McLure went to the farm for a few days' recreation.

21st Mr Baker, Mr Atkinson, and Mr Montgomery to dinner. A brilliant moonlight night. [*James Atkinson: a Sydney solicitor, who, in 1839, bought practically the whole of Port Fairy at £1 an acre.*]

23rd Continuous rain.

24th Mr James Boyd and Mr Fennell came early [*Robert Fennell, who was married to Maria Batman, became Port Phillip manager for Benjamin Boyd*]; and Mr Benjamin Boyd arrived with Mr Heriot in time for dinner. [*Benjamin Boyd: egoist, banker, and wholesale land-speculator, whose desperate enterprises were a principal cause of the depression in his time.*] Mr Benjamin had rubbed his shoes, and was still smoothing his hair when I received him. He is Rubens over again. Tells me he went to a *bal masqué* as Rubens with his broad-leafed hat, and was considered *comme il faut*. At the moment, he has just arrived from South America in his yacht the *Wanderer* which is anchored down the bay.

[G. G. McC., *the diarist's son, speaking of Boyd as the first man to run steamers between Sydney and Melbourne, mentions a highly varnished lithograph of his s.s. "Sea-Horse"; and, hoisted at the main, a house-flag, with two honey-bees, gules, on a field argent: the bees, doubled, symbolizing the initials of the proprietary name. Also, he alludes to a picture of "Lofty", Boyd's celebrated Clydesdale, "led by a groom in a broad blue bonnet". "Both of these used to hang in a recess under the stairs, at 'Mayfield', exactly over my bed." The same writer records his impression of the "Wanderer": "She was a smart, topsail schooner, much on the lines of the African slaver of the period, mounting six broadside guns, beside one large pivot-gun amidships. The crew were armed like men-o'-war's men." After Boyd's disappearance at Guadalcanar, in 1851, the "Wanderer" seems to have borne about with her the bad luck of her owner, and finally went to pieces crossing the bar of the Macquarie River, New South Wales.*

*John Webster wrote from Opononi, N.Z., 28th March 1910, to George Gordon McCrae as follows: "In 1854 I had the honour of shewing my water-colours to Her Majesty Queen Victoria. I was introduced by Lord Mandeville; and Colonel Phipps was gentleman-in-waiting. The Queen was much interested, and, on retiring, I was told by Colonel Phipps not to shew my back to her, but to take notice of where the door was as I withdrew, and to bow at every third step. The paintings I shewed to Her Majesty had to do with a cruise I made with Benjamin Boyd who was killed in the Solomon Islands. He was well known in Sydney. I have paintings of the cruise in my house at Hokianga."]

25th Sent Archie to Kirk's, to order the gig for Mrs B. and myself to make some calls. Archie brought word that "The gig has been sold, and the roads are too rough to allow of any lighter carriage being sent out for us."

26th Mrs Bunbury laid up with influenza. [*Epidemic in New*

South Wales, at least. "There have been three general attacks of in-fluenza since 1827."—SAMUEL BUTLER, *1837.*]

28th A fine frosty morning.

29th Mr Brierly, the marine artist, who travelled with the Boyds, and Mr Ashurst to dinner. They stayed all night. . . . Mrs Bunbury up again.

[*George McCrae imitated Brierly's voice: "Wha-a-ale o-i-l!" "For-ty pounds a ton!" "For-ty pounds a ton!" Then, to Hotson Ebden: "You're not the on-ly per-son who is going to be dis-gust-ing-ly rich!" Oswald Brierly was a pleasant, comfort-loving man; at this juncture, troubled with tired eyes and, consequently, unable to paint. Boyd said, in front of Georgiana, "We must get him away from ships." That was the first suggestion. The next she heard of it was, when Dr Greeves talked about Brierly's appointment as manager to Boyd's fishery, at Twofold Bay. But it was the artist's fault that he could never stop in one place for an unlimited length of time; and he had only completed a year's service in this employ when he resigned, to join a survey expedition to North Australia, led by Captain Owen, H.M.S. "Rattlesnake". During this trip, Owen vainly called an island after Brierly; vainly, because it had already been Christened "Dadda Hai". Soon after, Brierly returned to England where the Queen, his admirer, made much of him, giving him numerous commissions. In '67, as a member of the Duke of Edinburgh's staff, he dined and painted his way back to the colonies; then did the same home again, in time to transfer to the suite of the Prince of Wales, on tour in the Mediterranean. In '74 he was appointed marine painter to Her Majesty, and to the Royal Yacht Squadron; also, in '81, curator of The Painted Hall, Greenwich. Brierly died at London, on 14th December 1894.*]

JULY

July 1st Pouring rain. Captain Bunbury arrived.

2nd Mr Clark to dinner. Mr McLure returned in the evening.

3rd Captain, and Mrs Bunbury, and Harry left for "Stanney".

4th Ellen Hume, Jane Shanks, and little Farquhar rode in the dray to Melbourne to bring the boys home to their school duties.

5th Rode to town to Captain Roach's, Great Bourke Street West, to try the two pianos commissioned from London by Dr

Sandford; one of these, Captain Roach offers to Mr McCrae for a debt due to the firm at £50; I made my choice and was glad to learn that the other was the one the doctor liked best.

6th Captain and Mrs Lonsdale visited us.

[*Captain William Lonsdale (4th King's Own): first superintendent, police magistrate, and general Panjandrum of the settlement; amiable, conscientious, and hard-working, aged thirty-six; salary £250 per an.; with an extra fifty thrown in at the end of the year. On arrival, the soldiers bunked at Batman's store. During October and November Lonsdale himself stayed on board H.M.S. "Rattlesnake", but in December he occupied the box-shaped house that had been brought across from Sydney. This house, the future Government headquarters, was situated on the corner of Little Collins Street and Spencer Street; the whole encampment, administrative offices, barracks, guardroom, work-shops, prison, hospital, and so forth, being gathered together on four blocks bound, east, west, south, and north, by King Street, Spencer Street, Collins Street, and Lonsdale Street. Lonsdale confirmed Batman's choice ("Here is the place for a village.") and made Melbourne, or Bearbrass, the official site of the settlement, principally on account of an assured water-supply at the Yarra Yarra falls. This decision scotched William's Town—Governor Bourke's fancy. Lonsdale did not have much power vested in himself; he might have had a person arrested for beating a carpet in the street, or blasting a rock within the limits of the town, but little else. Every important movement was referred to Sydney, and nothing determined without sanction of the New South Wales Executive. These hard-and-fast rules, as well as the desire to make of Melbourne a convict rookery, set fire to that idea, which blazed up, and became Separation.*

At the date of the visit recorded in our diary, Lonsdale was forty-two years old. Mrs Lonsdale talked of Little Bourke Street, a rutty lane, barricaded with fallen gum-trees, "where there was still some holing and burning to be done".]

7th Rode to Newtown to see Mrs Eyre Williams. Lauchlan Mackinnon [*of Mount Fyans*] rode back with me.

8th Baby not well. Piano arrived.

9th Mr McCrae left early for Mr Malcolm's to stay till Monday, but his horse knocked up, so he came back at 5 p.m. [*James Malcolm: a Separationist, and the wealthiest man in early Melbourne. His estate was near the Merri Creek.*]

10th Mr McCrae, Mr McLure, and I rode to Merri Creek, and returned by Newtown to call on Mrs Montgomery.

11th Archie and Jane went to town. On the way back, the dray stuck in the swamp and they didn't reach home till past five o'clock. . . . Willie's pig was shot!

12th Rode to town. Called on Mrs Ailsa Craig, Mrs Meek, and Mrs James Smith.

13th Rode across to see Mrs La Trobe and Mrs Lonsdale. [*The Lonsdales, having given up their Little Collins Street cottage, now resided in the same area with the Superintendent, at Jolimont.*]

14th Mrs Thomas and Mary Anne came to look at our garden; surprised at the progress it had made.

16th Dr Thomas drove out for his wife, but left his sister for a few days to help me arrange the books in the book-shelves.

21st Mr and Mrs Edward Cotton, shipmates of Mary Anne and Sarah, and Mr Francis Lavie, of Highgate, came to see us.

22nd News (by letter from Edinburgh) of the death of our dear good friend, William Stewart—14th February.

26th to *30th* Heavy rain. River rising rapidly.

31st Rode to St James's Church. Charles Thomas and Ward Cole came out in the afternoon. River half-way up the bank.

AUGUST

August 1st Mary Anne Thomas went to town on my pony, as Mrs Thomas is far from well.

2nd Rode to town to call on Mrs Le Souef and Mrs Hoddle, and, returning, called on Mrs Eyre Williams.

3rd Dr Thomas vaccinated baby, and dined with us.

4th Anstruther Myer to dinner. The river now 16 feet above its usual level.

5th Mr Myer left. Captain Reid arrived. River falling.

6th   George ready to start for "Erin Cottage" for the birthday party, but in vain—an even downpour of rain having set in.

7th   Still raining heavily. Could not go to church.

8th   A letter from Mr Knox telling me of his wife's death. A kind soul, always loving to me.

9th   Mr La Trobe came to show Osmond how to plant the vine cuttings "obliquely to the sun, each cutting to have three joints and 'eyes'—one of these to be above ground, the second level with the surface, the third to be rubbed off to make way for the root." [*Osmond, the "Mayfield" gardener. It is his wife who helps Mrs McCrae with the boy's winter suits.*] River rising again.

10th   Mr Sydney Smith to dinner, and to stay the night.

11th   River rather lower today.

15th   Heavy gale, and pouring rain again.

17th   Deluge of rain and hail; Mr McCrae forty-two today.

> *Rain, rain, rattle-stanes,*
> *Dinna rain on me.*

19th   Still raining.

20th   Fair! Rode to Melbourne. Called on Mrs Denne. Mr McLure and the boys spend the day at "Erin Cottage".

21st   Rode to church, and, in the afternoon, with Mr McCrae, to Mr Gisborne's camp on the Merri. [*Native word for "stone".*]

22nd   Raining again. Cut out five pairs of trowsers, and nearly completed one pair.

23rd   And following days busy tailoring.

28th   Steady rain. None of us able to go to church.

31st   Rode to town on the Timor pony—an awkward creature; coming unexpectedly upon a blackfellow, he shied and nearly sent me over his head, close to the town boundary-post.

SEPTEMBER

September 1st   Arranged the larger room at the end of the house for the nursery, and Jane moved her bed and baggage into it. Still raining heavily night and day.

2nd, 5th, 6th   Thermometer (average) 55°.

7th After a visit to Jolimont, I told Mr McCrae what I had heard. Madame (speaking in her husband's presence) said of him, "He has too many irons on the fire"; whereupon he made this rejoinder: "Not *too* many, my dear, but some that should be tolerably hot ones when it comes to the handling." Mr McCrae, who wasn't in his best humour, compared Mr La Trobe to Major Davidson's hen—that hopped from one egg to another, so that the whole setting became addled!

[*The Superintendent's detractors seldom spoke of vacillation under any other name than that of "La Trobism"; yet, now and again, he was a man imperceptibly having his own way. "In the Jolimont garden, he nipped rosebuds and solved governmental difficulties at the same time. Suspected of indetermination, he showed himself resolute by refusing to allow felons to land from the transport 'Randolph', August 8, 1849; through which act the settlement was saved from convictism, and from the slur that must ever after have clung to it." M.S.S. (anonymous source)—collected from scrap-book.*

With regard to the above piece of history, H. G. Turner says the Superintendent did not act on his own responsibility. The governor, Sir Charles FitzRoy, was visiting Melbourne at the time and, before he went away, he "authorised Mr La Trobe to order the 'Randolph' to Sydney".

La T.'s habitual attitude (stated, with resignation, by the "Journal of Australasia"): "The people all disposed to act; the Superintendent remaining passive."

Because he was always in a ferment about people's feelings, La Trobe couldn't manage the wild-beast show that represented Victoria in 1852, so he never got anything done. The exasperated public decided he didn't exist, and the poor man was humbled every day by the appearance of an "Argus" advertisement which had for its caption—

WANTED: A GOVERNOR

Apply to the people of Victoria

This bludgeon-wit also grieved Mr Edward Bell (La Trobe's Achates), though, no doubt, his stable-boy guffawed when the barman at the corner house opined that "Charles Joey" had been "sent 'ere to look after black-

MELBOURNE IN 1851
From the original in the William Dixson Gallery, Sydney

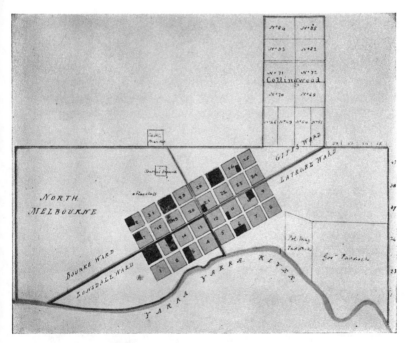

AN EARLY MAP OF MELBOURNE
Supposed to have been the work of Robert Russell

VIEW FROM FLAGSTAFF HILL, SEPTEMBER 1841
From a sketch by Georgiana

FLAGSTAFF HILL BEFORE THE
DAYS OF TELEGRAPH

Reading the list of arrivals on the board
at the Flagstaff
From a pen-drawing by George
Gordon McCrae

*fellows", and "governin' civilized people—like you 'n' me, Jack—
is a different thing!" The barman was right. La Trobe packed up his traps
and left—for ever, Australia ("Felix", perhaps, to some others) "infelix"
to him. N.B.—The blackfellow gibe was a general mockery, founded on
the fact that one of La Trobe's former employments had been to inquire
into the welfare of negroes at the West Indies.*

*R. H. Horne's criticism of La Trobe: "His Excellency. . . . courteous
to a provoking degree."*

*Captain Foster Fyans was a friend of La Trobe's, yet he tells funny
stories about him—good naturedly—as he might, in that mood, of himself.
Here is one, double-shotted, bagging the brilliant Wentworth as well:
"I shall never forget Mr Wentworth (the watch-house is not fitted for
gentlemen), and his bow to his Honour, the Superintendent, who was
sitting in the corner of the slab hut on a stool with three legs; his Honour's
graceful recognition of the salute: his Honour rising with dignity, when
the stool upset, making a noise, to the disgust of Mr Pat McKeever, chief
constable of Little Pedlington."—"Letters from Victorian Pioneers".*

*A death notice. "That many Victorians will recall with regret the
pleasant days spent under the rule of Charles Joseph La Trobe cannot be
doubted; and this, notwithstanding the prosperity they have since enjoyed.
In manner, he was kind and genial, and the faults of his government were
owing to his advisers, rather than to himself. He was wise enough and
honest enough to retire from a position for which he felt himself unequal,
and passed a life of sterling integrity." La Trobe died at Clapham House,
South Downs, England, on 4th December 1875.]*

11th Tried the paces of Mr Power's mare. Find her *saccadée*, and
hard in her mouth.

13th The Bunburys went to live at William's Town, the captain
having been appointed harbour-master there. Little Harry stays
with us till they are settled.

17th In the evening, Mr Redmond Barry to musical supper.
Mr B's voice a high bass; he sang "Love's Witchcraft" . . . his
favourite song. [*Redmond Barry: thirty-six years of age. It wasn't until
he reached forty that he presided over the Court of Request, a tribunal
which held its sessions in the billiard-room of the "Lamb Inn". The judge's
stipend, £100 per annum.*]

G

20th The plaster in the large room being dry, we brought the dining-room furniture into it. Mr William Ryrie to dinner. Mr Pohlman came during the evening. [*Henry Gyles Turner, after explaining a plot by Separationists, in 1848, not to have Port Phillip district represented on the Sydney Council, tells this dramatic climax: "When the returning officer, Mr R. W. Pohlman (afterwards judge) demanded the names of the candidates, he was met by a great outcry of 'No election!' and had to return his writ endorsed to that effect."*]

21st Arranged old dining-room as my bedroom. Mr Locke came. [*Locke, of Devil's River.*]

23rd Dr Myer came to see Harry Bunbury. Had Mr McLure's things removed upstairs.

24th The first day of summer; Dr Munro, Mr Morehead, and Mr Hunter to dinner. In the afternoon, Mrs Henry Moor and Miss Grylls visited us. Miss G. being on the eve of marriage with D. S. Campbell's medical brother, William.

[*Daughter of the Rev. J. C. Grylls, the first Anglican minister in Melbourne. Mrs Moor, wife of Henry Moor, solicitor, friend of Robert Jamieson and William Ryrie. Moor bought "Yalloak", Jamieson's station, at the head of Western Port. Rich, popular, irreproachable, despite of the "Argus" calling him "a double-faced, unprincipled schemer", he found himself Mayor of a very unfinancial Melbourne, in 1844; accordingly, he made his job an honorary one, and went in, head over heels, for cutting down expenses. He established new systems, showed money the right way round, and simplified procedures. One evening, in '46, the noise of a sectarian riot (cat-calls, howls, and pistol-shots) roused him out of his sleep, whereupon he put a black "capuchin" over his night-gown and, going out, read the Riot Act in the street.*]

25th A pleasant ride on "Don", his canter delightful. Mr McCrae went to dine at Captain Cole's and to remain until to-morrow.

26th Lauchlan Mackinnon to dinner. In the evening, delighted him (and myself) not a little, by playing several old Gaelic lilts. *Cela est dans le sang.* [*For solace of the heart, Montaigne prescribes "villanelles, homely gigs, and country songs."*]

27th Rode to town. Saw Mr and Mrs John Hawdon and Mrs

Joseph Hawdon, at Captain Cole's. [*John Hawdon owned, and worked, Mount Greenock Station, 1839. Joseph Hawdon, in 1836, headed the first overlanding expedition in which stock started from the Sydney-side, and after many difficulties safely arrived at the Port Phillip settlement. Hawdon took up ground south of the Yarra, and established there the first cattle station in Australia Felix. Before she married, Mrs Joseph Hawdon had been Miss Outhwaite, of an old Yorkshire family.*] Eliza went out to "Stanney" with Harry Bunbury, whence he will be taken to William's Town. Captain Cole and Dr Myer left for Sydney.

28th Planted a number of flower-roots from Sydney. Rain and thunder.

29th Letters from Mr Cummins, Richard, and Milty in reply to ours of January!

30th Mr Cavenagh, Mrs Hazard, and Mrs D. S. Campbell to see us.

OCTOBER

October 1st Attended service in the church of St James—now open for the use of the congregation. Remained for communion.

[*The old box-shaped chapel of 1838 has been described by George Arden as "a small wooden building with a ship's bell suspended from a gallows-like structure". On the present date, in the new church, Parson Thomson took for his text, II Chronicles, "Now mine eyes shall be open, and mine ears attent unto the prayer that is made in this place." Collection £11 18s. 3d.*

St James's old cathedral takes us back to the very beginning of Victoria's history. A piece of land near the corner of Little Collins and William streets was presented to the Church of England so that a building could be erected as a place of worship. The first structure was of wood, with a seating capacity of about 100 persons. Previous to this, the Old Court House had been used.

Drawings of the new stone church had been prepared by Melbourne's first architect, Robert Russell, and on 9th November 1839, the foundation stone was laid by Governor La Trobe. The church was opened in 1842, and a few years later Bishop Perry arrived and made the structure a cathedral. Melbourne was created a city at the same time.]

Few craftsmen being available at this time, no inscription was cut on the stone, but one was written on parchment, and together with coins and other documents was placed in a hollow in the stone and another larger stone placed upon it.

Two boxes are provided, one for the Governor-General, and the other for the Governor. St James's is the only church in Melbourne which has made special provision for the Governors.

The acoustic properties of the cathedral are perfect, and it is exceedingly well ventilated and lighted.

St James's is Melbourne's first church, its first cathedral, and was designed by its first architect; therefore, it stands as Melbourne's greatest memorial to the early pioneers of a great city—Melbourne "Herald".]

On my return home found Dr Munro, Mr Dunlop, and Mr Morehead who had arrived for early dinner. [*Dunlop became a member of the first parliament. Selby says he moved "that its meetings be opened with prayer". How this proposal was received history does not relate, but, in June 1934, the Premier of New South Wales having broached the same subject to the House, the Opposition hailed him with chirrups and jeers.*]

3rd Mr Lamb from Sydney and D. C. Macarthur to dinner. [*Mr John Lamb, "his coat dragged back over his shoulders": a member of the Legislative Council of New South Wales from 1844, and, after dissolution, again in 1848.*]

4th Walked across to Mrs La Trobe's, and, thence, to see Mrs Sheriff Mackenzie in Mr Kemmis's old house.

5th High winds, with clouds of dust.

6th Gardening. The cooking stove set in the apology for a kitchen.

7th Mrs Laidlaw brought Nancy to be with me as housemaid. The bullocks astray again.

8th The boys, Mr McLure, and I walked via Richmond to Melbourne.

9th Captain McLachlan to dinner. Ellen pleased with her cooking "convayniance". It cost me £20 in London.

11th Mrs Cole came to early dinner. Afterwards we both called on Mrs Curr.

12th Mrs Campbell Dunmore to dinner. In the evening she sang to my playing.

14th Mrs Urquhart, Mr Alison, and Mr McKnight to dinner.

16th Ward Cole brought the gig, and Mrs Cole returned with him.

18th Pouring rain all day.

19th A fair day, but rain again at night.

20th Piercing cold wind; rain, thunder, lightning. Hail at night.

22nd The river, today, 18 feet above the summer level; the top of our peach-tree just visible over the water.

24th Mr Ballingall to dinner. James Grahame and Mr Freeman rode out to see us.

25th Dr Thomas detained here all night on account of heavy rain.

26th Rain and thunder. River continues to rise.

27th A fine bright day. River subsiding a little.

28th A lovely warm day.

29th Very sultry.

30th In the forenoon, thunder and rain. Called on Mrs Palmer.

NOVEMBER

November 1st A fine, bright, warm day. Cut out and made window-blinds for all the front windows.

2nd Thunder and rain. Mr George Were rode out to say Mr McCrae was detained in town by business.

4th Mr McCrae came to breakfast; tells me that Mr Westgarth has failed; also, that we, ourselves, are likely to be reduced to the same condition, through the insolvency of the clients of the firm.

[*In November 1850, his term of office having expired, Earl Grey, absentee-representative of Melbourne in the Sydney council, left the seat empty, although no emptier than it had been during the last two years. A fresh election put William Westgarth into the vacant place. Then, when Victoria had become free, Westgarth returned to the new home-colony, and was chosen to represent the city in her parliament. At the same time he carried on secretarial duties for the Melbourne branch of the Australasian Anti-transportation League. Between '53 and '54 he spent* twelve months in England, and came back at the middle of the turmoil caused by the miners' insurrection. He was chairman of the committee that inquired into the Eureka Stockade tragedy, also chairman of the Gold-finding Board. In '57 he again journeyed to the old country, staying there for thirty odd years. At the end of that time he re-visited Melbourne, but in 1889 was home again in London, where he died. "Westgarth was essentially a business organizer, and was both first president of the Melbourne chamber of commerce (1851) and a founder of the present London chamber of commerce." Quotation from the "Australian Encyclopaedia".*]

5th   The three Montgomery boys came out with George to keep Guy Fawkes Day in the old-world fashion.

[Guy Fawkes, or Gunpowder, Day: kept up especially among the Scots, to perpetuate their spite against the man who justified his attempt upon the houses of parliament by saying he had only wished "to blow those Scotch so-and-sos back to their barren heaths!" Even during the eighties, we, of another generation, signalized November like cannibals, and singing "Hang him up high!" chucked our grotesque effigy into the fire.

> "The Gunpowder plot
> Will never be forgot
> While Edinburgh Castle stan's upon a rock."]

6th   A very hot day; could not go to church.

7th   Stribling arrived with his tools to make a coffin for Thomas's baby. It died today. Three days ago his mother was out here with him in her arms, and he appeared the picture of health. Infantile cholera and dysentery are just now decimating the young children.

8th   Ward Cole came, and, in the evening, we had some music.

9th   Oppressively warm day.

10th   Walked to Mrs La Trobe's . . . Mrs Myer there. Thence to Mrs O'Cock's, and, by the way, met Mrs Bunbury going to Jolimont.

[Mrs O'Cock was the wife of "Richard O'Cock, solicitor, legal adviser to several men prominent in the life of Melbourne in the forties".—Professor Ernest Scott. The Police Establishment for Melbourne, in 1841, was as

* 1927.

follows: Magistrate (Mr James Simpson), £300 per annum; clerk to the bench (Mr Richard O'Cock), £150 per annum.]

12th Ward Cole gone for a holiday to Geelong.

13th Rode to church, calling first at Captain Cole's.

14th Henry Montgomery and Donald Mackinnon (from the Loddon) arrived to "pot luck", which proved to be "nae luck at a' ". But, in the evening, a few "auld-warld ditties" made Donald fancy himself in his dear native isle.

17th Mark Nicholson and Dr Myer to dinner.

18th A very hot day. Baby has two teeth through.

20th Rode to the Moonee Ponds. Home by three.

21st Rode to town with Mr McCrae. Left my habit-skirt with Mrs Myer, and, in the afternoon, called on Mrs George Smythe in Collins Street.

23rd Jane Shanks went to Geelong to stay a few days with her cousin. By desire, I wrote to invite Captain Reid's wife to stay here with her two little boys—to be near Dr Myer—as Captain Reid can't afford to take lodgings.

[*"By desire" implicated Mr McCrae, and, although '42 was a disastrous year, Captain Reid should have been able to afford a lodging. At his station, Tichingorook (on the further side of Mount Martha), there were huts, haystacks, stockyards, paddocks, and garden-lands galore. This kind, hospitable, uncertain-tempered man seems to have looked twice at every penny he had got, and his hullabaloo about the loss of a cart-whip has been recorded (12th May 1844). In point of fact, Georgiana and her husband were worse off than the Reids; see entry of 3rd November: "We are likely to fail through the insolvency of the clients of the firm"; again, elsewhere: "spending our tradesmen's money".*]

24th While preparations were being made to plaster the attics, a large snake crawled out of the rolled-up carpet which had been standing beside Mr McLure's bedroom door ever since the carpet was beaten. I remember it came on to rain, but, as the carpet was rolled up and sheltered by a tree, it was left behind until the weather mended. However, we forgot it until the next day, when it was carried to the attic. The plasterer struck at the snake, and missed it.

He saw it crawl along the wall-plate of the roof of the nursery, and thence drop itself down the partition. Rev. James Forbes visited us; Captain Webster to dinner, and storm stayed by thunder, lightning, and heavy rain.

25th Both Timor ponies strayed during last night's storm; Mark Nicholson to dinner and to stop the night.

29th Thermometer 90°.

30th Thermometer 80°. A sultry, stifling night. To sleep, or to lie in bed, an utter impossibility. Sandy, six years old.

DECEMBER

December 1st A fine, refreshing morning.

3rd Went to Mrs George Smythe's . . . found her, with her husband, sitting beside their dying boy. "Congestion of the brain."

4th A deluge of rain. Only Mr McLure ventured to church.

6th George and his carpet-bag ready to start for Newtown, when Mr and Mrs La Trobe called to say they will drive him to Captain Cole's tomorrow, as Mrs Montgomery cannot come to town.

7th Mrs Curr and her daughter came to visit us.

8th A cold, damp, cloudy day. Letters from Mr and Mrs Fenning and Mrs Irvine of June 4. At night thermometer 47°, and this, the Australian midsummer! The boasted climate is a myth, and requires a constitution of india-rubber elasticity to sustain it.

9th Mr McCrae angry because Condell has been elected Mayor of Melbourne. In the evening, Mr McLure played on his flute "A prey to tender anguish" (Dr Hadyn) . . . at my request.

[*Henry Condell, brewer: elected first Mayor of Melbourne, 9th December 1842. In the following year, he became Dr Lang's instrument, when he defeated Edward Curr, candidate for Melbourne in the New South Wales Legislative Council.*]

10th Walked across to Campbellfield. Mr Jones Agnew Smith to dinner.

11th A hot wind. Mr Quarry married to Miss Bowman, of Sydney. Mr and Mrs Eyre Williams came to tea.

12th Cleaned picture-frames, ready for hanging.

13th [*A single-line entry obliterated. On this day, Mayor Condell marched with drums and brass instruments to the Supreme Court, where he was administered the oath of office by Judge ·Willis, that notorious fire-eater, and (according to Captain Fyans) "disreputable old rip". Mr Condell, not yet officially fledged, wore a scarlet cloak which, flapping in the wind, caused a panic among the bullock-teams in Collins Street.*]

14th Mr Mackinnon, Dr Black, and Mr Montgomery to dinner. [*Dr Thomas Black: proud of being a friend of Admiral King. He was treasurer of the Port Phillip Medical Association, founded 1846.*]

16th "Murray" brought us a live "tuan-tuan"—a sort of flying-squirrel, with extremely soft fur (like chinchilla, but no so long).

17th Dr Munro and his brother, and Archie McLachlan came to dinner. In the evening, the doctor treated us to some songs to my accompaniment. He has a fine, yet somewhat tearful voice, and sings with feeling. He goes to New Zealand. [*Rabelais says, "like a cicada, musically trying his voice in the dog-days".*]

18th Thermometer 108°. Frightfully close. The sun the colour of turmeric. No one could go to church. Late in the evening, Captain Cole and Mr Simpson came out from town. A letter from Octavius Browne, only eight months after date of ours.

19th The boys and I spent the day at Campbellfield, and Mr McCrae came to late dinner. I took occasion to remind Lyon Campbell that we had already met in the "auld countree" at Kinfauns, one day, when he and the Pattersons had ridden over from Castle Huntly to call on Lord and Lady Gray. "There was, at the time," said Lady Gray, "a sough that the young captain was likely to carry off one of the Patterson belles."

[*Although he generally galloped, J. D. Lyon Campbell lived within easy trotting distance of "Mayfield". My father remembered him as a hearty young man tearing about the country on horseback. His favourite mount was so spirited that the boys called him "The Unicorn", and, whenever the two appeared, they would shout, "Here comes the lion and the unicorn!" The unicorn's real name was "Clifton". Before Campbell settled in Australia he had been attached to the "9th Queen's Royal Lancers". He was of affluent fortune, and owned several properties, the largest of*] *these being Bullarook, upon the edge of Birch and Irvine's station, known as Seven Hills. When he died, at thirty-five, he left his new "Outside Car" (see entry of 8th December 1844) to Mr La Trobe who, until that period, had always used "The Marrowbone Stage". The Superintendent once got into a row for having allegedly ordered a government road to be made to Campbell's house at Campbellfield; and this act formed one of the charges brought against him by Fawkner at the Melbourne Town Hall Council, when La Trobe was asked to resign. Here are the exact words used in the indictment: "That Mr La Trobe had wasted the public money, in having expended £450 on a private road leading to the house of Mr Lyon Campbell, a particular friend; and only a paltry £50 on the Sydney Road."]*

21st Mr McLure left; to be absent for a fortnight.

22nd Mr Crawford Mollison and Mr Stephenson to dinner. Thomas brought the cedar presses for the lobby.

24th Mrs Cole gave birth to a son at 4 a.m. Dr Thomas brought the news, and dined with us.

Sunday, 25th Mr McCrae quite *hors de combat.* Captain Murchison dropped in at dinner-time. Jane returned from Geelong.

26th Mr Simpson sent me a dish of ripe strawberries. Dr Thomas and his wife, Ward Cole, Donald Mackinnon, Mr Simpson, and Jones Agnew Smith to dinner.

28th An intensely hot day. . . . *Nuit blanche.*

29th Lucia one year old today. Mr McCrae walked out with Mrs Ailsa Craig. Mr Craig to dinner.

30th Mr McCrae sent Archie to town for "Don". Found one of the clerks has taken him out early this morning, so his master had to start on foot.

31st Mr McCrae showed me Mr Montgomery's letter proposing to dissolve their partnership. Felt thankful at the prospect of returning home, even on small means, as the boys' prospects in the old country should be greatly superior to any that may offer for them here. Hope on. . . . Hope ever.

[*1842*]

THE men (Thomas and Stribling) engaged to build the walls of the house at "Mayfield" were paid 10s. 6d. per perch.

The window-frames, doors, and skirting-boards were made of Manning River cedar, and the floors were laid with very narrow shaved pine boards. The roof of the house was covered with slates of the size called "Countesses". At first we had temporary deal window-frames on which unbleached cotton was stretched for the window spaces, as no glass of the dimension required was procurable in Melbourne. After the woodwork was completed, Thomas used up some of the cedar that was left in making a pair of frames for Brierly's prints of "*The Royal Adelaide*" and "*The Pique*".

1843

JANUARY

January, Sunday 1st A hot and sultry morning, changing to a rainy afternoon. Mr, Mrs, and Miss Montgomery came to early dinner. Our men brought back the two Timor ponies.

2nd Willie left to go to Brighton with Mrs Montgomery.

3rd Mrs Edward Curr spent the day with me. Mr Hamilton to dinner.

[*Thomas Ferrier Hamilton: son of John Hamilton, colonel in the 3rd Dragoon Guards, and, on his mother's side, grandson of Charles, second Viscount Gort. At the age of sixteen, he left Scotland by the "Abingdon", and reached Sydney in '39; from Sydney, he overlanded to the Port Phillip country, where he and his friend, Thomas Carre Riddell, took up land along the Rocky Water Holes (the Sunbury of today). Here, at breakfast time, following Black Thursday, he sheltered and fed a burnt-out government survey party, including among its members a freckled-faced boy called McCrae (G. G. McC.). Besides the R.-W.-H. property, Hamilton acquired Cairnhill and Elderslie. A member of the Victorian Legislative Council, he was, also, for some while, president of the Melbourne Club. In 1853, he married Elizabeth, daughter of Sidney Stephen, Chief Justice of New Zealand. Died 7th August 1905.*

Black Thursday. "The fire was so near Melbourne that the sky seemed to be a mass of floating fragments of bark and leaves ablaze with the intense heat. We could hardly breathe the air. The dropping embers even set on fire ships in the bay."—W. Kaye.]

4th A frightfully hot day. Mr McLure returned from the farm.

5th Mr Sprott and young Robert Craig came out with Mr McCrae.

[*"A new-chum called Sprott."—Jim Hunter. In the Sprott versus Fyans case, 14th August 1845, Sprott was awarded damages to the tune of £200; but the successful litigant, having established the principle he was aiming at, relinquished all claims.*]

6th I rode to town. Called on Mrs Myer and Mrs J. F. Palmer.

7th Mr Brodribb to dinner. In the evening, Mrs Craig and the two little girls came to fetch Robert home. [*Without the help of initials, we suggest that this man was Albert Brodribb, whose overlanding, with cattle, in five days had been hailed as a paramount feat.*]

8th Rode to Heidelberg [*scrubby ground and thinly-timbered, undulating country*]; called at Mrs Curr's on the way home. Our black allies, Murray, Mooni, and Margaret, busy all day chopping wood and drawing water for Ellen.

9th Rode to town. Dined with Mrs Cole. In the evening, Mr Simpson took Mary Anne, Sarah Thomas, and ourselves to the Oratorio in the Wesleyan Chapel. The singers acquitted themselves well, especially Mr Blundell. It was past eleven before we got back to "Mayfield" with Mr Simpson.

10th Rode to town. Called on Mrs Jeffery from Kyneton and she, with Mary Anne and Sarah, walked out beside my pony to spend the day with us and remain for the night.

11th Mrs Jeffery left early. Mr Hogue, Claud Farie, and Mr Sprott to dinner.

[*At this time, Mr Sprott would be trying to live down the ridicule attached to his pistol-fight with Mr Campbell of the western district. The duellists had crossed the South Australian border, whence, after a couple of reciprocative pops, they came home again, their worst experience being a little stiffness resultant from their four hundred miles' ride. In '49, Dr Thomas entered into a more serious business which took place near Abbotsford, at 6 a.m. "His hat shook with the impact, and stayed shaking for some seconds. Then, when it finally fell off his head, a bunch of loose hair, clipped by the bullet, went whisking away."*

"I rode from Campbell's to Hamilton and Donald's, along with three of the tallest fellows I ever knew: 'Long' McNeil (6 ft 7 ins), Claud Farie (6 ft 5 ins), and Richardson (6 ft 5 ins)."—Aleck Hunter.]

12th Ill and shivering; and baby has a cold. Dr Thomas ordered me to stay in bed.

13th A letter from dear Aunt Fanny announcing the death of her half-sister, Katharine, at Nice in December, 1841; also, the marriage of Sir James A. Gordon's eldest daughter to a barrister, whose name she does not mention; and, yet again, the marriage of his third daughter to a young clergyman, the son of Sir William Barnett, M.D.

Colonel Charles Edward Gordon's only daughter was married, at Dublin (where the colonel holds an appointment), to a Mr Duckett, of Carlow. He has £3000 a year income, and "not a stiver in debt".

Aunt Fanny's own nephew, Tom Birch, formerly a lieutenant in the *Pique* during her perilous voyage, now Captain Commander R.N., has lately married a Miss Stephenson with £10,000; and his eldest brother, the Rev. Charles Birch, M.A. Oxon. has married the second daughter of Tom Burnett, Aberdeen, commonly called "Duke of Keppleton" (Keppleton being the name of their residence out of town). This recalls merry days at Wardhouse. Charles, not then ordained, but engaged to marry Miss Burnett as soon as he should have a "living". Charles offered to marry me gratis whenever I should require his aid. He was ordained in July 1830, but madame wouldn't allow me to claim his attendance in September of the same year.

14th Still in bed. Dr Thomas stopped the night.

15th Dr Thomas and Mr McCrae left for town early.

17th A hot wind. Ward Cole came out. Dr Thomas and Mr McCrae returned from Brighton.

18th Mrs Osmond came to help me with clothing for the voyage home. Captain Cole to tea.

19th Mrs Ailsa Craig, Miss Ballingale, and Mrs Bunbury to see us.

20th Mr McCrae laid up. Dr Thomas came in the evening.

21st Oppressively warm day. Mr Urquhart to dinner.

23rd Ward Cole to dinner. Captain McLachlan to tea.

24th Rode to Dr Thomas's; thence to Brighton. Left Brighton at a quarter to four—home at "Mayfield" by 6 p.m.

25th A hot wind. Mrs Thomas Walker, Miss Walker, and R. H. Horne. [*Richard Hengist Horne: author of "Orion", and friend of Elizabeth Barrett Browning; recognized as a great poet by Edgar Allan Poe, Robert Browning, and Thomas Carlyle. Setting aside the poet, Horne belonged to the educated pirate type, and, although he experienced adventures, he imagined more than there were. Similarly, my father, despite his milder nature, began to tell the family how once upon a time he had run away to sea. Bewildered children exclaimed their astonishment at never having heard the tale before; whereupon he protested, "I did, indeed!" I asked "How far did you go?" He paused, then said: "To the end of the street. . . ." Horne knew the same street.*]

27th Frank Cobham tells me that there is a man in possession at the Moonee Ponds, and another one seized the horse on which Frank was riding as Dr McCrae's property; so Frank had to walk to Melbourne. Mr McCrae left for Merri Creek to canvass for Dr Nicholson.

28th The sheriff and Mrs Mackenzie, also Dr and Mrs Thomas to dinner.

29th Mr Westgarth came out with Mr McCrae.

30th Mr McKillop and Mr McCrae started early for the Darebin. Mrs Lyon Campbell to early dinner.

31st Mary Anne and Sarah Thomas went to Great Bourke Street, as Baby Cole is to be baptized tomorrow.

FEBRUARY

February 1st Mr McCrae went to stand godfather for his nephew. Returned in disgust at the second edition of the names of "George Ward". I cannot see that it is worse than the second edition of "Andrew Murison"!

SUPPLEMENT

At this time, our contract with Mortimer, the butcher, for beef and mutton was at the rate of three ha'pence the pound; veal, pork, etc. at fourpence. The cart used to bring us a side of mutton twice a week, with a shin of beef for soup. The driver invariably added a sheep's head and pluck for the dogs, but Ellen prepared these Scots fashion for the master and allowed the dogs the leavings. The mutton was so fat, Ellen used to make candles for her own use and for the nursery of it. On Friday afternoons, troops of blackfellows and their gins used to assemble at the slaughter-houses to collect sheeps' heads and plucks which they roasted at their fires by the Merri Creek.

*　　*　　*

2nd　A fierce, hot wind continued through the day and night.

3rd　Mrs Thomas came to spend a few days as she is grieved at the thought of our going home.

4th　Mr Westgarth came out till Monday.

5th　A hot wind. No one ventured to church.

6th　Mr Westgarth left. Captain Reid to dinner.

7th　Rode to town, and went to the bank.

8th　Busy cutting out shirts for the boys.

9th　On account of Mr McCrae's recent quarrel with his brother Farquhar, his little namesake is henceforth only to be called by his second name, "Peregrine"—an awkward name to utter: "Peerie", the Shetland word for *small*, would be more euphonious. At Gravesend, the child was called "Master Paragon". An insect stung Perry's eye and gave him considerable pain. Luckily Drs Thomas and D'Purrier came in the evening and prescribed for him.

10th　Henry Montgomery came out to dinner. In the evening, *"Brewer's Natural Magic"* [*a discreet euphemism*] gave rise to a discussion which ended in remarks on H.M.'s brother, with accusations which Henry refuted. Retired to my room. Mr McCrae not only *suspects*, but openly accuses his partner of taking more than his share of the profits of the firm. On the other hand, Mr Montgomery complains that he is left to do all the work while Mr McCrae is amusing himself. Mr McCrae retorts that he himself created the business and kept it alive through civilities to all the clients.

11th　A fine, fresh morning, after a heavy storm of thunder. Mr McCrae, in a desponding mood, tells me (what I had a suspicion of

BEDFORD HOUSE, A PRINCIPAL INN DURING THE FORTIES
The vehicle before the door looks like being first cousin to Kirk's phaeton of the diary

THE OLD GOVERNMENT HOUSE, WILLIAM STREET, MELBOURNE

WATER-CART OF 1841
From a drawing by Robert Russell after the original by George Gordon McCrae

THE CHALET, SUPERINTENDENT LA TROBE'S COTTAGE AT JOLIMONT
From a sketch by Hugh McCrae

two days ago) that, after all my outlay and preparations, our prospect of leaving Australia Felix is becoming day by day more indistinct.

12th Mr McLure took George to the Kirk. Dr Thomas came out, and his wife returned with him to town. Heard of the death of dear Jeanie Farquhar (Mrs Mitchell) eight days after giving birth to a little girl who survives.

13th An intensely hot day. Archie killed a snake four feet long.

14th Mrs Thomas came out to stay a few days.

15th Captain and Mrs Reid arrived from their station. George and Willie rode on their Timors to Mr Curr's.

16th Mr McCrae tells me—Mr Montgomery wishes him to remain here to collect the debts due to the firm. At dinner, I fainted, just after carving. Dr Thomas and Charles came in at the same moment and attended to me.

17th Mr McCrae and Captain Reid left for Tichingorook. Dr Myer to dinner. Dr Thomas drove out for his wife.

18th Busy renovating the boys' Glengarry caps, as new hats are out of the question.

19th A steaming hot day. The boys could not go to church.

20th Dr Myer came to see Mrs Reid as she is to be his patient a few days hence.

21st After tea, while the toddy-kettle was still on the tray, the boys ran outside to exercise in the shade; and George, noticing a large snake below the doorstep, shouted to Archie, who struck at it with his crow-bar; yet it was protected in such a way by the wood-work that it remained unharmed. So I poured the whole kettleful of boiling water over the place, a ruse which effectually brought the snake into the open, when, with a mighty effort, it flung itself forth from beneath the step, and Archie gave it the *coup de grâce*. This was almost certainly the snake that had been seen by the plasterers, and it was fortunate the creature had not tried to escape through one of the rooms, as none of the skirting-boards was yet put in.

22nd Dr Thomas came in the evening; told me Mamie Cobham had met with a serious accident.

23rd Stunned by the prospect before me.

24th Mr McCrae returned from Cape Schanck in rather better spirits than when he left as *"he thinks* he sees his way to obtain a run next the Jamieson's Survey".

[*"Special Surveys were blocks of land containing eight square miles, or rather more than five thousand acres, which were sold in the early forties at £1 per acre to any persons who paid the amount into the Colonial Office at London."—"Victorian Historical Magazine".*]

25th A day of pouring rain and thorough discomfort.

26th Rain again. Only Mr McLure went to church.

27th Captain Reid arrived with Wattie, Johnnie, and Jane Scott, their servant, to stay here until after Mrs Reid's confinement is well over. They have their quarters in the upstairs rooms.

28th It appears that Dr Nicholson proposes that Mr McCrae shall give up this house to him; the land still being unpaid for. And that we shall pay him £100 a year rent for it, pending it being purchased. The price he asks for house and land is £1400. Dr Nicholson came to dinner.

MARCH

March 1st Willie eight years old today. Captain Reid took his boys to see the town for the first time in their little lives. The news brought out by the captain is that, yesterday afternoon, Mrs Q——y attempted suicide by cutting the vein in her arm and taking laudanum. After this, poor Mr Q. will look more like a ghost than ever!

[*Poor Mr Q. (high cheekbones and black hair), was a lady-chaser who stalked his feminine game dressed in a tall "Caroline" hat, a Willy-Wagtail coat with brass buttons, flowered vest, and white trousers strapped under Wellington boots.*]

2nd Mr and Mrs Pohlman on their way to the Campaspe *à cheval*. Mr Pohlman, well-macassared, managing a leather hat-box (perhaps the receptacle of madame's best *cheveux*!). Mr McLure amused us by remarking: "What an attentive *son* she has!"

[*Mr Pohlman: diffident and unobtrusive. He spoke with a lisp. As an M.L.C., in Strutt's picture of the opening of the first Victorian Legislative*

*Council by La Trobe, he can be observed seated "bodkin" between Ebden
and Ross in the front lefthand row, looking towards the governor.]*

3rd Captain Reid left for his station. Dr Thomas came to
prescribe for Lucy. His wife has gone out to "La Rose" to keep
Agnes company.

5th Mr McCrae unable to go to town today. Dr Nicholson, Dr
Thomas, and Mr William Ryrie to dinner. Conjectures as to nature
of luminous appearance observed in the west last night. Mrs Bunbury gave birth to a daughter this morning.

*[On 28th March this comet was seen at Greenwich. Its place, as found by
rough comparison with 63 Eridanus, was nearly as follows: Right
ascension 4 hours, 21 minutes, 35 seconds. North Polar distance 96
degrees 51 minutes.—G. B. Airey.]*

6th Awakened at 3 a.m. by Dr Myer's arrival, and, a few
minutes later, the cry of the new-born babe! Rose, and did what
I could for the little stranger—a fine "lass bairn"; and returned to
bed at 4 a.m.

7th Dr Myer to dinner. The comet distinctly seen, and most
brilliant. Mr McCrae, gazing at it, stumbled over the wheelbarrow
and had to hurry inside to doctor his broken shin! A sad outcome
of star-gazing.

> *[For he that strives to touch a starre
> Oft stombles at a straw. . . .]*

8th Captain and Miss McLachlan came early to spend the day.
The comet appears larger and brighter; it resembles the one of 1811,
but its tail is longer. The earlier comet was right overhead, and, at
home, the sky was darker blue than here.

*[During three appearances, Georgiana's comet had traversed thirty-two
degrees eastward. A. C. Le Souef described its effect upon a tribe of
aborigines, who broke camp in the middle of the night. "They thought
the comet had been sent against them by the Ovens blacks, to do them
injury."]*

13th Captain Reid arrived. The weather very trying.
14th Lucy feverish.

16th Took my miniatures out of the tin box, to have them ready for showing to Mr Westgarth. Then began to cut Perry's hair, and had got one side (only) done when the visitor arrived.

17th The fuchsia-plant given to me by Mrs Howitt has been destroyed in the night. Mr McCrae blames Archie for allowing our cow to rove. Finished cutting Perry's hair.

30th Captain Reid left. Intensely hot night.

31st Hot, moist, and oppressive all day long. Dr Thomas came.

APRIL

April 1st C. H. McKnight and James Irvine to dinner. Eliza gave me notice that she wishes to leave three weeks hence to go to Launceston.

2nd Eliza took George and Willie to St James's Church.

3rd Dr Thomas tells me I have "low fever"—or "swamp fever"—which just now is raging at Back Brighton.

4th Perry and Lucy both suffering from feverish symptoms.

5th Rose from my bed this afternoon. Mr McCrae full of perplexities.

6th Up at noon. Mr Westgarth, Mrs Thomson, and Dr Thomas to dinner.

7th "*Me voilà sans sou! mais non sans soucis*" . . . Mrs Derrett called for her accompt, and I *had* to borrow the sovereigns out of the purse dear Aunt Fanny netted me, given by her to each of the boys "to purchase an [*indecipherable*] each", but their papa never could make the investment *en bloc*. No sooner had I paid off Mrs Derrett, than Mr Mackenzie, the clerk, came out with a note from Mr McCrae desiring me to send "every pound, shilling, and sou that I could muster" by bearer. Sent three good promissory-notes, two for £9 10s. each; and one for £30—another for £27. In the evening, I learnt that owing to Mr Montgomery having advocated the claim of Donovan, the builder of the new Union Bank premises (in accordance with Mr McLaggan, the architect's report), Thomas Elder Boyd, the manager of the Bank, sends to give *Montgomery and McCrae* warning that "unless they pay £160 before twelve today he shall summon them", thus forcing Mr McCrae to discount bills he had set apart for tradesmen's accompts, besides compelling him to give a bill for £30 to make up the amount, as no money is to be had at this time from any of the clients in or near Melbourne. [*Boyd could bleed a stone. If the stone dried up, he pulverized it. James Montgomery was the first Crown Solicitor (£200 per annum), but, after a lot of rasping and rubbing up against Judge Willis, he resigned in favour of Henry Field Gurner. Montgomery's next move was to form a partnership with Mr McCrae: an arrangement which lasted until the end of '44.*] The scarcity of actual coin is remarkable. It is said that Cashmore, No. 1 Collins Street East, is the only man in town who can give you the full change of a five pound note. [*Michael Cashmore: a member of the city council, inspector of the meat market, draper, amateur actor, etc. During the forties, people made appointments to meet each other at "Cashmore's Corner" (Collins and Elizabeth streets), where Michael Cashmore kept his store—opposite a dust-heap through the summer, but a lake in winter, quite Venetian to behold!*]

8th Found in my desk a purse containing twenty hoarded shillings: a fortune to me in these impecunious days. The sheriff gave Mr McCrae a hint that Dr Thomas would be in danger of capture on Tuesday next should he not be able to pay up £30 in the meantime.

9th Mr McCrae rode to church. The boys unable to go for want of summer hats to protect their heads from sunstroke.

11th The *Enmore* came in. Received bill of lading for my box from London. Luckily, the marble mantelpieces were not sent. Ellen begged the price of a pair of boots "to keep her feet off the ground". Let her have eight of my bright shillings.

12th Lush brought his bill. I gave him my William the Fourth sovereign in payment. A bill of £20 was dishonoured yesterday. While carving a leg of mutton at early dinner, the guard of the fork gave way and the knife cut clean through the first joint of my forefinger, horizontally. . . . *à l'instant*; bound it up tightly with my pocket handkerchief. Nearly fainted. Could not sleep all night for the throbbing pain in the nerve which is divided at the tip of the finger.

13th Mr McCrae left for the Camerons, leaving us an order for flour.

14th Good Friday. Mrs Montgomery gave me a cast in the trap to church. Learnt from Mrs Cole that Agnes Bruce gave birth to a son on January 5 . . . "Andrew Murison".

15th Heavy rain; said to be the first of the winter rains.

16th Walked to Newtown, whence Mrs Montgomery gave me a cast to church (Easter Day).

17th Letter from Mr Moffatt, Montreal. George and Willie went to spend their Easter Monday at Newtown. Captain Reid arrived and told us of his troubles *en route!*

18th Mrs Reid and the children spent the day at Newtown.

19th Dr Myer came to tell me his wife had given birth to a fine girl this morning. Watty Reid threw a piece of slate at Perry and cut his forehead. Dr Myer dressed the wound which was dangerously near the temple.

20th The Reids preparing to start homewards. Captain Reid took the boys to town early, but found he could not leave till tomorrow.

21st A lovely morning. At noon Captain and Mrs Reid, the baby, and Jane Scott left for Tichingorook. Thunder and rain during the evening.

22nd Archie brought out the box; it is well the contents were paid for in advance.

23rd, 24th Mr McCrae laid up at home.

25th Unpacked my box; found a brown merino dress and cape, a straw-bonnet ready trimmed, two dozen gloves, an umbrella, cap-ribbons, tapes, cottons, needles and pins, two frocks for Lucia from her godmother, Mrs Cummins, and a quantity of books for distribution.

27th Miss Gavan and Mrs Montgomery came to see me.

28th While we were in Nicholson's paddock, Willie killed at a single stroke from his cane a curious little cinnamon-coloured snake about fifteen inches long; on examining it, we found two protuberances like finger-ends, or fins. . . . Mr La Trobe, when he saw it, said it was a pity Willie had killed it, as it is a harmless creature of the lizard family—by name *Pseudopus*, or "false-footed".

30th Mr McCrae, returning from church, called on Mr Locke, who gave him a book he had picked up on the road to Melbourne, supposing it belonged to us. It proved to be one of the books from Martha Cummins that I had given to Aleck McCrae.

MAY

May 1st   Mr Montgomery was thrown from his horse. Mr McCrae laughed!

2nd   Sarah Thomas came to see my new things.

3rd   Went to Mrs Myer's to offer some of the gloves, ribbons, and artificial flowers for sale "at prime cost", for ready cash only.

4th   Suffering from "blight" in my eyes.

6th   Sarah making frocks for Lucia. Miss Gavan to dinner.

8th   Incessant rain. Needlework all day.

9th   Dr Thomas came for Sarah, as Mrs Thomas has gone with Agnes to "La Rose" today, Dr McCrae having departed for Sydney.

[*Kerr's "Directory" for 1842. Physician: Farquhar McCrae, J.P., "La Rose", Moonee Moonee Ponds, Melbourne. Edmund Finn describes McCrae as "a squatting doctor", and thinks he dabbled too much in land and politics. He tells the story of his departure for Sydney, where he died, 20th April 1850, at the early age of forty-three.*]

11th   Captain and Mrs Cole, and the baby; Mr and Mrs Edward Cotton; and Mr and Mrs Pohlman came.

13th   Walked to Bourke Street, then home again.

14th   Mr McCrae rode to church, and I walked with the boys. Returning, Mr McCrae took Perry on the saddle before him, while I stopped at Dr Myer's, to rest. Then Elliot Heriot came out with me to dinner.

15th   Captain and Mrs Eddrington came to bespeak our good offices for Donald Macpherson and his wife, old servants of theirs, now residing in the cottage half-way between this and Mr Cavenagh's. Macpherson's wife is in a dying condition, and they are very badly off.

16th   George, and Lucia, and I walked across the swamp, and Lucia lost one of her shoes in a mud-hole by the way. Found the poor woman in the last stage of consumption; beside her, a child

of a year and a half old. The mother, just delivered of a dead homun-
culus—her long arms and drawn features most painful to look
upon. She had been a bright-eyed bonnie lass; but, from too-long
nursing Mrs Eddrington's sucklings (and probably not on a
sufficiently nourishing diet) she is so exhausted as hardly to be able
to speak above her breath. The husband took advantage of my
being beside his wife to go to Richmond for a few articles of food.
In the evening, I sent Jane across with a basket of needful things,
and some Port wine. Jane returned much interested in Mrs Macpherson, whose parents were respectable farmer folk; and her
husband has "aye been a weel-deeing lad". *Entre nous*; it behoved
Mrs Eddrington, more than ourselves, to see to this poor woman's
dying wants.

17th Lucia and I crossed the swamp and found the woman
sinking rapidly. Called at Mrs La Trobe's, and Mrs O'Cock's, and
Dr Myer's. On returning home, found a letter from Madame
[*the Duchess of Gordon*], dated at Pau, November 1, 1842.

19th Borrowed £2 from Jane Shanks to pay Mr McCrae's
servant at the office. A miserably cold day.

20th Elliot and Ancrum Heriot to dinner.

21st Wrote a long and particular letter to Madame, urging her
to purchase this house and land as a permanent home for myself
and my children; enclosed a plan of the ground and the house,
with an elevation of the front. By advancing me the £1400 for the
property *now*, the outlay will be worth double to me what the sum
would be, at her decease; so I feel hopeful she will see fit to invest
so much in the hands of the trustees for me.

22nd It appears I must go to the ball. Began to arrange my best
black satin.

23rd Dr Thomas drove out in his gig and took me to town.
At 10 p.m. we went *en masse* to the Mechanics' Institute. All the
élite of the colony assembled, and in full swing, including Mr and
Mrs La Trobe; the Mayor, Mr Condell; [*a brewer, whose ale was
stronger in the head than he was, in magisterial ability*] and his niece,
dressed in Mantis green, not unlike the insect itself in the waltz
attitude. Mr C. H. Ebden's movements somewhat eccentric, now
and then cannoning among his neighbours.

[*Charles Hotson Ebden: a better business man than a dancer. At the first government land sale he acquired three half-acre town-lots for £136 and two years later re-sold them by public auction for £10,244. Again, in 1851, he purchased Moorabee station, holding it for three months only; at the end of this time, J. H. Paterson bought him out for an exorbitant figure. Meanwhile, he had taken over Sugarloaf Creek, then, having made money out of it, passed on to Carlsruhe. His dandyism was so excessive that his black boy copied his gait and speech. James Hunter of Devil's River describes the latter as an aboriginal bored with Australia, and records his pet phrase: "I'm going home to England, directly"; then adds, "He is from Ebden's station, and he and Charlie are as like as two peas." One of the first representatives of the Port Phillip district on the Sydney Legislative Council, Ebden fought for separation, and, upon a successful issue, rose to be auditor-general of the new colony.*]

Major and Miss Davidson, Mr and Mrs Curr, Mr and Mrs D. L. C. G. Erskine, Major and Mrs St John, the Sheriff and Mrs Mackenzie; the two Misses Fenwick, from Corio; Mr and Mrs John Cotton, and a brace of Misses; Mr and Mrs Edward Cotton, Mr and Mrs Lyon Campbell, Mr and Mrs Verner, Mrs Flintoff, Captain and Mrs Cole, Dr and Mrs Thomas, Mary Anne, and Sarah; and several others unknown to us. Dancing was kept up briskly till after 1 a.m.

[*With high spirits, and plenty of good humour, Port Phillipians were losing their Englishness. Compare the above with Crabbe Robinson's description of the waltz as it was danced in 1801.*

"Rolling or turning; though the rolling is not horizontal, but perpendicular. Yet Werter, after his first waltz with Charlotte, says—and I say so too—'I felt that, were I married, my wife should waltz (or roll) with no one but myself.' Judge: The man places the palms of his hands gently against the sides of his partner, not far from the arm-pit. His partner does the same, and instantly with as much velocity as possible they turn round and at the same time gradually glide round the room."]

24th After luncheon, came back from Melbourne.

26th Dr Owen arrived from Sydney bringing a letter of introduction from Dr Nicholson; oddly enough, it seems Dr Owen was long ago acquainted with Dr McCrae and William Bruce in Edinburgh.

27th Treated myself to a day of sketching out of doors.

28th Dr Owen to dinner. During the afternoon, we watched the coolies (at Major Davidson's, opposite) go through their club exercises. The doctor remembered the major in India, where his sobriquet was "The Devil on Two Sticks" (satirizing his irascible temper, and the Malacca canes he used to lean upon). Later on, Dr Owen accompanied us on a visit to Mrs Davidson and Carrie. Mrs Davidson showed us over her husband's tent, and exhibited the Indian goats in their compound. The doctor talked Hindustani with the coolies, and learnt that the major gives them half a rupee each, per month, with rations. It was pitiable to see these finely developed men grovelling in the dust with their foreheads at the feet of the man with the awe-inspiring name. [*A year earlier, 1842, Sir George Gipps refused a speculating company the right to import coolies into Australia.*]

SUPPLEMENT

About this time our neighbour, Mr James Simpson, designed a piece of roadmaking from the western corner of our allotment, past George Smith's and "The Grange". Our share of the cost was £40. There was also a raised footpath, about four feet wide, with sloping sides and a ditch to carry off rainwater. The sides of this path, in springtime, were gay with orchids and other strange flowers, while in the ditch next the roadway, slender frogs disported themselves, silent by day, but at sunset deafening us with their vespers.

In 1844, the "whins" I had planted across the allotment behind the house—from the gate of Nicholson's paddock to the fence of the "reserve" for the roadway to the bridge—had become a thick hedge some five feet high. The allotment is now intersected at this point by Murray Street, leading from Church Street, west across.

* * *

29th Royal Oak Day. George completes his tenth year. Lyon Campbell's three boys and the two Montgomerys came to spend the day. While I was sketching the house from the west end, Mrs Lyon came and carried off her boys *sans façon*.

30th Perry unwell. Mr McLure and the boys went to spend the day at Newtown.

31st Heavy rain all day long. Mary Anne McLachlan [*afterwards Mrs Charles Le Souef*] and the boys arranging scraps for Willie Montgomery's scrap-book.

JUNE

June 1st Mary Anne and I went to see Mrs Curr and the Davidsons. Captain McLachlan came for his little girl. Mr Dalgety, Mr Montefiore, and J. L. Foster to dinner. A very rainy night; but only Mr Foster remained.

3rd Mr McLaggan to dinner. Mr Dalgety, wading across the swamp last night, lost his favourite stick; it was made of ringed gidgee wood, and he had kept it for five years.

4th Mr McCrae home all day; so we read to the children. Mr H. Perry to dinner and stayed the night. His father is shortly to arrive here as the deputy surveyor-general, and will probably rent this house and land. Perry senior was *locum-tenens* while Sir T. L. Mitchell was on leave in England for two years—1839-40.

5th Mr McCrae very feverish; sent for Dr Thomas, and he and Dr Owen came together.

7th The *Alicia* arrived from England.

8th Mr McCrae out of bed. The sheriff and Mrs M. called.

9th Mr McLure and the boys went to town for the home letters and newspapers. Mr Montefiore took leave of us, as he goes tomorrow to Sydney. Dr Owen, Dr Thomas, and Charles came out to late dinner.

10th A wild, wet morning. Mr McCrae rode to town.

11th Pouring rain. Nobody able to go to church.

12th A dreary evening. Mr McCrae works out Mr McLure's chess problem: white to move, and mate in four moves. *J'ai le nez enchifrène* and would enjoy a sneeze.

[*Wretched entertainment. So it was with every phase of society; bad enough in town, but worse in the bush. . . . Just bread, alone; and never any circuses. One man said, "I got six months' pay in a day, and blued the whole lot up in drink!"*]

16th Still raining heavily. Dr Myer came to dinner.

17th My pulse scarcely perceptible. Mr Mollison to dinner.

19th Dr Thomas says I have "low fever" again. Mr McCrae went to dine at Captain Cole's, and to talk business.

20th Agnes La Trobe came early this forenoon, to stay with me during her mama's confinement, as Mr La Trobe's dressing-room has to be given up to that "of all hated, the most hateful of women" —the monthly nurse.

21st Mr La Trobe came to tell me Madame gave birth to a daughter (Cecile) last night.

22nd Jane Shanks laid up with a feverish attack. Mr La Trobe rode across and took Agnes on the saddle before him to see her mama's new baby, and returned with her in time to ride into town with Mr McCrae.

23rd Our familiar aborigines spent the day here. Betty, or *"Yellambourrime"* (Rough-haired) exchanged names with Lucia. This is a native compliment to be received with good grace. In the afternoon I walked across to see Mrs La Trobe and the baby.

24th Midsummer day. Cold and wintry. Mr La Trobe came to see Agnes; told us Judge Willis had been dismissed, and Judge Jeffcott appointed in his stead. Dr Myer and Mr Stawell (of the Pigeon Ponds and Chetwynd country) to dinner. In the evening, much talk about England.

[*Georgiana was entertaining a future Chief Justice, unawares. Sir William Foster Stawell, a Trinity College, Dublin, man, reached Port Phillip in '42, and, during a later period, as Attorney General to our first parliament, distinguished himself for logical acuteness, combined with penetration and iron force of will. "His diction was fluent and rapid; so much so, indeed, as to render it, at times, difficult to follow him." In 1857 he became Chief Justice, a position which he held until 1886. Next year Stawell was appointed Lieutenant Governor; nevertheless, he left Melbourne in 1889 and, following the instructive adage, repaired to Naples; saw it, and—died.*]

25th Ill with cold. These swamps, and river damps, don't agree with me.

26th Busy writing letters to be forwarded by the outward-bound ship.

27th Pouring rain. Mr McCrae dined at Captain Cole's.

28th Major and Mrs Davidson came to see me; also Mr La Trobe "to know how Agnes has been behaving". Mr La Trobe says that some 800 partisans of Judge Willis have signed a protest against the authority of Sir G. Gipps to depose his judgeship. Poor man! In Jamaica, and elsewhere, he was never considered quite sane, though *sometimes* rational in his conduct, both public and private.

[*"A disreputable old rip, who, I think, was in consort with the devil."*— *Captain Foster Fyans.*

John Walpole Willis, the fire-eating son of an eighteenth-century Captain of Dragoons, began life as a barrister. He was twice married: the first Mrs W. (a daughter of Earl Strathmore, who had her espousal quashed through Act of Parliament) being succeeded by a Miss Bund. In 1828 Willis became Judge of the Court of Chancery in Canada, but lost that office within twelve months. His next employment was in British Guiana, where he remained till 1837, when he was appointed one of the judges of the Supreme Court of New South Wales. Willis's cross-grained nature made him unpopular; consequently, in '41, the not-very-much-sought-after position of resident judge of Port Phillip going begging, he had it given to him, not only on account of evident ability, but also that his associates might be rid of a scurrilous tongue.]

29th Mr McCrae went to town to attend the meeting of Mr La Trobe's friends, to consider how they can best remove the blame endeavoured to be cast upon him by Willis's supporters. Enclosed, with a letter to Mrs Jeffery, a packet of choice flower-seeds from our garden. Mr McCrae wrote a note to Dr Thomson, of Geelong, who, he considered, "has misrepresented his exertions for Sir T. L. Mitchell in a most amazing manner".

[*If Thomson had misrepresented McCrae, it was without effect upon Mitchell, as witness the following excerpt taken from a letter of Sir Thomas Mitchell's addressed to Georgiana: "Fifty-five, Hans Place,*

Sloane Street, London. . . . Surely our stars, and yours, are under some favourable influence, for when I think of what Mr McCrae did for me; and, indeed, the colony, with Blackwood; I must ever feel indebted to him. The encouragement now proposed will certainly determine me to take out barometers; models of bridges; etc. for that country which, before, I rather paused about doing." Thomas Livingstone Mitchell reached Sydney on 23rd September 1827, and began duty as deputy surveyor-general, under Oxley. Oxley's death occurred on 25th May 1828, when Mitchell succeeded to the higher position, and, surviving his predecessor for twenty-seven years, died at Darling Point, Sydney, on 9th October 1855. (Kt. Bach. 1838.)]

Mark Nicholson arrived so completely drenched with rain that he had to be supplied with a whole suit of dry clothing. Mr McCrae taken ill during the night, complaining of languor and sinking.

30th Mr La Trobe brought flower-roots for my garden, and inquired about Agnes. Agnes is quite at home here, has her lessons and writes her copy under Mr McLure's eye, and plays with the boys. Their favourite game is "Parrots up a gum-tree". There you may see them all perched on different branches and chattering to each other. Agnes has dubbed George a "politer", Sandy a "circumventor", and Willie a "schemer". She is very volatile, and quick, like Willie; so it's diamond cut diamond between them.

JULY

July 2nd Mr McCrae rode to church, and Mr La Trobe came early and took Agnes *à cheval* to dine with her mama. George and Sandy covered with nettle-rash. Dr Thomas came out with Mr McCrae.

3rd Mr Mackinnon tells me that the "ladies" were very riotous at the "North Star" ball the other evening and that, on Mr La Trobe's health being proposed, an individual demurred, calling Mr La Trobe "a humbug".

[No doubt, the "individual" thought he shouted truth. Many people imagined a vain thing; because La Trabe seemed flexible; whereas, in

fact, he was firm—a firmness spoilt by the desire to be friends with both sides. In his most passionate moments he never "over-roared" the gentlest sucking dove.]

4th   Mr McCrae unable to go to town. Mr Mackinnon remained here to talk over business matters.

5th   Mr R. Campbell came out to dine with Mr McLure.

6th   Mr William Walker to dinner.

7th   Miss Gavan came to stay a few days. Letter from Dr Owen.

8th   The *Mary Lyon* sailed for England with our letters.

9th   Mrs Curr and her daughter came. In the evening, Mrs Cole arrived, bringing with her sundry bags of old letters belonging to Mr McCrae, found on the removal of his mother's wardrobe.

10th   Mr McCrae busy sorting and burning letters. *Tout sage qu'il est!*

11th   Mr McCrae planted the vine-cuttings from Skene Craig's vineyard in Collins Street West. Judge Jeffcott arrived from Sydney.

[*The blandiloquent and thoroughly accomplished second Resident Judge came to Port Phillip in the revenue cutter "Prince George". He was a member of the Irish bar, and had been Law Adviser at Dublin. Unlike his predecessor, who had often arrived late at court, Jeffcott took his seat punctually to time, and soon gave the impression of a wide-awake, thoroughbred man.*]

12th   Mrs W——t came across to affix her signature to a document (for raising the wind) to avoid the éclat of appearing at Mr McCrae's office. I stood by to see her write her name—not that I had any doubt of her being well accustomed to do so, but because Mrs L. C. is circulating a report (on the authority of her maid who was dismissed ·from "H——n" for improper conduct) that Mr W——t married his cook and that she can neither read nor write! Anyone can see at a glance that Mrs W——t is a born gentlewoman. Before she married Mr W——t, a solicitor, belonging to an old Church of England family in Yorkshire, she had been Miss Felicia B., an authoress, and a communicant.

I can now enlighten Mrs L. C., by positive proof, of the absurdity of her servants' assertions; and shall take care to contradict all who amuse themselves by repeating them. It requires proof positive to convince some people of their error, when once they have taken up an idea to the prejudice of others.

List of Flower-seeds and Esculents in the Garden at "Mayfield"

Toker Beans: fine new long-pod bean; Maltese Cabbage; Torsi: the Maltese Turnip; Ocra Hibiscus Esculentus: Maltese Cauliflower; Maltese Lettuce; Sea Kale: Dark-coloured Nasturtium; Choice Capsicums, from Cape of Good Hope; Bignonia Stans; Malope Trifida; Iris; Sweet Pease; Indian Shot; Teak-tree; Almond-tree; *Thistle from Fyvie Castle*: and whins from Hill of Gourden. *Gigantic Lily from Botany Bay.* Cassia, from Hartlands. Tulips. Spanish Broom. Laburnum. Cypress. Bigonia. White Lupin tree. Hollyhock. 10 weeks Stock. Dark Wallflower. Carnations. Convolvolus Minor. Palma Christi, or Castor-oil Plant. Alyssum. Indian Pinks. Marvel of Peru, or Four O'clock, Jamaica. Love Lies Bleeding. Eschscholtzia (Californian) Nemophylle. Summer Cypress. Sunflower. Full-eyed ditto. Giant Sunflower. Poppies. Cape Joy. Ixias. Borage. Millefoil Rue. Tansy. Crown Narcissus, from Miss Gavan, grown in Ireland; 22 flowers on one stem. Crocuses. Gladioli. Jonquils. Narcissus. Violets, and Pansies. Neither Buttercups nor Daisies.

List of Varieties of Vines

Pedro Quinanes. Sweetwater. Claret-grape. Hamburgh Muscatel.

13th Perry's face and hands covered with "Dibble Dibble" again.

14th Put in the flower-bulbs from Mr Curr's; and those Miss Gavan brought from Ireland. Also, she gave me two ash-leaved potatoes which have been planted out.

15th Judge Jeffcott arrived to inspect the house; he is of the opinion it is too far from town. [*The punctuality complex. Meanwhile, he lodged at the Prince of Wales Hotel, Little Flinders Street East; dear and exclusive; the best of that time.*] Mr La Trobe came for Agnes after dinner, as the *garde-malade* has left.

16th Miss Gavan took Willie and Sandy to church. George went with Mr McLure to the Rév. Mr Gunn. Mr McCrae rode to "Stanney" to dine with the Bunburys. Mr R. H. Brown to tea.

SUPERINTENDENT LA TROBE
From a sketch by Hugh McCrae

When he became superintendent, La Trobe, who had travelled a lot, solaced himself with reading books by discoverers and explorers, or else took part in competition against Lyon Campbell to see who could grow the finest fuchsia, the reddest geranium . . . for, although he wore a ceremonial uniform, he was anything but military-minded. From the beginning he provided for posterity, taking care to withhold areas of land from sale—areas that later grew into sanctuaries of quietness and rest, not one of which is honoured with his name.

CAPTAIN FOSTER FYANS
IN HIS OLD AGE
From a sketch by Hugh McCrae

Captain Fyans, Crown Lands Commissioner, has a mountain, as well as a bridge and a ford, named after him. His reports to La Trobe are full of vital egotism; for instance: "I ordered *my* two constables to load, and *my* ten convicts to fall in, close to *my* hut." Without much sympathy for the squatter, Fyans divided them into three classes, namely, "Gentlemen, shopboys, and shepherds."

ROBERT HODDLE
From a sketch by Hugh McCrae

Hoddle was Senior Surveyor at Port Phillip, and in 1837 he laid out the township of Melbourne. On 1st June of the same year he acted as auctioneer at the first land sale.

JOSEPH HAWDON
From a sketch by Hugh McCrae

"Mr Hawdon, to whose enterprise the district is indebted for having opened a communication by land to South Australia." (*Port Phillip Gazette*, 5th January 1838.)

17th Miss Gavan left. Dr Thomas came to see Perry. In the evening, thunder, lightning and rain.

18th Archie Grahame and Elizabeth Impey have a holiday on account of Archie's marriage with Jane Scott (Mr Reid's nurse-girl), at St James's. Mrs Montgomery came on horseback for me, and I rode beside her to Collins Street. Called at Mrs Skene Craig's, Captain Cole's, Mrs Ailsa Craig's, and Dr Thomas's, then to Dr Myer's, where we found Captain Bunbury. [*In a list of those on board the brig "Sterlingshire", arriving at Port Phillip, 5th October 1836, we read the name of Skene Craig, commissariat officer. Skene Craig afterwards was put in charge of the post office. He died in 1837.*] Detained by squalls and rain, and had to stay all night at Mr Montgomery's.

19th Crossed the swamp, early, to "Mayfield".

20th Wrote to Mr La Trobe, recommending Captain McCrae for a magistracy.

21st Headache all day.

22nd Mr Shadforth [*Judge's Associate*], Mr Bernard, and Dr Myer to dinner.

23rd Mr La Trobe, with Agnes, to see me. Mr La Trobe says that, although nothing is available at present, he will do all he can to assist Captain McCrae. In the meanwhile, he has invited him to be one of the District Council.

24th Sketched Lucia, in the old grey bonnet.

25th Went to Campbellfield to enquire for Mrs Lyon, whose baby died when two days old.

26th Miss Gavan and the Montgomerys called.

27th Margaret Murison Thomas baptized at St James's.

28th Mr McCrae in bed all day; Dr Thomas, Henry Montgomery, and Mr Burke came out.

29th A bitterly cold day. Dr Thomas came to see his "patient", who refused the medicines prescribed for him. George went with Jane Shanks to the Kirk.

30th Letter from Mrs Jeffery with two books for Sandy. Read the memoirs of the Emperor Alexander, also an account of the gentle wife of Mr Shepherd and her intercession on behalf of Lord Byron. Head very bad: the result of perpetual worry.

I

AUGUST

August 1st   Miss Montgomery and Mr Burke married at St James's, then at St Francis's.

2nd   Mr McLure took the boys to town. Dr Myer called.

3rd   Harry Bunbury arrived, in charge of a constable and one of the boat's crew.

[*This doesn't mean he was arrested, though no doubt he deserved to be. John Hunter, in a letter dated 7th May 1842, writes: "Hawka was driving Mrs Bunbury's tandem, and the first night we went to Murchison's, where Master Bunbury kicked up the Devil's Delight and astonished the quiet young Murchisons." Very likely the constable who brought Harry would be an old man, dressed in civilian clothes, with a belt, or saddle-girth, to hang his truncheon from; on his head, a cabbage-tree hat, marked, like a zoological specimen,* MELBOURNE POLICE. *It wasn't till '51, when Sturt became police magistrate of the city, that members of the force began to be chosen for character and physique. These men looked pachydermatous in bulky uniforms, especially during winter-time, when they wore "Long Tom" overcoats reaching to the heels of their Wellington boots. We can imagine their appearance through a Yarra fog, with lanterns strapped to their waists, feeling for their batons down the legs of their trousers, and ready to spring enormous rattles which could be heard as far as from Cole's Wharf to Dr McCrae's house in Great Bourke Street West.*]

4th   Mrs Montgomery brought cake and gloves from Mr and Mrs Burke.

5th   Letter from Sir Thomas L. Mitchell.

6th   George, Willie, and Sandy went to Kirk in their newly-made tartan suits.

7th   Mr Clark and Mr Powlett to dine and stay the night.

8th   Dr Thomas and Mr Bernard.

9th, 10th, 11th   Needlework.

12th   Letter from Sydney saying the clerkship Mr McCrae applied for was already disposed of.

15th   While Mr McCrae was absent making some arrangement with Mr Montgomery, I drew from the bank my half year's pay, £50.

16th On giving it to Mr McLure, he returned £10 into my hand, and insisted he would not take more in these times. . . "Indeed, if you cannot afford so much, £40 will suffice." This is most kind and considerate, and so utterly unexpected.

[*If ever Nature plagiarized character from a book, she honoured Fielding when she caught up the mould he had used for making "Parson Adams", and cast another, calling it "McLure".*]

19th Captain Bunbury took Harry with him back to William's Town.

20th The boys accompanied Mr McLure to the Kirk.

22nd Mr John Cotton and his eldest son to breakfast; afterwards, with Mr McCrae for *la chasse aux petits oiseaux*. Mr Dunbar, read as a peony, and late for dinner. He had been round by Campbellfield to offer a gold watch, and his hand, to Mrs Lyon Campbell's maid (Miss Menzies), but she would have neither, because she had already promised to marry Mr McLure's namesake who keeps the school across the swamp.

SUPPLEMENT

Mr Dunbar was a son of Professor Dunbar of Edinburgh University; his brother, William Dunbar, a barrister, became a great favourite of Uncle John Morison and a frequent guest to Abercromby Place, but was disliked by Dr McCrae on account of his attentions to Agnes, then a girl of sixteen.

Mr McLure's school was kept in the then new stone cottage opposite where the gas-works now stand. The old tumbled-down house, lately demolished, has been carted holus-bolus to the bank on the west side of Hawthorn Bridge.

*   *   *

23rd Captain and Mrs Bunbury and Baby "Louise Comtessa".
25th Bought shoes for the boys.
26th Everybody taken ill during the night.
27th No one able to go to church today.

28th Dr Thomas's diagnosis of my case: "Intercostal Rheumatism." He orders warm baths and sudorifics.

29th Remain in bed.

30th All the patients better. Rain and sleet.

31st Captain Reid lamenting that he had lost, out of his cart, the two "Bullan-Bullan"* tails he was bringing as a present for me.

SEPTEMBER

September 1st Mr John Cotton to breakfast.

2nd Captain Reid tells me Dr Nicholson has lost his motion, the majority opposing the appointment of a paid agent for Port Phillip at present. [*At that date, 1843, Nicholson (without a title) was representing Port Phillip in the Sydney Legislative Council. Later on he helped to found the University of Sydney, of which he was elected vice-provost in 1851, and delivered the inaugural address at the official opening on 11th October 1852. He was provost from 1859 to 1861, and chancellor in 1861-2. Died in England 1903. (Kt. Bach., 1852; first Australian baronet, 1859.)*]

3rd Rained obstinately all day.

4th Mrs Donald Mackinnon to dinner.

5th Mr John, and Mr Edward Cotton, and two Misses Cotton, to early dinner; wet up to their ankles in crossing the bog. Miss Cotton sang: "O lovely night"; and played for us. [*The irony of it!*]

6th It appears Dr Nicholson's motion was not lost, but referred to a committee. *Nil desperandum.*

7th Farquhar Perry's birthday; his papa gave him the foal of the brown pony. Letters from Octavius Browne and Martha Cummins telling me their marriage is to take place in August.

8th Rain cleared off. Had a walk through the garden.

9th Captain Dunbar to breakfast. Captain Reid, Captain West, and Captain Bell, a cousin to Henri Bell, to dinner. So many captains!

[*Halfpay officers of the army, or navy, swarmed to Port Phillip, and small wonder, since the money they paid to acquire Crown Land was subject to remissions, proportional to their rank and length of service.*]

* Lyre-bird or buln-buln.

10th Church out of the question. Mrs Musgrove and her sister, Mrs O'Cock, came to see us.

12th Sandy took a fall off the brown pony and hit his head against the projecting root of a gum-tree. Received Blunt's *Beauty of the Heavens*: a present for the boys from Octavius Browne.

13th Dr Thomas came to see Sandy.

14th Sandy recovered, but not likely to trust himself on the back of a Timor for some while to come.

15th Furbishing the children's clothes.

16th Mr Campbell came out early, and, after dinner, started with Mr McLure for a long walk. Mr McCrae went to town to have the ponies shod, and returned with a letter from Dr Nicholson saying, 'In consequence of the utter uselessnes of an agent at this time, and the strenuous opposition of Dr Lang, he (Dr N.) had withdrawn the motion." He also desires Mr McCrae "to seek a purchaser for this house *without delay*".

[*Nicholson's was Hobson's choice. Later, after uselessly sending representatives to the Sydney Council, where their speeches were allowed but always shelved, Port Phillipians decided to boycott that chamber and to deputize nobody at all. However, lack of unanimity compelling different tactics, a public meeting was held, in the course of which Dr Greeves proposed the return of Earl Grey. A poll was held on the following day, when Earl Grey won by a hundred and two votes from John L. Foster.*]

17th The boys went to the Kirk to contribute their mite towards the Kirk Extension Fund. Mr McCrae took me for a ride to Merri Creek.

18th Dr and Mrs Myer told us that Bishop Broughton leaves Sydney on October 12 for Melbourne; also that Octavius Browne proposed, while in Melbourne, to Miss Stevens, but was not accepted. (Miss Stevens afterwards married Mr George Airey, and died in her first confinement.)*

20th Mr McCrae tells me to make up my mind to go to the bush, as we must leave this house in a week or two. Mr La Trobe and Agnes visited us. Mr McLure took the boys to Captain Eddrington's so that they might enjoy the fine spring day.

* Added later by Georgiana.

21st Put in some melon seeds ... For whom shall they bear fruit?

22nd Everybody suffering from sore eyes.

23rd Received a parcel of fine new stockings—a present from Mr Gittins-Bucknall, Mr Clissold's cousin.

24th Put in Indian flower seeds.

26th Mr Westgarth to breakfast. I rode to town, met Captain Newby, called at Captain Dunbar's, and, thence, to Newtown to see Mrs Eyre Williams.

27th Made confirmation-caps for Mary Anne and Sarah Thomas.

28th Called at Dr Howitt's. Mrs Howitt tells me that her sister, Miss Bakewell, is a patient of Dr Jephson at Leamington, and has just been baptized into the Church of England there; Dr and Mrs Jephson her sponsors. Mary Murray, sister of Admiral Sir Arthur Farquhar's late wife, is also at Leamington, and talks much to Miss Bakewell of her cousin Mrs Farquhar McCrae at Melbourne.

29th Hot wind all through the night. A sultry morning, then cold and rainy in the afternoon!

30th Mrs John Cotton and three daughters, Major Webb, Captain Reid, and Mr Westgarth to dinner.

OCTOBER

October 1st Mr McCrae *hors de combat*, from having, *par politesse*, walked all the way to Great Bourke Street West, next to Mr Hoddle's, with Mrs Cotton and the young ladies, then back again to "Mayfield", last night.

2nd Icy cold morning. A large party for the Kirk today.

3rd Mr Westgarth brought me fine samples of notepaper; most acceptable at this time. Major and Miss Webb to dinner. While we were at table Mrs Cobham, Mamie, and James Grahame were announced, and, after a quarter of an hour's ceremonious conversation, they all left.

4th Mr McCrae and Captain Lonsdale went to steamer to meet and welcome Bishop Broughton, then to luncheon at the Rev. A. C. Thomson's.

5th Visited Mrs Henri Bell and Mrs George Thomas.

8th Mr Westgarth and Mr McCrae rode to Cooper's Hill.

10th Called on Mrs John Cotton; found her packing up for the bush, and short of the packing-cases she had lent to Mrs Thomas and to me. The contents of a sea-chest (young children's underclothing) most acceptable.

11th Mr and Mrs George Thomas to dinner. Find that Mr Westgarth was for some years a clerk in a wine merchant's at Bordeaux, and, in 1829, in an establishment at Cadiz, and lastly at *Xeres de la frontera*. In the evening refreshed his memory with some old familiar Spanish songs and boleros.

12th Rode with Mr McCrae to call on the Bishop at Captain Cole's house which he has lent, with servants, for the prelate's accommodation. We were most graciously received, the Bishop having heard of me by letters from friends at Home, and from the Sconces.

13th The boys travelled to town in Tuck's cart, and I rode in to get a parcel from Mr Knox (2 vols of Channing's Sermons). In the evening heard the Bishop preach from *Galatians* iii, 17. I slept at Dr Thomas's, and Mr McCrae at Captain Cole's.

14th In town all day.

15th Perry rode in, and Mr McLure and the rest of the boys walked to hear the Bishop preach *Zephaniah* iii, 16 and 17 in aid of the fund for paying off the £1000 still owing for St James's Church. The collection only amounted to £27. At church in the afternoon; the Bishop gave us an excellent sermon from *Ephesians* vi, 10, in the course of which he dwelt on the duty of discouraging evil; the neglect of so doing he considers equal to the commission of sin.

16th The Church Committee met—the Bishop in the chair. After the building questions had been disposed of, Davis the auctioneer rose, with a preface, and expression of pain at being called by his conscience to state that the Rev. A. C. Thomson is considered deficient in religious knowledge, careless of the performance of his clerical duties, and guilty of conduct unbecoming to a clergyman, all of which charges, he, Davis, was ready to substantiate. He then moved that a vote of want of confidence in Mr Thomson should be carried. The Bishop told Mr Davis that he, the Bishop, is Mr Thomson's judge, and that he could not entertain such a matter in such a place; but, if Mr Davis had complaints to make, the Bishop was ready to receive them in private. Report says Mr J. F. Palmer seemed to know beforehand what Davis was going to say; and that a certain "Super" was not taken by surprise. Dr Myer rose to pass a vote of censure on Mr Davis; but whether for the matter, or manner of the accusation, did not appear. The Bishop remarked that this affair of Davis had given him great concern; and everyone agrees that it was exceedingly ill-timed. At 5 p.m. rode out with Mr McCrae to "Mayfield".

[*Davis became Mayor of Melbourne in 1856. Commenting on his election, the "Journal of Australasia" said: "We do not profess any special admiration for the new mayor, but are ready to give him credit for having been a very useful member of the council for some time past. His particular line has been the detection and exposure of jobs and other abuses; and, in this department, for which he seems to have a call, he has rendered good service." Georgiana's diary bears witness to the "seemingness" of the call.*]

17th The Bishop tells me his wife is a daughter of the Rev. Dr Francis of Tunbridge. Her sisters were Mrs Southcombe and Mrs Tolfrey, both widows. A son of Mr Tolfrey devoted himself, while in Ceylon, to the translation of the Scriptures into the native language. He had got so far as *John*, when his health failed, and he died at the Cape of Good Hope on his passage Home. (This young Tolfrey was a nephew to Mrs Dr Christie, the Major's mother.)*
In my student days I was acquainted with Mrs Southcombe, and occasionally saw Mrs Tolfrey when at her sister's abode in London. The Bishop told me he had once met my father at dinner at Lambeth Palace, with the Earl of Aberdeen. Howley, the then Primate, had been tutor to the Earl, and, the conversation turning on over-study at College, the Archbishop remarked that he himself had been very much the worse for over application, and that he had studied so hard because his father was a poor man and denied himself in order to afford his son the advantages of College. (Howley's father, who was a purveyor of butcher-meat, resided in a street off Caven-

* Added later by Georgiana.

dish Square; and his mother was formerly housekeeper in a high family.)* Howley, while Bishop of London, confirmed me at St James's Church, Piccadilly.

18th The Bishop explains we have no evidence of the apostle Luke, or others, being in the fullness of glory, and that to pray to them is useless and shows a want of confidence in the Almighty. The Millenial period not to be revealed to man. . . . Nay! Not to the angels in heaven! The excessive and desultory reading of novels and periodicals hurtful, and a bar to the more solid exercises which invigorate the mind.

20th Mr McCrae, Mr McLure, the boys, and I went to Mr La Trobe's pew at St James's to witness the confirmation of Mary Anne Thomas (Sarah was too ill to leave her bed), Mamie Cobham, and ninety other young people. After the laying on of hands the Bishop preached from the text "The bread which came down from heaven . . . that man may eat thereof, and not die", clearly showing how our Church holds *the Body and the Blood* as typical, and the transelementation as a spiritual remembrance; for, were the actual Body received into the mouth of man, Christ would be made to dwell in the midst of sin. A solemn exhortation and warning was then addressed to the newly confirmed.

In the evening, Mrs D. A. C. G. Erskine gave a Quadrille party for the young people; but Mary Anne Thomas, holding fast to her Home notions, would not go to the dance; nevertheless, the Cobhams and John Cottons went, because those from Goulburn do not often have opportunities for dancing.

21st Hot wind. Poor Sarah alarmingly ill.

22nd An excellent sermon from *Hebrews* x, 10. Mary Anne and ourselves at early communion. After church, Mrs Cobham called at Dr McCrae's to ask him to look at her limb where she had a pricking pain. . . . On examination by microscopic glass, the doctor discovered the presence of a needle, just above the knee, and speedily drew it forth, discoloured by its long lodgement. Mrs Cobham recollected being at work when hourly expecting her brother Alexander to return from his first campaign. Hearing his well-known knock at the house-door she rushed to open it,

* Added later by Georgiana.

and in her haste fell downstairs, work in hand; she must have fallen on it. The pain only began a few weeks since, though the needle had been embedded for over twenty years.

23rd Sarah Thomas much worse; the ailment is chiefly in the brain and spine. Charles Thomas arrived.

24th The Bishop has given his bond for £300 as security for the Rev. A. C. Thomson. On my way, today, I met the Rev. P. B. Geoghegan, who gave me his benediction as usual.

26th I visited Mrs Hutton. Mrs Cole took Agnes McCrae to call on the Bishop who gave her a letter for me to forward to Lady Saltoun's protégé, c/o Mrs Stiles at Windsor, enabling me to come at all particulars regarding Mrs Fraser and her family. Sarah's convulsions returned. I sat with her till midnight, then Mary Anne took my place till six, when I resumed watching. Sarah, by this time, exhausted but tranquil.

27th The Bishop has invited Dr McCrae and Agnes to stay with his family at Woolloomooloo until they can settle themselves in Sydney. Maggie Hawdon, Ward Cole, Charles Thomas, and ourselves went in to St James's for morning service; text "Be kindly affectioned one towards another" evidently preached at the more rebellious part of Mr Thomson's congregation. After service, the Bishop told us he had received a letter (from his friend Dr Pusey) which he said might be read and interpreted in two or three different ways. Our friend considers that Newman has done more harm than Pusey has.

28th A frosty morning. Visited Mrs Eyre Williams and saw her second son, now a fortnight old. Mrs O'Cock gave me a cast home in her carriage.

29th Sermon: "In the latter days, perilous times shall come."

30th Mr McCrae breakfasted with Mr Simpson at "The Grange".

31st Bishop Broughton and Mrs James Smith to luncheon; the pole of their carriage broke on the way to Pentridge, where he found a congregation of fifty persons; one of these, a woman, forty-four years old to be baptized!

NOVEMBER

November 1st Mr and Mrs Hawdon drove out for Maggie, since they have to be ready to leave Brighton in time to catch the *Shamrock* for Sydney on the 4th. The Rev. Mr Gunn, just returned from his travels in the interior of New South Wales. His usual journey forty-five miles a day: one day sixty miles through rough bush . . . crossed a river in a bark canoe paddled by a black who squatted on the gunwale not an inch above water. "No fright you?" said the pilot; and, by the manipulation of a bit of gum-bough, they arrived at the opposite bank. . . . Mr La Trobe called on his way home. Louise Fraser to early dinner, and afterwards to "St Helier's", to see Mr Curr's new house. Mr Curr offered to drive me in to St Francis's to hear Father Geoghegan's lecture on "Purgatory".

2nd Blistering wind. Mr Simpson and Mr Jamieson to dinner. In the evening Mrs Bunbury and Mrs Thomas visited us.

3rd Thunder, lightning, and enormous hailstones. In the evening Mr McCrae listened to Bishop Broughton's diatribe against the doctrines of Dr P. B. Geoghegan.

4th Mr McLure and the boys went to town.

5th Perry and I walked to St James's. In his sermon the Bishop exonerated the Popish party from the blame of the Gunpowder Plot. After church Mrs Bunbury and I stayed to luncheon and tea with him. Being alone here, he misses the society of his wife and daughter, so we did not hurry away. I played, and Mrs Bunbury sang, some sacred songs; then when it became time to go he asked us to stay all night in the spare-room; but Mrs B. had to go home; and I went to Dr Thomas, as his wife had gone to "La Rose". Sarah is convalescent, but still in bed.

6th Perry and I went aboard the steamer at noon, and, in one hour and ten minutes, were off William's Town. Captain Bunbury rowed off for us.

7th Captain Bunbury went to Melbourne. I copied some old-time songs for the Bishop. Went for a walk with Mrs B. and Perry, and enjoyed a sniff of the sea.

8th Helped Mrs B. to modernize the sleeves of her pretty Challi dress.

9th A freezing, rainy day. Captain Bunbury unable to go to the Brighton picnic. Perry and myself tied to the house all day.

10th Grigsby arrived with the bullocks . . . and then went on. Captain B. left for Melbourne. Mason slept here.

[*Note. Grigsby and Mason came out with the Bunburys. The cattle were for Captain B.'s run "on the Grampian hills." Mason was subsequently Mayor of William's Town . . . and Grigsby J.P.*]

One day, Captain Bunbury showed me as many as thirteen ships in the Bay, among them a large vessel called the *Admiral*.

11th Went to the Back Beach in search of shells. Perry within an ace of treading on a snake which I killed with the stick of my parasol. Perry went in for his bath in the sea. This day, three years ago, the Bunburys joined us at Plymouth.

12th Captain Bunbury's men rowed us across to the Liardets'; and we traipsed along the banks of the Yarra to opposite Cole's Wharf where we paid pennies to be ferried over in Hill's boat. Late for church! The sermon was from *Matthew*, xxiv, 24, showing that miracles ceased with the apostles . . . and that the so-called miracles of today are the work of "the man of sin". I took Perry home, with Eliza and Sandy. The Bunburys and I went to luncheon with the Bishop. Dr Thomas laid up with "swamp fever". Sarah at church for the first time since her illness. Returned to the boat and rowed all the way down the river; when we got as far as the junction the wind was right in our teeth, and Mrs Bunbury "uncomfortable". . . . . The *Morayshire* coming in after twenty-four days from Sydney.

13th Heard that Mrs and Miss Scott and the fiancé, Dr Edward Barker, had called on us at "Mayfield". A hot wind. After today, the Bishop will have nothing to detain him here. He wishes to visit the Bishop of Tasmania, but no sailing ship is advertised for V.D. land and he will not go by steamboat.

14th Started at 2 p.m. with Captain and Mrs Bunbury in the boat, and arrived at Cole's Wharf by 4 p.m. Mr McCrae met me and we walked all the way to "Mayfield".

15th Mr Simpson and Mr McCrae attended the meeting at the Mechanics' Institute.

20th The Bishop talked of the increase of the Democratic Spirit and the decline of loyalty ... mentioned "The Conversations of Sir T. More" by Coleridge as a piece of prophetic excellence, then, alluding to Agnes, he said, "We have a Scots girl who shall attend on the doctor's children, so that Mrs McCrae may go to church with us, every day in the week."

21st A bitterly cold day. Letter from the Rev. Mr Stiles (concerning Mrs Fraser and her two children) which I shall forward to Lady Saltoun per first ship. Lyon Campbell has invited the boys to spend Saturday at Campbellfield. Willie played two of Steibell's lessons to let him hear what progress he had made in music.

22nd Rode to town early; had a long talk with the Bishop on secular matters. Heard of Dr Myer's appointment to the Lunatic Asylum at Jericho, Van Diemen's Land, with £150 salary, free house, and assigned servants. [*During this period convicts were being poured into Tasmania at the rate of 4000 a year.*] Archibald Cunninghame, and Dr Kilgour (agent for Dr Nicholson), met Mr McCrae to talk over arrangements relating to this house.

N.B. The land was to have been paid for at the end of five years, but, owing to bad times, Dr Nicholson would not wait beyond three years. Had he allowed the five years to elapse matters could have been satisfactorily arranged. On my way out from town, I overtook Mr Westgarth. In the evening a letter came from Dr Nicholson desiring Mr McCrae to send up the deeds. He will cancel the mortgage and obligation, so that we may be tenants here at £100 a year rent; and the doctor retains his acres and the house for £1400 (the price of the land, and £500 advanced to Mr McCrae).

23rd Mr and Mrs Henry Smythe to dine and stay the night. Thomas brought the valuation of the house to send to Dr N. Our aborigines here today. They call Henry Smythe "Dareem", and his brother Lory, the surveyor, "Mamghie". Dr Kilgour and Major Wentworth came and stayed all night, the doctor very considerate towards me.

24th Sent our bees' house to Mrs La Trobe.

25th Mr Westgarth and Mr McCrae started for Captain Reid's. The boys went to Campbellfield.

27th Grasshopper plague. Spring-cleaning. Carpets beaten; floors washed; carpets re-laid. Tired out by tea-time.

28th Arranged books in recess-shelves. Miss Gavan came to console me on having to give up "Mayfield". I told her of the permission we had to stay, so long as the place remained unsold; also, of my hope that Madame might advance me the wherewithal to purchase it.

29th The grasshoppers have increased by thousands, myriads even convering the walls of the house for two feet above the ground; crows and magpies snap them up in Nicholson's paddock, but, where once our vegetable-garden was, today there isn't a potato-top or a blade of cabbage to be seen! Mr Simpson tells me that pigs "scotch" the larvae; also, that flockmasters drive sheep among the grasshoppers, and the sheep, trampling, destroy them.

[*Grasshoppers, known to the entomologist as* Chortoicetes terminifera, *have a span of life of three months. They are able to fly up to 100 miles a day, and farther with a tail wind. They hatch out in millions in a few days, and when in search of food might travel 500 miles in a couple of days. And they will eat almost anything.—Note stolen from the Sydney* "Sun" *of 16th August 1934.*]

DECEMBER

December 1st [*Dr McCrae assaulted by J. L. Foster in Queen Street, Melbourne.*]

9th Glad Agnes has decided to go to Sydney. Sent her Farquhar's ring.

10th Mr McLure and the boys go to church.

11th The *Midlothian* sailed with Bishop Broughton, Dr McCrae, Agnes, and their children for Sydney.

12th Rode to Heidelberg. Called at "Hartlands" to see Mrs Brown, then on to D. C. Macarthur's, to spend the day. Began my return journey at seven, and, having forded the river in a very bad light, got to "Mayfield" by dark.

13th Letter from Mrs Cummins, telling of Martha's marriage to Octavius Browne. Letter-date, August 14, just four months since.

15th Mrs George Thomas, with her brother Mr Locke, also her aunt, came to see us. Mrs James Smith and Miss Nellie, in the evening.

16th Tuck started for Captain Reid's, and Mr McCrae left for Kinlochewe where he has a few acres, for which Mr Malcolm offers him *two tons and a half of flour!* [*Mr Malcolm arrived from Van Diemen's Land with Gellibrand, January 1836. In 1840 flour was sold ta £100 per ton. Wath it cost in 1843 I am unable to say.*] Returning, Mr McCrae called on Mr Gittins-Bucknall (Mr Clissold's cousin). Malcolm's offer accepted . . . A letter from Dr Nicholson, saying he will sell the house and land for £1300; and £105 is the rent he expects. Mr McCrae wrote in reply that he cannot pay the rent. So we most prepare to leave as soon as possible.

17th Walked with the boys and Mr McLure to the Scots Church, then back again. Very tired when we arrived home. Captain and Mrs Cole came in the afternoon.

19th Copied sketches of "Mayfield" to send to Mr O. Browne.

20th Mrs La Trobe and Miss Franklin (Sir John's daughter, by his first wife), to see me. Mrs La Trobe says the *Rajah* will not sail till after Christmas, consequently Sir John and his family will have their Christmas dinner at Jolimont.

22nd Eliza Impey saw a snake in the lobby, and Mr McCrae killed it. A note from Mrs Jeffery regretting she must put off her visit till Easter.

23rd Busy at my Saturday work till 11 p.m.

24th The boys all at church.

25th Christmas. A tremendously hot day. Mr Westgarth came to stay for a day or two.

26th Visit from Dr Thomas.

27th Packed native seeds to send Home. Eliza Impey took the tin box to have it soldered.

28th Went to Jolimont with my pacquet for the *Rajah*, and took leave of Miss Franklin. Sir John and Lady Franklin gone to town.

29th Dr Thomas, Mrs Thomas, and the baby to see us. Lucia two years old today, and far from well.

30th Lucia still an invalid.

31st Mr McCrae very feverish and out of sorts. The boys went to Kirk with Mr McLure. . . .

A rainy night. So dies this year!

SUPPLEMENT

In November, 1836, the population of Port Phillip was 284 souls.

Mount Eliza was named after Mrs Batman.

Mount Martha in honour of Mrs Captain Lonsdale.

1837. Sir Richard Bourke, then Governor of New South Wales, came to Port Phillip, and, on March 5, named the settlement in honour of Lord Melbourne. Bourke Street was named after the Governor himself.

The Hopkins River near Warrnambool had been named by Sir T. L. Mitchell, Surveyor-General of New South Wales in honour of his friend John Paul Hopkins, major in the 56th Foot, son of Captain Hopkins, R.N., killed by a cannon-ball at the battle of the Nile.

1840. Anthony's Nose was so named by C. J. La Trobe, the Superintendent, from its strong resemblance to Anthony's Point on the Hudson River, United States. The Saintship was probably added by the neighbouring lime-burners, chiefly men from Ireland, more conversant with the history of St Anthony than with that of the Anthony after whom the American Point had been named.

1843. Simpson's Road was named from the fact that Mr James Simpson at his own cost (and the cost of his two neighbours), made a footpath and road along the frontages of "Mayfield", Smith's paddock, and "The Grange".

★   ★   ★

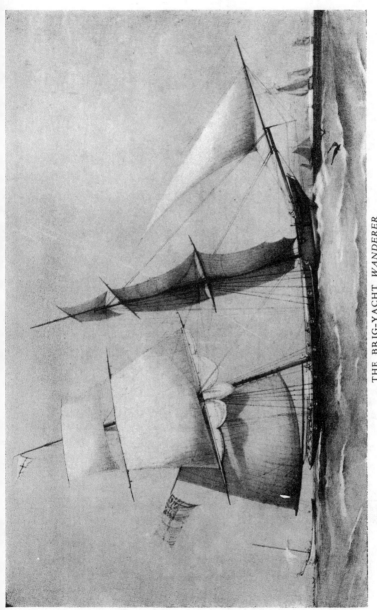

THE BRIG-YACHT *WANDERER*
Benjamin Boyd Esq.
From a lithograph by Oswald Walters Brierly

MAYFIELD, JUNE 1843
From a sketch by Georgiana

1844

JANUARY

January 1st A gently falling rain. Arrival of the *London* from that ilk, bringing satisfactory accounts to shippers of their sales of Port Phillip tallow and bark. [*William Hull, a town magistrate, first began the exportation of bark. He was a neighbour of Georgiana's, and famous for his roses: "Hull's Abbotsford Queen."*] The *Rajah* delayed.

2nd Agnes La Trobe sat for me: *chez elle.*

3rd Unable to go to Jolimont; sent my apologies. Captain Reid in the evening.

4th Rode to Jolimont. Madame in bed with one of her violent toothaches. Had a long sitting from Agnes, Marie Rose keeping her steady. Mrs Myer came to take leave of Agnes before "going to Jericho"! (Van Diemen's Land). Judge Jeffcott and Mr La Trobe invaded us, and so ended our sitting.

5th Agnes here, to give me another long sitting. Mr Mackinnon to dinner. Dr Myer bade us good-bye. At night Captain Reid visited us. He gave us an account of Sir John's and Lady Franklin's stay at Tichingorook [*Ghosts in the frogs*]; and of their journey thence to Arthur's Seat, guided by himself. [*Georgiana's own husband was one of the Arthur's Seat party on this occasion, yet, for some reason, she suppressed the fact.*] Lady Franklin rode from the foot of the mountain to the first point, and walked the rest of the way. At the summit, Sir John remarked that it was many years since he (then a very young man, sailing with Flinders) had stood on the self-same spot surveying the panoramic view of the then uninhabited wilderness. Sir John had his tents pitched in Captain Reid's compound. Madame—rather *exigeante*—used to send her china tea-pot to be filled from the kettle in the kitchen. . . . Sir John "a thorough gentleman and a prayerful Christian."

[*Henry Gyles Turner in "A History of the Colony of Victoria" has analysed Sir John's report upon the Flinders Island Aboriginal Settlements, and found it "tedious and verbose . . . permeated with the mellifluous language of the Christian philanthropist"; and so forth. Yet, Franklin was a great humanitarian, and a prime mover for the act which brought about the abolition of convictism.*]

6th Mr McCrae interviewed Dr Kilgour who urged him, on my account, to remain here so long as the property stays unsold or un-let, because, in any case, someone will have to be left to take care of the house. But Mr McCrae was obdurate. For my own part, I would rather continue here than go to the bush before there is a place for us to occupy.

7th The boys and Eliza Impey went with Mr McLure to the Kirk. A breathlessly hot day. Captain Cole in the evening.

8th Heavy downpour during the whole of the forenoon. Altered summer frocks for Lucia.

9th The *Rajah* sailed with Sir John, Lady, and Miss Franklin, also with our despatches for London.

10th Mr McCrae, accompanied by George, "Murray", and "Tommy", went by Palmer's Punt to shoot birds; returned at 4 p.m. with seven pigeons and a wattle-bird. [*Palmer's Punt used to operate where Hawthorn Bridge is now.*]

11th A severely hot day. Lucia feverish.

12th Made three dozen muslin bags to protect the peaches against locusts. Suffering from hot-weather headache. [*Sir John and Lady Franklin sailed for England.*]

13th Oppressive heat . . . not a breeze stirring. In the evening, thunder and lightning which continued with great violence till 2 a.m.

14th Raining cat and dogs. Return storm at night.

15th Cold and dank. Upset by change of temperature.

16th A steamy day. Mr McCrae remained in town very late.

17th Boisterous weather. Busy with my sewing.

18th, 19th Mr McCrae out of sorts. Dr Kilgour to see him.

20th Mr McCrae away with Willie, and "Murray" and "Tommy", at Walpoles and Goggs, shooting pigeons. On their return the blacks came about the house to beg or steal gewgaws for tonight's corroboree. Jane Shanks, Mr McLure, and the boys went to the flat beyond Campbellfield to see the corroboree.

21st Captain Cain to dinner. Eliza Impey and the boys walked to St James's church.

22nd Rode to town, to Dr Thomas's, to see Mary Anne. Heard of Jeanie Morison's marriage to John Summers, the minister's son.

23rd To Jolimont, where I had a good sitting of Nellie. After luncheon, to Captain Lonsdale's to take leave of Mrs Henry Smythe. As I feared, the Myers don't feel at ease in the penal colony, surrounded by "canaries!" [*Convict servants called "canaries" on account of their yellow uniforms.*]

24th, 25th Days of incessant rain and domestic discomfort.

26th Dull overcast sky. Busy all day.

27th A clear morning, everything fresh and *riant*. Went to Jolimont and had a successful sitting of Nellie.

28th On their way from church Jane and the boys were overtaken by a hurricane "strong enough to blow the Devil's horns off"! At least that was how Tuck expressed himself when they ran to his hut for shelter.

29th Henry Montgomery brought news of Mrs Bunbury's having gone to "Woodlands" to stay with Mrs Greene, for change of air.

30th Report says Sir Eardley Wilmot was appointed to Van Diemen's Land after having galloped through his fortune. He abandoned his wife in London, and has irritated the *pur sang* by entertaining at Government House persons of either sex never before considered presentable. [*The story is biased; and it is possible that Sir Eardley copied Macquarie in Sydney, who expected "pure merinos" to mingle with "emancipists": circiter 1810.*] "As for this scheme of government, he takes the salary, and leaves the Colonial Secretary to wind up the work he sends Home as well as he can." George and Tuck have been told off to bring Nellie La Trobe and her *sac de nuit*.

31st A frightfully hot day. Lucia peevish.

FEBRUARY

February 1st Mr La Trobe came to see Nellie, and brought with him Judge Jeffcott to see my portrait of her. Mr Matson, D. C. Macarthur, and Mr Simpson to dinner. Dr Kilgour arrived too late.

3rd Mr McCrae brought me my half-year's money from the bank. Notice from the Port Phillip Club warning Mr McCrae that he, in common with other members, must contribute £15 as his share towards settling with the tradesmen and various creditors of the club.

[*According to Mr Thomas O'Callaghan, "The club was wound up in 1843 (perhaps it was '44?), and, on March 15 of that year, the wines, spirits, furniture, and fittings (including, no doubt, Georgiana's stair-rods) were sold. In July, 1850, it was licensed as the 'Port Phillip Club Hotel'. Much of the original building remains; but there have been alterations and additions."*]

4th Captain Reid, Mr McLure and the boys at the Kirk. Dr Thomas to see us.

5th Handed Mr McLure £40, of which he immediately returned £10, excusing himself from taking more on account of the bad times. I paid Jane the £10. (Mr McLure's generosity is like that of his prototype James Story, who has been likened to "Dominie Sampson" himself.)

6th Mr McCrae has determined that we must cover the journey to Captain Reid's on horseback, although I have told him how hazardous it is for me to travel far on the Timor pony. He says he can't afford to pay for a conveyance, so I, *and mine*, must take our chance. Dr and Mrs Thomas, with the baby, arrived early, and, at 5 p.m. Captain Reid, Mr McCrae, and I started for Tichingorook, crossing the Yarra by Palmer's Punt to Glenferry, then across the scrub, nine miles, to Brighton Road, but not by a direct route, because, even with the aid of his compass, Captain Reid thinks we ran the risk of being bushed for the night. Got to Fleming, the blacksmith's, at 7 p.m. Had tea there, and waited for the moon to rise, then stretched away for *Mordialloc* [*Moordy-Yallock: sixteen and a half miles from Melbourne*], going at a sober pace and arrived at the Travellers' Rest, 11 p.m.

7th A morning of cold drifting rain, with little or no prospect of clearing up. The captain busy inspecting and mustering Major Fraser's cattle. Mr Horsfall and James Fraser came in at dinner-time. At 2 p.m. moving off with Mr McCrae, I suffered a good deal from the effects of a canter. At 5 p.m. crossed the difficult Carronyulk Creek, and afterwards enjoyed a fine retrospect view of the ten-mile beach and mountainous distance from highlands near Hungry Flat. Here Mr Jamieson and Captain Reid overtook us. Mr Jamieson didn't remain long, but struck across to Captain Baxter's. We came to Tichingorook by half-past seven—myself, wearied to death by an uneasy saddle and the chafing of a too-long stirrup-leather.

8th Cramped-feeling eased by a night's rest in a comfortable bed. Heard Wattie and Johnnie Reid their lessons, while their mother saw to the dinner. (Mr McCrae reading *Lady Sale's Journal*.) "Dorothea" and her foal, after some days' absence, wandered back, to the captain's delight. In the afternoon he showed me his fine potato crop, following which he and Mr McCrae went for a stroll. I helped Mrs Reid to cut out and fit on a set of new chair-covers to brighten up her room.

9th Suffering from lumbago. Tuck called, on his way to "May-field". Just before dinner (3 p.m.) Dr and Mrs Barker drove up in their tandem on their way to Melbourne; pressed us all to pay the wedding visit on their return to Barrabang. To provide fresh meat during our stay, Captain Reid shot a bullock.

10th Captain Reid and Mr McCrae inspected that part of Jamieson's survey which allows a small run to be taken up. We had four chair-covers completed before they returned.

11th Hot wind. Reading all the forenoon. After dinner, strolled to the opposite hill, the site fixed on by Captain Reid for his future house. While admiring the prospect from it, Simon came to tell the captain that Dr Clutterbuck and another gentleman had arrived from Melbourne. [*Dr J. B. Clutterbuck came from London, but, not prospering in Melbourne, he announced in the "Herald" his intention to practise at Kilmore. Unfortunately, he spelled this place-name with two ells.*] The "other gentleman" proved to be Captain Dunbar who finds it expedient to be out of town, as well as to divert his mind from dwelling *too* much on his recent loss of £5000 cash.

In the evening Captain Reid told stories about a certain Baron de Busche of the Ceylonese Infantry; his picaresque adventures in smuggling gold chains and some six thousand pounds' worth of coffee. His subsequent mercantile transactions—Brummagem chains —and disgrace, brought to my mind the wife and daughter of the said burly Baron, left alone in London, and guests of Mrs H. Clissold, our clergyman's wife, at Stockwell, 1837.

[*There seems to have been a trade in gold chains. A Victorian pastoralist, James Malcolm, owner of 60,000 acres of land, 30,000 sheep, and having an income of £3000 a year, bought a "gold chain" in India (1851), and found out, too late, it was a brass one!*]

12th Tuck arrived from "Mayfield" with a letter from Mrs Thomas giving a good account of the children. Thermometer 85°. Captain and Mrs Reid rode with us to Stony Point [*Now "Schnapper" Point . . . so named after the Dutch frigate.*] and the Tanti Creek. Home by 4 p.m. Found Johnnie in disgrace, for having allowed Wattie to chop off the first joint of his forefinger with an axe. Luckily, Dr Clutterbuck was at hand, and, as the cut had not severed the skin, soon had it to rights again.

13th Saw the orphan lamb being suckled by Tuck's "mother-dog". Dr Clutterbuck left for town; and Mr McCrae and Captain Reid went to the creek to fish. After tea, Mr Horsfall gave notice of his approach by sundry flourishes on his Cornopean, and subsequently rendered a programme of familiar tunes, alfresco. Nothing talked of but the Alfred Langhorne's, and Boyd's, muster of cattle-lifting arrest; etc. I had a dreadful night of spasmodic *étouffement*. [*Paragraph not clear.*]

14th A crystalline morning. Thermometer 80°. Mr Horsfall rode with Mr McCrae as far as Tanti; caught my pony, and Mrs Reid's "Maggie" and foal, as well as young "Traveller". Weddell, here, resting Mr Simpson's cows on their way to "The Grange": wrote a note for Weddell to leave for Mr McLure. The Barkers have returned from Mrs Scott's, so I trimmed Mrs Reid's bonnet against our visit to Barrabang. Mr Jamieson and Mr Gorringe arrived towards evening.

15th At 6 p.m. the thermometer down to 48°. *Quel climat!*

Mr Gorringe and Mr Horsfall left before breakfast. At eleven Captain and Mrs Reid and Mr Jamieson, Mr McCrae and myself went on horseback to inspect the Survey. Alighted at "Kangarong House", and saw Mrs Newby and her two little girls; she complains of loneliness during the captain's absences at sea, and is terrified by the way the wind " 'owls down the chimney-'ole at night"; and "sometimes, the dingoes, too!" "Never a soul to speak to." Further on, Captain Reid took me to see his stand-by Bakmadarroway Creek. After leaving the Survey, came upon the land Mr Powlett had alluded to. Delighted with its position and sea-view. Rode along the sands while the others were washing their horses in the surf. Suddenly my pony propped, and I had just time to disengage my limb from the pommel before he started to roll himself on the beach. Mr McCrae wouldn't allow me to remount, but took off the Timor's saddle and put it on "Don". Meanwhile, I had slipped away to make a sketch of "St Anthony's Nose" and Mount Martha. Afterwards, we had luncheon under the trees. Thermometer 90°. A soft wind from the sea. Returning over the hill, Mr Jamieson was able to identify some of his own bullocks, among strangers, quietly at graze, whereupon, he and Captain Reid, with much shouting and cracking of whips, proceeded to "cut them out" from the mob. An exhilarating sight, full of novelty for me.

As I rode up the steep path, beyond Saltwater Creek, Mr McCrae called to me to "look to Don's feet", which I immediately did, with disastrous results, because, in doing so, I missed seeing a branch of the she-oak on a level with my head. The impact brought me out of the saddle, but, by good fortune, I took some part of the bough in my hand, and thus saved myself from falling to the ground. "Don" stood motionless where he was, while Mrs Reid cooeed for Mr McCrae to come to my aid—a clumsy rescuer, who, instead of lowering me, insisted on hoisting me up again, and gave me such a twist that I couldn't thereafter sit in any other way than *à califourchon*. Accordingly, I walked "Don" the six miles back to Captain Reid's. (After seven hours in the saddle, exposed to the scorching sun, I felt knocked up, and had reason to dread the effects of the wrench in my side.)

6th A beautiful morning, which I should have enjoyed more f my knee had not continued to pain; my back, too, so racked me that I reclined on the sofa all day.

17th At 7 a.m. Mrs Reid and I started for Barrabang in the family cart, driven by Mr Barker's George, Mr McCrae and the Captain, on horseback, taking turns to lead old "Jack". Stopped at Mrs Newby's, and further on came across the miamia put together by Thomson the shepherd's wife, with the help of her little son, for a temporary lodging, on the chance that a dray might happen that way and carry then and their gear to town! Here I had my first view of grass-trees, and almost immediately afterwards, saw six or seven kangaroos hopping along. By noon, we alighted at Maurice Meyrick's deserted hut, took out the canteen, spread our napery on a square table, and used stools and boxes for seats. About three miles before coming to Barrabang we climbed out of the cart and walked up one of the "cups", or sand-dunes, whence we took in a majestic view of Point Nepean across a finely wooded middle-distance and fore-ground. [*It was in one of these "cups", immensely deep, and three miles in circumference, that John Barker's brother Edward fought a duel with Meyrick of "Boneo". Out of the wind, and lighted by the rays of a hidden sun, the men stood, pistols in hand, ten paces apart. Meyrick fired first, and the bullet flipped his enemy's ear; whereupon Barker, taking aim, not at Meyrick, but at a gull on the wing, killed it . . . in terrorem.*] The men rode on, and we joined them, *after seven hours spent in travelling a distance of twenty-two miles.* Found Miss Elvidge and Georgiana Scot at Mr Barker's; had some fine old songs out of "Grandma's Book", and didn't go to bed till past eleven.

[*This is John Barker, barrister, "holder of the first land order presented in Melbourne, and, it is believed, the first issued by the Commissioners". Coming to Australia in 1840, he selected land at Cape Schanck. In 1851 La Trobe deputed him to adjust the boundaries of runs in the southern part of Victoria; was appointed Clerk of the first Victorian Legislature, and, for over forty years, remained chief of the parliamentary staff.—* "Victorian Historical Magazine".]

18th A hot wind. Rested on sofa. Miss Elvidge stayed at home to keep me company while the others visited Mr Dod's station.

19th Rose at 5 a.m. Travelled to Cape Schanck, where I made several sketches. On our way back, Dr Barker and Mr McCrae put up a kangaroo-doe, or "flier" as it is called, and soon had the dogs in full chase. I spurred "Don" after them and was just in time for "the kill". Dr Barker calculated the weight of the kangaroo at about 70 lb. Returned to *déjeuner à la fourchette*. In the afternoon, a nephew of Rogers, the cutler (Mr Turner, from the Schanck), took Mr McCrae to see the view at Western Port Bay. During dinner-time, Captain Reid came to loggerheads with Dr Barker; and it was only through the tactful intervention of our hostess that peace was restored.

20th With Mrs Reid, in the family cart, to Meyrick's hut, which we reached at 3 p.m. The men, *à cheval*. The shepherd's wife absent from her miamia, and not likely to return. Making for home, our "chariot" overtook Captain Reid who told us he had cut off the branch of the she-oak responsible for my accident.

21st Weather cold and boisterous. A sea-captain to dinner, who spoke a good deal that was interesting about King's Island; but many of his remarks inaudible, on account of terrific claps of thunder.

22nd At "Halfway Flat", on the road to Mr Wedge's, I surprised some native turkeys: a contretemps, too much for my Timor pony, who lay down in the scrub, hardly giving me time to get to security. After dinner, at Mr Horsfall's, Dr Jamieson arrived from "Weerool". Had an enjoyable confab with him about the "Auld Countree", Spey—fishings, and so forth.

23rd A cloudless day. "Budgeree Tom", and others of his tribe, arrived from Gippsland. Mr Horsfall's gig not available for the journey to Mr Clow's at Dandenong (native word for "Big Hill"). Went instead to "No-Good Damper" and reached the inn at 4 p.m. [*A lime-carter, after a night in the bush, noticed one of his bags thrown down and the contents poured over the grass. Assured that some wild animal had done this, he adjusted everything and continued along the road, but had hardly gone a hundred yards when there appeared an aboriginal, who called out "That p'feller no good damper!" meaning, of course, that he had taken the lime and tried it as flour. In this way, De*

Villiers's Inn came by its name.] Passed "Lotus" and her foal, by the way; also, "Tom Jones". My Timor so bone-lazy, it has taken him five hours to walk fifteen miles. Mrs McKie, hostess of the inn, loud in her lamentations about the kangaroos raiding her melons and cucumbers. My bed-place, or bunk, a narrow frame of wood, much too short and hard, yet clean and tidy. For dinner, three courses of veal. Rain hammering on the roof.

24th Cool and fine. Rose, tolerably well rested, at seven. Mr Horsfall came along at 1 p.m. At 2 p.m. said good-bye to Mrs McKie (who gave me her written recipe for *infallible yeast*), and took the road for the South Yarra pound, where we arrived at three, thence across the river by Palmer's Punt, and so home to "Mayfield", by four in the afternoon. George "colded". Willie pale, others looking well. Read of Sir Arthur Farquhar's death at Carlogie, Aberdeenshire, October 25, 1843.

Sunday, 25th A day of thorough physical rest. Mr and Mrs Eyre Williams came to tea.

26th Letters from Mrs Bunbury and Mrs Sconce, with a white frock for Lucia.

27th Letter from Sir A. Morison, saying Fyvie was still in Scotland, and quite well.

28th Called on Mrs Howitt, and Mrs Thomas.

29th Mr Westgarth came out. He and Mr McCrae went to fish for freshwater herring. They returned with a basketful of . . . nothingness.

MARCH

March 1st Willie and Edward Howitt came to keep up Willie's birthday. Mr Jamieson in evening.

2nd A crackling hot day. Mr McCrae called at Mr Locke's to see the Ashursts; found the young couple had already left for their own house at the Moonee Ponds. George, returning from town with the newspapers, was thrown by the brown pony, although, luckily, not much damage was done.

Sunday, 3rd All the boys, except George, at church. Mrs Lyon Campbell came to apologize for her children's absence from

Willie's birthday party. Six weeks hence she expects to sail for England.

4th Mrs Bunbury heard of the death (from consumption) of her only sister, Mrs Liddell.

5th Mr and Mrs Ashurst and Charles Thomas to dine with us.

6th Walked to Newtown and back.

7th A very hot day. Suffering from pain in my side. Dr Thomas tells me the pain is a result of the twist I experienced at Saltwater Creek, and advises me to be careful.

8th Mr McLure left for a few days at Heidelberg.

9th Frank Cobham of age today. Mr La Trobe came to know if I can give him any information regarding the Collegiate Church of St Katharine, London, which has been demolished, to make room for the New Docks? In fulfilment of a commission he had given them, Mr La Trobe's friends have purchased, and consigned to him, a marble font with pedestal complete; this font formerly belonged to St Katharine's Church (not the original one, but a modern replica). Handed Mr La Trobe *The Mirror*, vol. 6, which describes the pulling down of the church and other particulars. He carried the book home to read at his leisure.

[*This font was presented to St James's Church, Melbourne, on the occasion of the baptism of La Trobe's only son, Charles Joseph, in 1845.*]

Sunday, 10th Wind like the blast from a furnace. In the absence of Mr McLure, the boys stayed away from church.

11th Mr McLure back in time for breakfast.

12th Mr McLure took George and Willie to the Mechanics' Institute Museum under promise to return by themselves. George and Willie kept their word, but hardly reached the house before a torrential downpour set in. Late at night Mr McLure arrived, his boots over their collars in mud, so that he was forced to leave them on the dirty-shoe mat outside!

13th Lanty Cheyney passed through. He told me he had recognized Mr McCrae on this side of Brighton, at noon on Tuesday.

14th Lanty brought from town a summons for Mr McCrae

to be in Melbourne by the 27th on Mr Crawley's business. Sent the summons, care of Lanty.

15th Enter my fortieth year today. *Like everyone else*, the boys have forgotten me.

16th Mr McLure walked with his pupils to the Merri Creek.

Sunday, 17th George and Willie at church. Sandy and Perry, my patients, at home. After morning service Mrs Cole took George, as her guest, to Brighton.

18th Augusta Curr came to see me.

19th Cut out and made velvet bonnet for Lucia, also another, for Mrs Reid's little Ellen. Thunder in evening.

20th A return-storm, which lasted until noon. Henry Montgomery filled me with envy when he told me he expected to sail for London by the *Aden*.

21st Tuck arrived with a letter, and a horse for Mr Powlett, who starts with Mr Simpson, tomorrow, for Captain Reid's.

22nd Copied sketches to send Home per *Aden*.

23rd Heard through the Thomases of Mrs Bruce's safe delivery of a daughter. Peggy McLure, from across the flat, came to help me make window curtains.

24th Willie and I walked to St James's. Sermon from *Exodus* iii. We remained all night at Dr Thomas's.

25th A letter from Mr and Mrs Fenning, with a versification of my own letter to Mrs F. by Mr F., concluding with an additional stanza, which shall, I trust, prove true.

> But hark! I hear a soft voice say
>   "Pilgrim, be patient: yet once more,
> Shall you retrace the watery way
>   And end your days on Britain's shore."
>
> WM. F. FENNING.
Stockwell, October 1842.

For many years, I believed the last verse *would* be prophetic; but now—*qu'importe?*)*

Willie and I walked out to "Mayfield" for early dinner.

26th The pain still in my side.

* Added later by Georgiana.

27th Mr Westgarth has invited us to go coal-hunting with him (in the *Vesta*, tomorrow) at the foot of Mount Eliza.

[*Mr Westgarth anticipated a time (1854) when the government—vainly—would send experts to the neighbouring Mount Martha. In those days, the only practicable coalfield was one at Western Port, and that not so practicable, since there were no tramways, and breakwaters were yet to be constructed. Discoveries had often been announced, and, in 1839, the very spot on which the Victorian Assembly afterwards stood had been "declared carboniferous".*]

28th Mr McLure started at 6 a.m., but returned after breakfast, the day being too turbulent for the trip.

29th Rain all the forenoon. In the evening Mr McLure and Mrs Thomas attended Dr Wilmot's lecture.

[*Dr William Bryam Wilmot (first coroner, not only of Melbourne, but of the whole county of Bourke): fat and placid, well dressed and habitually amusing. Once upon a time, when he arrived to make a post mortem at the Melbourne Hospital, he was told by the resident surgeon he had come too late, that the subject had been buried, and so forth. "Pray, don't let that trouble you," murmured Wilmot, "any old body will do!"*]

30th Letter from Dr Beattie, and some Home newspapers.
31st All the boys went with Mr McLure to the Kirk.

APRIL

April 1st School resumed after four weeks of holidays.

2nd Mr Westgarth impatient to make a fresh start.

3rd Mr McCrae and Tuck came on horseback from Arthur's Seat, bringing several ducks and a kangaroo-tail. At night Captain Reid arrived.

4th Weighed out twelve pounds of tea for Tuck. Mr Westgarth explained his plans for the lignite expedition and says the *Vesta* will proceed down the bay tomorrow.

5th Captain Reid and Mr McLure sailed in the *Vesta* this morning. At about 11 p.m. only Mr McLure returned . . . willing to talk on any subject, except the result of their adventure.

[*Perhaps Mr Westgarth's coal-find tallied with that other, which was discovered at Apoinga; subsequently supposed to have been dropped off drays, and to have been washed into drifts by the floods.*]

6th No Captain Reid yet! Mr McCrae and Tuck away in town, while I busied myself looking out bed-linen etc. for the hut at "Wango".

7th Easter Day. Sandy and I walked from "Mayfield" to Dr Thomas's *in one hour exactly*. At church morning and evening.

8th Captain Reid arrived after everybody had gone to bed.

9th Visit from Mrs Curr.

10th Captain McCrae is in great straits for want of ready cash. He confided to Captain Reid that Dr McCrae declares his inability to repay £125 lent to him over ten years ago. This McCrae estrangement cuts me to the quick, but, unfortunately, I am not in a situation to offer any practical help.

11th Mr McCrae bought Captain Reid's spring-cart for £11. After he had gone to bed, Captain Reid went to Mr McCrae and talked seriously to him on the subject of his brother's pressing wants.

12th Mr McCrae wrote a letter to Captain Reid, *for him to show to Captain McCrae*, hoping thereby to create a better feeling, and, if possible, to persuade Alexander to let his boys come to us. This letter drew an immediate reply from the Captain in the course of which he went on to say that the position taken up, and so obstinately held, against his wife, compelled him to ignore any such arrangement . . . however, the warmth of his feelings towards his brother and myself is undiminished. Willie and I visited Mrs Scot and Mrs Ed. Barker at their apartments in the Clarence Hotel, Collins Street. The town all agog for an early hearing of the Dr McCrae versus J. L. Foster case.

[*The forties were horse-whipping days. Only a short while before the Doctor's affair, a Mr Hogue had publicly beaten a Mr Carrington; which assault was followed up by young Mr Kinchella, of Sydney, larruping the scurrile (soi-disant "Major") Mudie; a business assessed by law at 20s. a blow, wherefore K. was mulcted £50. John Leslie Foster, nephew of Lord Fitzgerald, and defendant, in the present instance, suc-*

ceeded Lonsdale as Colonial Secretary, and administered the government
in the interval between La Trobe and Hotham. He was not popular. His
quarrel with McCrae, or, rather, McCrae's quarrel with him, had a
money basis. On 17th April 1844, the case came before Judge Jeffcott
and a special jury of twelve. McCrae, who was represented by his friends,
Cunninghame and Williams, asked for £2000 damages. Foster, with
Redmond Barry, and Stawell, for counsel, admitted the assault, and paid
£10 into court. When the time arrived for the hearing, there wasn't a
seat unfilled; and we are told, in the journalese of the period, that "The
event caused considerable interest in the upper stratum of society to which
the individuals belonged." Here follows the story, crystallized into as
little space as possible. On 1st December 1843, Dr Farquhar McCrae,
riding up Queen Street, was intercepted by Foster who hammered both
horse and man so fiercely that McCrae became unseated. The Doctor ran
after Foster, who turned upon him, and, a second time, gave him the whip
over head and shoulders. The row began about a purchase of land from
McCrae by Foster. The transaction proved unsatisfactory to the buyer,
in consequence of which he said sharp things about sharp dealings, in the
club and round the town. Then, when McCrae asked Foster if it were
true that he had spoken in this way, the answer was "Yes." The Doctor
walked about for a while, and at last went home to write a letter; in this
letter he referred to the money which J.F. owed him. Foster, ignoring the
reference, issued a challenge instead. McCrae fiddled out neatly by saying
Foster, "as a man of honour, should first of all discharge his debts and,
afterwards, his pistols". That answer proved too much for the enemy,
and, since horsewhips had not been mentioned, he armed himself with one
of Dinwoodie's best, and used it on the Doctor as described above. Afterwards, McCrae's letters were produced in court, and, inasmuch as they
were held to be "couched in language of studied and covert affront",
damages dwindled from £2000 to £250. A week and four days after
the assault, the Doctor and his wife sailed for Sydney. At this time Mc-
Crae was forty years old; Foster was twenty-five, Irish-born, and educated at "T'thrinity" College, Dublin.]

In the evening Captain Reid told me he had spoken to Mr
Simpson about Captain McCrae, and at once Mr Simpson went to
entreat Mr La Trobe to afford him some employment, but, alas,

there is "nothing to be disposed of". Spent a sleepless night thinking of Alex, without a shilling to buy food for his children.

13th Mr W. Mollison, Mrs Scot, Mrs Ed. Barker, Miss Scot, and Dr Barker to dinner. At pudding-time, our cow "Balbirnie", being moon-blind, fell into the river and couldn't be extricated from the mud, so that we were forced to leave her all night. [*It is possible that this cow had been nicknamed after Mr Balbirnie, nephew of a Scottish earl, and lessee of the first bridge over the Yarra.*]

14th A piercing north wind. "Balbirnie" still mud-bound, but, in the afternoon, Stribling and Archie hunted her up the bank where she remained, too enfeebled to move. Mr McCrae, covered with rugs, nursed his cold by the fire, while Ellen stayed by the riverside to share some toddy with the cow!

15th "Balbirnie" walked to the shed, next the kitchen-hut.

[*From a letter on the same subject: "Mr McLure accompanied me to see what could be done. He pressed with his fingers upon the artery under the cow's jaw, feeling for some pulsation against the bone, but, his hands being still painful, he gave up. So it became my turn, and I counted fifty, or fifty-five."*]

16th Mr McCrae wrote to his brother enclosing a letter from me, and £10 from himself. True to my prophecy, Lizzie Cobham is engaged to be married to Mark Nicholson. Mrs Jeffery to early dinner. Archie Jamieson, with Mr McCrae, to late dinner. Mr McLure produced something he had written to the measure of "Hohenlinden" which Sandy recites so well.

> At Melbourne-town, some months ago,
> When stocks were selling very low . . .

A curious satirical endeavour, alluding to the recent establishment, at Batman's Hill, of abattoirs and boiling-down works.

> And now, on Yarra banks, are seen
> Deeds bloodier far than e'er had been
> At Linden, Prague, or Waterloo. . . .

[*At the Melbourne Melting Establishment, they accounted for three thousand sheep a week. W. Kyle, in his article written for the "Victorian Historical Magazine", says: "Boiling down gave the owners of sheep*

THE FIRST MELBOURNE LAND-SALE
Robert Hoddle on the rostrum

HOBSON'S FERRY

PRINCE'S BRIDGE, MELBOURNE

The second bridge of the name, constructed of granite, designed by David Lennox and built by Patrick Reid. It cost £15,000. "I remember old Prince's Bridge being built . . . at the town end of it, a shed occupied by David Lennox and his whitey-grey belltopper. Loads of stone from the Merri Creek; the noise of trowels; cracking of handkerchief lashes; columns of dust. . . ."—George Gordon McCrae.

MEN IN STOCKS OUTSIDE THE WOODEN POLICE-COURT DURING JAMES SIMPSON'S MAGISTRACY
Opposite to, and south of, the site of Scott's Hotel

VICTORIAN GOLD-LICENCE, 1854

stations a great advantage over the owners of cattle stations, enabling them to become independent of merchants, wool firms, and banking institutions." The idea emanated from the Australiarch, William Charles Wentworth; and Edward Curr, seeing it was good, established "works" at Port Phillip.]

17th Because I had objected to our run being called "Wango" (the native appellation of the survey), it has been decided to retain the name of Arthur's Seat, originally given to the mountain when it was first seen from the deck of Flinders's ship by Lieutenant Murray, forty years ago. The spring of water is already anticipatorily christened "St Anton's Well". Dr McCrae wins his case against J. L. Foster, and has been awarded £250 damages!

19th Wind and rain. Mr McCrae and Mr Jamieson started for Kangerong. Mr Mollison to dinner.

20th Mrs Jeffery gone. Letter from Alex McCrae, returning the money as he fears "it might inconvenience Andrew to part with it". I have re-enclosed the £10 under another cover, for Mr McLure to carry to "Sherwood" tomorrow.

SUPPLEMENT

At this time, legs of mutton, denuded of fat, were to be had at the boiling-down works for 5s. the dozen. Many sea-captains used them, salted, for victualling their ships, while not a few families bought legs for soup or cutlets.

*   *   *

21st Mr McLure executed my commission on his way to the Kirk. Captain Cole, Mrs Cole, and Mrs Thomas came out in the evening; . . . but, *to them*, not a word of Captain McCrae.

22nd A magnificent day. Mrs and Miss Skene Craig came to sit in the garden.

23rd A London fog! The boys walked through it to Jolimont with jonquil-bulbs for Mr La Trobe; thence, to Dr Howitt's. I paid Eliza her outlay in town: 10s. for coffee, 1s. 6d. for mending water-cans, and 3s. for milk, as "Balbirnie" is still useless. Mrs Jeffery arrived with a lot of Home letters.

25th Mrs Cole gave birth to a daughter this morning.

26th Eliza announced Captain McCrae, and the next moment I found myself folded in Alexander's arms, both weeping. I hadn't seen him for three years, but he looked ten years older. He was penniless, and had even sacrificed the whole of his father's library— including a folio edition of Cook's Voyages—by auction for a paltry £9. [*This copy of the Voyages is now in the Melbourne Public Library.*] Mrs Jeffery, having sneaked in from town, tragically surprised us, and when Alexander asked me to introduce him to her she flounced out of the room, but, after his departure, came back to exclaim in Sarah Siddons tones her surprise that "that man should be in *our* house!" and enquired whether I had it in my mind to visit his wife? I told her "yes", but further questioning was cut short by the arrival of Mrs Henri Bell. [*The Bells, William and Henri, both mentioned in this diary, belonged to the mercantile firm of Bells and Buchanan. William was fifth mayor of Melbourne.*]

N.B. Mrs J. has taken her cue from the Coles, and *Mrs* Thomas— *not* from David, because he has always been well-disposed towards the Captain. (When this fine lady next goes to town she will have quite a budget of rare news to communicate to her friends.)

27th Letter of advice from Mr Dobie saying that he had transmitted £157 16s., the amount of an old outstanding debt due to Mr McCrae from Rankin, W.S. Edinburgh. It arrives opportunely, because, with this in hand, we shall be able to stay on at "Mayfield" for the year, or until I hear from Madame. A letter from Sir Arthur Farquhar dated September 1, 1843, which had been preceded by news of his death some two months since, October 26, 1843. A message from the grave! Yet I feel glad to know that he still entertained kindly sentiments towards me and mine.

28th Prayed for rain, to prevent Mrs J. from going to town . . . and my prayer was granted. However, in the afternoon, Dr Thomas drove out for her; he told us of Bishop Broughton's eldest daughter Phoebe's marriage with Mr Boydell from Durham, but now a squatter on the "Sydney-side".

29th Mrs Jeffery being safely out of the house, Alexander came to call. He told me how Dr McCrae (despite of the heavy damages recently awarded him) still declares himself unable to pay any portion of the £125 he owes A., his excuse being that he has had to supply Captain Cole with money to help him purchase "St Ninian's" for Thomas Anne.

30th Delighted with the inclement weather which should certainly keep Mrs Jeffery at Mrs Cole's, for, although Dame Juliana is the daughter of a Northumbrian baronet, Sir Matthew White Ridley, and her brother Major Tower, an *habitué* at "The Doune", Rothiemurchus, at Cluny, and at Gordon Castle, she remains a voluptuous worldling . . . mightily inquisitive about other people's concerns and the true personification of *savoir-faire*. Like her brother, she is tall and handsome, with the *véritable air distingué*, now *passée*, seeing she has a son over thirty years old.

MAY

May 1st While Lucia slept her noonday sleep I hurried across to "Sherwood", where Maggie received me standing at the open door. She enjoyed my surprise-visit so much that I felt the same happiness myself, especially after I had renewed the offer to have her boys educated with our own. She gladly accepted, and I turned towards home, blithe as a lark, through the wind and the rain.

[*Considering the circumstances, "Sherwood" was, in all probability, "a portable one-roomed family mansion", of the kind advertised in the weekly prints. Pioneers, whose thoughts soared above the rough comfort of locally constructed "mansions", sent for theirs to outside countries. Thus Lonsdale, in no other way to be compared with a snail, brought his house, almost upon his back. J. M. Clow imported from Van Diemen's Land a two-story one, with a front veranda, and three windows in the roof. La Trobe's "The Châlet" (in French, "the carriage-house") is said to have arrived from Switzerland, but more likely it came from England. Sir Thomas Mitchell, in a letter to Georgiana, speaks of "Maning, of Holborn, who makes a business of building wooden houses in sections; for use in Australia." "He can prepare a five-roomed one for £125, at two week's notice. Freight out £30." The Hon. R. D. Murray says of the imported English houses that "their low roofs, combined with their wooden walls, afforded no shelter from the heated atmosphere". Further on in his book, the same author (laughing over the unscrupulous sale of lands without titles) tells about the cuteness of purchasers, who took the precaution to provide for themselves houses on wheels! The McCrae's own first habitation originated in Singapore, and, until their arrival, had been known as "Singapore Cottage"; but upon their occupancy, they changed its name to that of the ship they had travelled in—the "Argyle".]*

2nd Wrote to Alexander, asking him to bring his wife here on Monday. Dr and Miss Black to early dinner in the afternoon; I showed them the garden, which both admired very much.

3rd Tuck left with the loaded dray for Arthur's Seat.

4th Captain McCrae and baby Sally came in the afternoon.

5th Captain and Mrs Reid arrived towards evening, the Captain overjoyed at the result of his mediation.

6th Another deluge. The Captain's George so wet through he had to be new-dressed before he could sit down to his lessons.

7th Lent Mrs Reid my pony to get across the flat to town. Captain McCrae to early dinner. Mr Westgarth and Captain Reid in the evening.

8th Despite the weather, Mrs Jeffery came to say good-bye. Dr Thomas in the evening; he tells me Maggie is alarmingly ill, with little hope of recovery. Mark Nicholson had arrived in town to be married; but Mrs Cobham postponed the ceremony till another year. Mrs Henri Bell's baby boy died today.

9th Eliza brought word that Maggie Thomas is still alive.

10th Maggie better.

11th Mrs Turnbull and her daughters came to look at the house with a view to renting it, but she objects to our make-shift kitchen. Poor "Balbirnie" died today. Archie found that five of her ribs had been broken.

12th The boys at Kirk with Mr McLure. After dinner, I was surprised by the arrival of Captain and Mrs Reid, the former vehement concerning his 15s. whip which he had left in the spring-cart and which Mr McCrae imagined to be part of the bargain!

14th, 15th, 16th Days of illness spent in bed.

17th Mrs Montgomery tells me her husband has been required to pay up £900, due on their house at Newtown, by Thursday, and, since no money is available, this action must eventually bring him to the insolvency court.

18th Aleck went home to "Sherwood" to stay till Monday.

19th All the boys at Kirk in their old dresses, Perry very pale on his return. In the evening, Mr McLure brought news of Conrad Knowles's death. Knowles who was not yet thirty-four when he died had been a favourite Melbourne actor; indeed, Dr Black considered him one of the most tolerable comedians of the day, while even Mrs Jeffery allowed him some particle of merit.

20th An oppressive day, with a feeling of loneliness because Eliza had gone into town to enquire about Maggie Thomas. Late in the afternoon Dr and Miss Black came to see me, and they stayed sitting in the garden, until 9 p.m. The night dark, and a great deal of lightning without any rain.

[*Dr Thomas Black, "Pine Grove", Richmond: He owned three two-storied houses on the east side of Swanston Street, between Collins Street and Flinders Lane, which he knocked into one to provide premises for the proposed new Bank of Victoria. This brought him in £1500 per annum, for eleven years, at the end of which time the bank removed to other quarters—Information from "The Chronicles of Early Melbourne".*]

21st Captain and Mrs McCrae arrived. Mrs McCrae very much taken with little Lucia's appearance; her "lint-white locks" set off by a striped blue tabbinet frock, once part of an old dress of mine.

22nd Informed by Mrs Curr that Lyon Campbell is suffering dangerously from a heart-attack. Despite the fact that he had been warned against taking preparations of Mercury in any form, he broke the rule, and thus brought upon himself this present illness. Like the rest of us, he is just now in pecuniary difficulties.

23rd The boys and Mr McLure started early to spend the day at Captain McLachlan's. Captain McCrae and Maggie came to early dinner, after which Alexander and I walked to Campbellfield to enquire for L.C. To our surprise, we were received in the drawing-room by Mrs Lyon, who, by the way, is "one of those who cannot look on suffering" although, from the tone of her conversation, one would never suppose any serious malady threatened her husband. But when his faithful friend and attendant,

William Ryrie, came into the room, it was evident from what he said that Lyon's recovery is despaired of.

["*Fiery Ryrie*": *duellist. In the Ryrie-Snodgrass affair, hair-trigger pistols were used, almost for the first time. There was no knocking-in of flints; and Snodgrass handled his gun so windily that a premature explosion put a bullet through his foot. Thereupon, Ryrie fired a "dumb shot" into the air, and honour was satisfied.*]

24th Eliza visited Dr Thomas on my account, and returned with a bottle of brandy . . . a present from Mrs Thomas to be ready for any emergency.

25th A delicious morning. Watched Mr McLure passing under the trees to his usual Saturday walk.

Sunday, 26th On their way home, our church folk called at Campbellfield. . . . "Mr Campbell is better."

27th Cut out, and all but finished, Perry's dress. In the evening Tuck arrived, then Mr McCrae, drenched to the skin.

28th Tuck started early for town in the dray, Ellen with him to make purchases and visit her friends, *while she can be spared*. Eliza took orders about the cooking of our dinner from Ellen across the wheel. Captain McCrae to luncheon, but nothing well done. After luncheon I left the brothers *tête-à-tête* and went to my own room to complete Perry's dress.

29th George eleven years old today. The three elder Campbell boys, and Maggie and Alexander to dinner. In the afternoon, the Currs came across and while everybody talked I put the finishing touches to the tapestry I had begun while we were staying at Mrs Cummins's, then counted the stitches from end and side and found they amounted to no less than 40,000!

30th Mr McCrae walked to town with his brother. Eliza helped me bring the school-table into the drawing-room as our scholars are beginning to be cramped. This arrangement will do away with the necessity of having two fires during the winter.

31st Alexander called at Campbellfield, and learnt that poor Lyon died this morning.

JUNE

June 1st   Mr McCrae accompanied the Captain to the Separation meeting. C. H. McKnight and Snodgrass Buchanan have invited me to the Squatters' Ball; but ——! *"To them* that list the world's gay showes I leave."

[*The joke is, she was going to have a baby in less than four weeks' time.*

According to Professor Edward Shann, "When first used in Van Diemen's Land the term 'Squatter' had the same contemptuous ring in Australia as in America, and it long retained a suggestion of criminal origin—at least in the ears of the 'pure merinos' or 'free settlers'." William Campbell wrote lengthily on the subject, proposing that the offensive name should be changed to "Pastoral Tenants of the Crown".]

2nd   Mark Nicholson to dinner.

3rd   Lyon Campbell's funeral.

4th   Captain Reid and Mr McCrae mutually shocked at the Rev. A. C. Thomson for "mixing with, and encouraging the young bloods of the town". This happened at last night's ball, on the same day after he had read the burial service over poor Lyon Campbell. Mr McCrae loudly declared "Thomson shall never more be minister of mine!"

5th   On his return from town, Mr McCrae related how his friend Mr Moor had dined with the Verners of Heidelberg on Monday and had been surprised at finding himself *vis-à-vis* to Mrs Lyon! And she, with uncovered head, ... devoid of outward signs of sorrow. This, too, on the very day of her husband's obsequies.

If the parson's behaviour was reprehensible, what is Mrs Lyon's?

6th   Mr McCrae walked across to "Sherwood", Mrs McCrae [*the Captain's wife*] being ill.

7th   The Captain to dinner. *La fortune du pot!*

8th   Mr McCrae in town till late in the evening.

9th   The boys, with Mr McLure, to Kirk. Hugh Walker to dinner, and stayed all night.

10th   Mr McCrae and Mr Simpson in town all day.

11th   Mr and Mrs Damyon to see me.

12th   Mr La Trobe walked across from Jolimont. He brought flower-roots for Willie and Sandy, and asked after his book on Mexico which Mr McCrae had forgotten to return. He also advised me to encourage Australian flora in our garden.

13th Archie Jamieson and Captain McCrae to dinner.

14th Mr Jamieson and Mr McCrae started early for town. My head tortured with neuralgic pains.

15th The boys and Lucy went to Dr Howitt's, to return *Our Neighbours*; and Mrs Howitt sent me another of Miss Bremer's pleasant novels, *Family Cares and Joys*.

[*Godfrey Howitt, M.D., of a celebrated family, has been described by Christopher North as "ane o' the best botanists in England, an' a desperate beetle-hunter". The doctor came to Melbourne in 1839, bringing with him his house which he erected on land he had purchased, at the corner of Spring and Collins streets. Here he lived and practised his profession for over thirty years. Then, in 1869, he removed to "Rosemont", Balaclava, where eventually he died. In private life, Howitt loved to be alone, avoiding, politely, even a friend like Georgiana, who barely records his name. His son, William Godfrey, another doctor, married Captain Alexander McCrae's daughter, concerning whom there is an indirect reference in the diary, 29th November 1844: "Captain McCrae called for his George, who is wanted to rock the cradle just now." G. G. McC., remembering his boyhood, describes Howitt's home as "a low-browed one-story cottage, with a veranda, front and ends". He also says little about the doctor, although he relates how his wife had lent him story-books he might never otherwise have known—"thin little quarto volumes, bound in dark green cloth".*]

16th Only our servants at church today. (The effect of the Squatters' Ball!) Mr Malcolm, the Separationist, came out to dine.

17th Mr McCrae to luncheon at "Sherwood".

18th Unpleasant sort of day. Eliza not attentive to her work, seeming to have something on her mind.

19th Walked over to see Mrs McCrae and the children. On my return Eliza startled me by saying she "wishes to leave on the 26th of this month" when her half-year will be up. The reason is, she's to be married to Peggy McLure's brother William, a carpenter who has secured a contract for timber-splitting in Dandenong at

£3 a week. Their banns were put up last Sunday. This is vexatious
for me; Eliza *might* have given me notice earlier, or made her
young man wait until I can get about again. In the evening, Jane
told me that "poor Eliza hadn't known till last week that William
must leave at once, or lose the contract".

20th Agnes Laidlaw, who occasionally helped our Jane with
the children on board the *Argyle*, will be at liberty ten days hence,
and is most anxious to come to "Mayfield".

21st Captain McCrae "lumbagoed".

22nd Maggie to early dinner; George and Aleck went home
with her to "Sherwood" till Monday.

23rd Everybody at church except myself, so I went into the
garden where I read a little out of my Bible in the silver letter with
the Common Prayer.

24th Mr Heriot to dinner; felt uneasy during tea-time, but
did not like to ask our visitor to call at Dr Thomas's on his way
home. After Mr H. had left, the rain began to pour in torrents and,
at 2 a.m., I was forced to rouse Mr McCrae. . . . While he prepared himself for town, I woke Jane and Ellen in order to have a
fire put in my room.

25th Dr Thomas arrived at 4 a.m. and I suffered unusually,
owing to the strain I had experienced four months ago. However,
at a few minutes past twelve (noon), I was delivered of a fine girl.
No sooner had Jane dressed the child than Ellen carried her into the
drawing-room, where the boys were still at lessons. Mr McLure
took the baby in his arms to welcome her into the world.

26th Lanty arrived and was allowed to see the baby. Paid Eliza
Impey the balance of her wages, £10, and she left.

27th Dr and Mrs Thomas, and Willy Howitt, came out.

28th I had a shivering fit, and stayed ill all night long.

29th A letter from Mrs Cobham saying Lizzie is to be married
in October, and that Mrs C. herself, and Frank, are going with their
cattle to Port Fairy in November.

30th Awoke refreshed. Sat up for a time in the nursery while
my room was being aired.

JULY

July 1st Bright and clear. Jane went to Eliza's wedding, and returned at 4 p.m. Mr McCrae spent the day with the boys in town.

2nd Severe frost during the night. Mr Westgarth came out with the newspaper account of the wreck of the *Isabella*. The passengers, three days on the rocks at Flinders Island, at the end of which time they were safely taken off by the *Flying Fish*. All landed at Hobson's Bay yesterday afternoon.

[*She struck on a reef between Chapel and Badger islands. The ladies and a few male passengers were "most miraculously landed" in the ship's boats, while the remainder were lashed to the poop all night. Next morning, everybody having been safely brought ashore, the "Isabella" went to pieces. Nothing in the way of clothes or provisions was saved. During their enforced stay on the island the survivors were without fire or blankets, and lived on pumpkins which drifted from the ship, and a few crayfish they were able to catch. The following is a list of the "Isabella's" passengers, and cargo: Mrs Hardy and infant, Mrs French and child, Miss Scott, Messrs Broadfoot, John Hunter, Alexander Campbell, ——— McNeil (from Port Fairy), and Barry Cotter. Intermediate: Jack Ewart, G. Roach (Darebin Creek), H. Davis, and ——— Coffin, late of the ship "Wallace". Cargo: 260 bales of wool, 212 casks of tallow, 611 hides, 2 casks beef, 250 tons bark, 29 logs gum, 4 logs blackwood, 3 bales leather, 1 box swan skins, 2 bales seal skins, 5 boxes specimens natural history, 1 box works of art, 1 box pictures, 1 cask mutton hams, 1 box bird skins, 35 kegs nails, 4 trunks, 2 boxes apparel, 2 boxes books, 2 ditto documents, 1 case shoes, 9 bags horse-shoes, 2 casks mace, 1 China table, 7 cases wine, 7 hogsheads Geneva, 49 bags bark, and original cargo shipped at Sydney.*]

3rd Dr Thomas pronounces me "free from fever".

4th A cold raw dull day. Mr McCrae busy writing.

5th George and Lucy severely "colded". Letter from Agnes saying that as Sir James McGregor never took Farquhar's name off the Army List he is still eligible for a Surgency in the Regiment. He talks of going to London, should he not succeed in building up a practice at Sydney.

6th Sat by the fire all day. In the evening Captain McCrae brought letters from three of his superior officers for me to make copies of, which copies I am to send to Sydney Smith.

7th Very rainy. No one could go to church.

8th Up all day. Tuck arrived from Arthur's Seat.

9th A fine bright morning. Drew a plan for the house at Arthur's Seat. Planted cuttings sent by Mr La Trobe.

10th Tuck gone away again.

11th Piercingly cold. Even with a fire, and with mittens on, I can scarcely keep my hands warm enough to have my letters in time for the *Arab*.

12th, 13th, 14th, 15th Little to do, and very much depressed.

16th Rode to town through trees hidden by mist.

24th By advice, I wrote to Dr Nicholson regarding this place, and made him aware that as the house at Arthur's Seat is not nearly completed we cannot leave "Mayfield" earlier than Christmas.

25th Lanty very ill, so Mr McCrae had to go to town.

26th Captain McCrae to dinner. In the evening, Dr Thomas.

27th A ship having arrived from Launceston with mails from England, Mr McCrae went to enquire if it brings letters for us.

28th, 29th. . . .

30th Dense mist again. People who have been seven years here, say these are the first mists they have seen in this district, though such are prevalent in Van Diemen's Land at all seasons.

31st Lanty and Mr McCrae have gone across to see about fencing the ground next to Mr D. L. Campbell's. (The Captain's acre, and Dr McCrae's.)

AUGUST

August 1st Mr McCrae has arranged to go to Arthur's Seat with Mr Powlett on the 12th.

2nd Mr McCrae in town all day arranging his affairs.

3rd Captain McCrae brought me my half-year's money.

4th, 5th, 6th. . . .

7th Mr Foot [*the surveyor*] and Maggie McCrae came across early. At 3 p.m. the Rev. James Clow arrived and was ushered into the drawing-room, where he found among those already assembled

Mr Simpson, Captain McCrae, Mr McCrae, Mr McLure and the boys and Lucia. Jane carried in the baby, whom the minister solemnly baptized, after the Presbyterian rites, by the name of Margaret Martha. Afterwards, while Mr Clow was delivering a most impressive address, Perry, from his position near the window, called out that Mr C.'s mare had broken loose and was dashing up the carrots and the onions; but Mr Clow only paused for a moment, and then went on with his speech. After the ceremony concluded, all hands, except Mr McCrae, set out to catch the mare which proved not to be an easy matter. Eventually Jane, having handed the baby to me, secured the obstinate creature, so that Mr C. was able to go on his way in peace.

8th Rain bucketing down all day. Charles Thomas came.

9th Mr John Highett to dinner; when leaving, he put on Willie's hat by mistake and found it rather large . . . though Willie is only nine years old!

10th Copied out a list of debts due to the firm of Montgomery and McCrae.

11th A sunshine day; but the flat not dry enough for the boys to get across to church.

12th Mr J. F. Palmer called on his way to town.

13th, 14th Mr McCrae away all night, both nights.

15th A tranquil day. Packed seeds for Arthur's Seat.

17th Mr McCrae's forty-third birthday. Messrs Westgarth and Broadfoot rode out to dinner. [*Craig and Broadfoot, Merchants, Collins Street. Skene Craig, originally in charge of the Port Phillip Commissariat Department, went into partnership with A. A. Broadfoot. They "rowed"; and Craig challenged Broadfoot to a passage of arms, which Broadfoot accepted, although he was so scared that he sent for Dr Campbell and Dr Thomas to be present. The affair came off (appropriately) behind the morgue, at the foot of Batman's Hill. Craig missed Broadfoot, and Broadfoot missed Craig, whereupon they rushed forward to congratulate each other.*] I gave Mr Westgarth his choice of the shells and fossils I had brought from England, for the Museum of the Mechanics' Institute.

18th Lakes of water outside. George and Willie chanting "Anybody going to *swim* to church?"

19th Mr McLure went to court to testify to the character of Mr Lidemann, and he had hardly come home again, when Mr John Cotton arrived with an offer of £100 a year, if Mr McLure will consent to go to the Goulburn as tutor to his sons. Mr McLure excused himself on the grounds of ill health. . . . "I should even have to leave this family, with whom I am so happily situated, were it not for the fact that they are going to reside by the sea."

20th Dr Kilgour, to see Mr McLure; he will sail for England a month hence, on his way home to Aberdeen.

21st Recollecting Dr K.'s conversation of yesterday evening, he said the natives north of the Grampians talk about a species of Boa called *Mindi*, which lies in wait by waterholes, and, if an emu comes to drink, makes a meal of the complete bird! ["*The 'Mindi' often ascends the highest tree in the forest, and, like a ring-tailed possum, securing its hold, stretches itself over an extent of twenty and thirty miles."—William Thomas: Guardian of the Aborigines.*] Also, natives of the Upper Loddon describe an Ichthyosaurus, 12 to 18 feet long, haunting river beds, and able to swallow a tortoise with ease!

22nd Tomorrow, the *Delaware* will sail for Arthur's Seat. Worked all day on the plan of the house, and, when I had finished, put the sketch on the dining-table, ready for Mr McCrae to take with him in the morning.

23rd Rose early and prepared all the packages to send in. Mr McCrae started on horseback, but returned at 10 a.m., having omitted to take the plan of the house with him! He soon set off again; and we were imagining him well on the road, when he arrived a second time. "The wind is dead ahead, and the boat cannot sail today."

24th Neale brought word that the *Delaware* will leave by the morning-tide tomorrow. Mr McCrae surprised by a note from a gentleman who had failed to keep his appointment at the office! This unique piece of civility is from Mr Moule, son of a clergyman in England. Here, nobody thinks of being punctual, far less of apologizing for keeping a professional man waiting for hours at his office.

25th Mr McCrae rode in to start for Arthur's Seat. Miss Gavan came; Mr La Trobe, and Captain Lonsdale.

26th Lanty brought me a letter from Mr Cummins, and one from Mr Knox's solicitor telling me of the change Mr K. had made in the distribution of his property since his wife's death. "He has not left anything to his niece (a friend of Mrs R. D. Long's) Mrs Lane, and ordered all his books and collection of old classical music-books to be sold, and the amount realized for these, and his house, to be divided among his Scots cousins . . . so many in number, that some of them will only get £10 for their share. In the will made during Mrs Knox's lifetime, as they had no children, her niece was provided for, and a legacy mentioned for me; also he had promised to leave me certain music-books and his d'Osterwald Bible [*Mrs La Trobe was a great granddaughter of the Rev. John d'Osterwald, translator of the Swiss Bible*], but, after Mrs Knox died, he took a holiday in Berwickshire, to look up any blood relations he could find; the result was 'legion'—all strangers to him—and glad to claim him as their wealthy kinsman!"

> [*Women be forgetfull, children be unkinde,*
> *Executors be covetous; and take what they finde.*
> *If anybody asks where the dead's good became?*
> *"So God me helpe," they answer, "he dyed a poor man!"*]

27th. . . .

28th A letter from Dr McCrae telling the Captain he cannot let him have any money, having only taken eleven guineas since he arrived at Sydney [*nine months ago . . . 13th December 1843—28th November 1844*].

29th, 30th. . . .

31st Heard of the safe arrival of the party at Arthur's Seat.

SEPTEMBER

September 1st Kept to my room all day. Mr McLure read with the boys till dinner-time.

2nd Lanty carried in a bag of books to be forwarded by the *Delaware* for Arthur's Seat.

3rd A note from "Dame Juliana", to which I returned an answer by Mrs Thomas.

4th A sharp north wind. By Dr Nicholson's desire, Mr Easey, the auctioneer, arrived to examine the house. Captain McCrae and Sally to tea. Maggie had a letter from Lizzie Cobham engaging her to be bridesmaid-in-chief at her wedding.

5th Cold heavy rain, succeeded by sultry heat; and then thunder . . . with frost in the evening. *The weather of four seasons within twelve hours!*

6th Our chimneys swept for the first time since they were built.

> [*Ramoner-çi, ramoner-là,*
> *La cheminée de haut en bas.*]

7th "Mrs Chatterbox" called in, on her way to the Currs', to be first with the news that Edward Bell is to be married to Miss Fenwick! Also that George Sherbrook Airey is about to resign his commissionership in favour of Major St John. . . . [*George Sherbrook Airey: nephew of the celebrated English astronomer of that name. Airey's Inlet was called after one of this family.*] Perry six years old today.

8th Jane went to the Kirk, and the boys read service at home.

9th Dr Thomas drove out with his little Maggie, who looked well . . . the Quarry-Wilmett affair greatly talked of in town. . . .

[*Apparently the Quarrys were a soul-stirring couple. See entry for 1st March 1843, where Mrs Q. cuts a vein, and swallows laudanum: "Mr Q. will look more like a ghost than ever!" The husband first comes into this diary so far back as 25th October 1840, in a white squall off Tilbury Fort, helping Mrs McCrae's little Farquhar up the rope-ladder of an emigrant ship. Elsewhere, on a supplementary page, he has been described thus: "Jephson Quarry . . . 'Hurrah for Ould Oireland!' . . . the broth of a bhoy, very pugnacious, not prepossessing to look at. A pale-faced man dresst in a sheet, he would make a capital spook." Soon after marriage, Mrs Quarry, a handsome woman, began to tread her shoe awry; so carelessly, that Mr Quarry put her in charge of her sister's husband, Mr John Wilmett. Events quickly followed, and on 7th September 1844, during night-time, Casanova slid under the shadow of the Wilmett's veranda, where he was grabbed by Wilmett himself, who, however, with a pistol*] poking in his face, elected to let go. *Subsequently Quarry found a letter to his wife, signed Edward Hodgson; thus discovering the cuckold-maker's name. At once a duel was arranged, only to be stopped by the authorities, who had Hodgson arrested and bound to keep the peace. Quarry sailed fiercely to China, but the vessel he travelled on never got farther than Port Curtis, where she splintered on the rocks, 21 deg. 5 min. S., and 150 deg. E. After that, nothing was heard of him until a Jack Tar belonging to the wrecked ship appeared in Melbourne, and started what my father called "a painted picture-show". In this "painted picture-show" was to be seen a representation of Quarry's barque (aptly called "Peruvian") lying aground; and "figures on the sand". The sailor draughtsman said Jephson had escaped, but whither he went nobody knew. As for the wicked beauty, she continued to be romantic, and, even in her autumn forties, looked alluring—in the bar-room of a Collingwood hotel!*]

Mr McLure read in a Caithness newspaper, at the Rev. Mr Gunn's, notice of the death of Mr Bruce of Symbister.

10th Mrs Howitt sent me Mary Howitt's new book *Rural Life in Germany*.

11th A strong north wind. Everything bleak outside. Jane's bucket rattling about the yard. Sent word by Lanty to Mrs Thomas of Symbister's death.

Accidents and Misdeeds among the Children

12th On Thursday, the Captain's George (playing Humpty Dumpty) "had a great fall".

13th On Friday, the Captain's Aleck kicked our Sandy till he roared!

14th On Saturday, Lucia ran out to call the boys to morning-prayers just at the moment when the same Aleck, having his back towards her, flourished his spade. The edge of the spade struck against her mouth and drove in one of her teeth. Aleck's father, who had come to borrow "Don", was very angry, and would have beaten him, had I not begged him off. *Note:* "Don" refused to be caught.

15th Aleck sent back to "Sherwood" till Monday. Jane took the other boys to the Kirk.

NORTH MELBOURNE, LOOKING WEST, 1854
From a sketch by Georgiana

A VIEW OF QUEEN STREET, MELBOURNE, 1853
From a pen-drawing by Georgiana

THE GREAT FLOOD OF 1852
Sketched by Georgiana from her attic window at 144 Latrobe Street West

CAPTAIN REID'S STATION, TICHINGOROOK, FROM THE WEST, 1844
From a pencil sketch by Georgiana

THE MINISTER'S HOUSE, FROM DR THOMAS'S VERANDA,
BOURKE STREET WEST, 1843
From a pencil sketch by Georgiana

16th Sent newspapers and some books to be forwarded to Arthur's Seat, per *Delaware*.

17th Several heavy showers. These showers could be heard in the distance approaching from Campbellfield and, so soon as one had passed, another would follow, with intervals of about only five minutes between. Dr Thomas came to early dinner, and told me Mrs Cole had a letter from Agnes Bruce saying that her father-in-law died on March 27, and that they will soon leave Bigton to take up their residence at Symbister.

18th, 19th Rain, rain.

20th, 21st, 22nd Rain, rain, rain.

23rd Steadily falling rain all day long. Dull and dreary.

24th Letter from Arthur's Seat; Mr McCrae will be unable to travel for a few days yet on account of a log having fallen on his foot, but, for our wedding day, he sends some lines pencilled during the storm of Monday last.

25th Twice seven years a wife today. A letter from Mrs Octavius Browne dated at London, May 23.

26th In the evening, Mr McCrae arrived, very tired, after his journey. The Captain came across to tea.

27th Captain McCrae brought some correspondence received from Sydney.

28th Mr McCrae wrote to Agnes concerning the monies due to Captain McCrae.

29th Mr Westgarth to dinner. The river "up".

30th Mr Westgarth left. In the evening, the boys read in turns from *Rural Life in Germany*. All much interested in the ascent of the Brocken. Mr McCrae still laid up with his lame foot.

OCTOBER

October 1st The river much swollen owing to the interminable rain. By noon, the water had risen above 18 feet perpendicular, the highest flood-mark for 1842.

2nd The mark 3 inches lower today.

3rd Mr Westgarth, in sea-boots, telling us that the lower part of

Captain Cole's bonded store is under water, but a proportion of goods has been saved.

4th Mr McCrae rode to town to see how it fared with Mrs Cole, as Captain Cole is at Sydney. This afternoon, the river is 18 inches lower.

5th The water in Mrs Cole's dining-room at the wharf was up to the top of the table, while she herself looked for refuge in the upper floor of the house. [*The genesis of Melbourne's waterfront. Captain Cole built a wooden wharf, the first beside the Yarra (on land bought by himself at the Crown sale); 4th August 1841.*]

6th Mark Nicholson came. No one at church today. Lightning at night.

7th Mr Westgarth and Mark Nicholson left early for town.

8th A cloudy close morning. Mr McCrae's foot a nuisance to him.

9th Better weather. The sun shining across wet grass while Lucia helps Mr McCrae put in seeds of melons and pumpkins brought from "Sherwood" [*the Captain's place*].

10th Mr McLure and Lanty left for Arthur's Seat.

11th A cloudy day. Dr Thomas came in the afternoon.

12th Cold and damp. The river has subsided to the level of the palings at the foot of the bank; five panels carried away!

13th Jane paddles across the flat to church, and back. Mr Forbes, preaching the sermon, much disconcerted when the *other* Forbes' dog came down the aisle and barked.

> *Bells is ringin',*
> *Cats is singin',*
> *An' dogs is gannin' to chorch.*

14th Mrs Sconce has a son.

15th The boys took back to Mrs Howitt *Rural Life in Germany*, and brought home Miss Bremer's *President's Daughter*.

16th Received from Mrs Jeffery the goose eggs from Mount Macedon, for Ellen to set, as she wished for them.

18th A visit from Mr Gilfillan, who showed me his portfolio of sketches. [*Mr Gilfillan was one of the last men to wear a pigtail in the British Navy. He settled in New Zealand at Matarawa, six miles out*] *from Wanganui, where, some time in 1847, Maoris attacked his home-stead and killed his wife and three children; one other child escaped who lived to be eighty-three.*] Mr McCrae admired a view of the Bermudas, and spoke of "the clear water there", when Mr G. interrupted: "If you mean *sea*-water, well and good! But if you mean water *ashore*, it's as much as your life is worth to swallow it! Goat's milk is the only drink, or rain-water . . . at sixpence a pail!!"

22nd Dr Thomas borrowed Mr McCrae's spring-cart to take poor Mrs P. W. Welsh and her luggage to the steamer for Laun-ceston.

[*In 1843, "Paddy" Welsh had been declared bankrupt, his debts exceeding £29,000. Welsh was co-executor, with Farquhar McCrae and Sydney Stephen, of Henry Fysche Gisborne's will, and, when Welsh, in 1844, applied for a certificate of discharge, his fellow-executors entered a caveat against the certificate being granted. Subject matter taken from a paper by N. M. O'Donnell, M.B.*]

26th Boisterous day, with showers of hail.

27th Fine and clear, but the air very sharp. Captain and Mrs Cole, both muffled up, drove out to see us. It is exactly six months, and one week, since they last favoured me with their presence.

28th Willie practising his native spear in the paddock near the river.

29th The boys went to town for the newspaper. Perry and Lucia amused themselves indoors.

30th Soon after Mr McCrae had gone to town I heard George scream, and saw him running towards the house, in front of Willie and Sandy. Willie's spear had glanced off a tree and flown in George's direction, the point of it grazing his right eye. Sent Nancy off for Dr Thomas who arrived about 1 p.m. when the wound had begun to bleed. Dr Thomas said to keep it clean and it would all come right.

31st George heroic. Mr Westgarth brought a batch of letters for us. Mr McCrae gone to town on account of the Marquis of Ailsa's affairs. [*The Marquis of Ailsa, head of the Kennedy family, was in partnership with the Hunters.*]

NOVEMBER

November 1st   On the same business, Mr McCrae at Ailsa Craig's to breakfast, where he learnt that Mr Montgomery is not only purchasing sheep but that he has already been paid £900 odd for the land expenses of the Ailsa cause, a sum which Mr Montgomery had led Mr McCrae to believe would never be forthcoming. Mr McCrae and Mr Craig placed the accounts in the hands of Mr Henry Moor so that he may collect the debts and issue circulars which two months ago Mr McCrae left with Mr Montgomery and which he was told had been issued without success. Mr McCrae dined and slept at Mr Craig's.

2nd   Mr McCrae came out to breakfast, and returned to town to arrange with Mr Moor about the settlement of his own affairs, as proposed by Mr Montgomery.

3rd   Mr Westgarth to dinner. Nobody at church.

4th   Mark Nicholson brought Lizzie out to stay for a day or two.

5th   Mr McCrae sent letters for Mr McLure by James Simon who goes to "Kangerong".

6th   Learnt that Mr Kemp the Post Master, is going Home on halfpay (invalided), provided anyone will take his place for half the salary. Mr McCrae called on Mr La Trobe, who at once wrote to ask leave to appoint Captain McCrae at £200, and to allow Kemp £150 during his absence. An unsatisfactory meeting with Mr Montgomery, who refuses to submit the disputed accounts of the firm to arbitration.

7th   Mr McCrae to town early. Mr Montgomery "ready to take his oath that Mr Hunter is a client of the firm, and not of Mr McCrae's only".

8th   Dr and Miss Black drove out to "Mayfield"; they offered me a seat in their carriage whenever I wished to go to town. Major St John was thrown from his horse today.

9th   Mr McCrae and the boys at Ailsa Craig's all day.

[*This Ailsa was certain to have been named after the celebrated Craig, in Scotland. "Far, far away to the westward over our brown horizon, towered up, white and visible at the many miles of distance, a high irregular pyramid: 'Ailsa Craig'." "Reminiscences": Thomas Carlyle.*]

10th George, Willie, and Sandy went to St James's. Mr Westgarth and Captain B. Cain came out to dinner, the latter bringing me a letter from Mr O. Browne of June 12. [*The captain built the first ship in Melbourne: a brig called the "Jane Cain"; launched 27th January 1848, in the presence of six thousand people.*]

SUPPLEMENT

"Mayfield" was sold to Mr Allen for £1100. He built a new kitchen at the cost of £100, and sold the property to Sir Francis Murphy for £2000. Sir Francis divided the land and sold the five acres of whins (beyond the hedge to Simpson's Road) for £5000, and asked £6000 for the four acres next the river and the house. [*The whins were grown from seeds gathered at the Hill of Gourden, Fyvie.*] This *surely* would have been a safe investment for Madame's £1100!

> [*Ah! that for one she-hypocrite, you must
> Permit so many acres to be lost!*]

When the "explanation" came it was to the following effect: "In the present bad prospects of the colony the purchase of the house is not considered a safe investment, the £100 is for your immediate wants."

★ ★ ★

11th Mr Westgarth tells me that Phillip Hervey, formerly keeper of the Observatory on Flagstaff Hill, has got his ticket-of-leave and is employed occasionally to write in Mr La Trobe's office at a salary of 6s. a day. Hervey, in his first youth, was manager of Baring's Bank at Naples, after which he returned to London where he lived *en grand seigneur* until, drawing a bill to satisfy some persistent hanger-on, he was cast for transportation and came to Australia. Here he lay *perdu*, apparently quite satisfied to be out of the great world.

One evening Mr McCrae called at the Observatory and asked Hervey for a light for his cheroot which had gone out. Hervey immediately rose up to get the light, but, in doing so, let a book fall from his lap. Mr McCrae went to pick it up, and, to his great surprise, found it to be Aeschylus!

After a time, Hervey ceased to be seen in Melbourne, and, since no one heard of his death, it was generally thought he had slipped away to England.

[*The following parallel story, undated, is told by Isaac Selby in his "Memorial History of Melbourne".*

"When our cemetery was opened it became the Flagstaff Hill Signal Station for the ships entering port. Buckland, an ex-convict, had charge of it. He was a well-read man, and accumulated a library. There is generally a prejudice against a man who has been in prison, and it operated against him; and he had to give up his position. He went to live in Fitzroy. He sustained himself on what he had earned for some time, but when it was about expended he took his books down to the Mechanics' Institute and made a present of them to its library; then he went home and blew his brains out. They brought his body to the cemetery in a cart, and buried it on the eastern side, near the fence, but they did not dig the grave deep enough, and, when it rained, the coffin was disinterred, and he had to be buried a second time. Now he sleeps in a nameless grave."

Can it be that Hervey and Buckland represent the same man? An alias might account for the difference.

Describing his own boyhood, George McCrae, the diarist's son, mentions gratefully how Hervey would often let him peep through his field telescope. "One morning, we found him with his glass trained towards the east, where there was congregated a large crowd of people about a rust-coloured sandstone building. He told us it was 'Hanging Day' at the new gaol on the hill, and that the number of silk parasols slanting above the crowd was 'something astonishing'."]

12th Mr John Cotton came out with Mr McCrae to dinner.

13th Mamie Cobham's engagement to James Grahame is announced—the event to take place next year. I had the English bulbs lifted.

14th Sent in my saddle for Mamie to ride out with James Grahame to dine with us; they told me they had seen Captain Cain's and Miss Williamson's wedding party going to the church this forenoon.

15th Mr McCrae returned from Kinlochewe. Lanty brought home the piebald pony.

16th Returned to Dr Clutterbuck his Brande's *Manual of Chemistry*. Thunder and rain!

17th Pouring rain. Nobody able to go to church. Mr Westgarth brought me a letter from Mr Cummins enclosing a bank-bill for £100 from Madame without a word of explanation. [*For subsequent explanation, see Supplement to entry of 10th November.*] Mrs E. Cotton came to say "Adieu" as she goes to Balkham Hill tomorrow.

18th Mr Jamieson and Mr Westgarth arrived in the evening.

19th The boys went to town to see Mr Yaldwyn's collection of birds brought from England. Strange, it appears to me, that a man past forty-six years of age, with a fine old property, "Blackrock", Sussex, held by his ancestors for seven hundred years, should sell his paternal acres and transplant his family to Australia! Mrs Yaldwyn and the children remain for the present in England; Mrs Y's sister, Miss Bowles, has come out with Mr Yaldwyn; and Mark Nicholson tells me we shall soon have her for our neighbour at "The Grange" . . . *tant mieux pour vous.* [*Possibly this Mr Yaldwyn was W.H. of that ilk, a member of the Separation Deputation to London in 1841.*]

20th As Mr Westgarth was leaving, the door blew inward behind him and filled the house with rain.

21st Mr McCrae brought Lizzie Cobham to dinner.

22nd On his return from town today, Mr McCrae told me "There is prospect of an arrangement being arrived at soon."

23rd Mark Nicholson came out with Mr Yaldwyn.

24th Nobody at church.

25th Mark and Lizzie rode to town.

26th The Rev. James Forbes came to see us.

[*Rev. James Forbes: later on, a secessionist from the Church of Scotland. He built the John Knox Church, opposite the Melbourne Public Library, and edited the "Port Phillip Christian Herald". A week before his death,*

12th August 1851, having been apprised of his condition, the good man sent for his infant son, only a few days old, and not only baptized him but entered his name in the Family Register. After this had been done, he said: "I have performed the last act of my ministry", and straightway died; a gentleman of Christ.]

27th A "brick-fielder!"

28th Mark Nicholson left for Macedon. Thunder and rain in the afternoon.

29th A cold rainy day. Captain McCrae called for his George, who is wanted to rock the cradle just now.

30th St Andrew's Day. Sandy eight years old.

DECEMBER

December 1st Lizzie Cobham and the boys went to church. James Grahame returned with them.

2nd Quite a summer day. Lanty left for Arthur's Seat.

3rd The boys put on their new linen blouses to escort Lizzie to town for making her wedding purchases.

4th Like yesterday . . . a lovely day of cloudless sky . . . and the song, or "whizz", of the cicadas incessant.

5th A halcyon morning . . . too beautiful to stay indoors!

6th Mr McCrae quite knocked up. Tuck went to town to make preparations for going to Arthur's Seat. Mr McLure returned in high feather, charmed with the prospect of our new home.

7th A letter from Mr McLaren which breaks down all hope of employment from the Union Bank. Mr Westgarth to dinner.

8th Nobody at church in the forenoon. Mr La Trobe arrived in his new "outside-car" (once the property of poor Lyon Campbell) to take me across the flat to Jolimont. *Mem*: To ask Mr Mc-Crae to procure a spar for a flagstaff to set up at Mr La Trobe's bathing "loge" at the Heads.

9th Mrs Howitt, Willie, and Edward, came to spend the day. Mrs H. helped me to draw the seams of my new 5s. dress.

10th The boys spent the day with the Howitts, and I completed my print dress.

11th Mr McCrae arrived in the afternoon, angry and dirty, from floundering in the swamp, "Carrum Carrum", next Mr Horsefall's. Mr Westgarth came out.

12th Mr J. F. Palmer to see me, with a box of ripe cherries, the first of this season.

13th Paid Mortimer's account (out of my £100) £41.

14th Disagreeable weather. Captain McCrae came across. Blustering south wind at night, and heavy rain.

15th George and Mr McLure at Kirk. Mr Westgarth returned with them. In the evening James Grahame told us Mrs Thomas gave birth to a daughter last night.

16th Mr McCrae went in to see his new niece and her mother.

17th Walsh called on his way to Cape Schanck.

18th Mr McCrae learnt today that Mr Moor has effected an arrangement with Mr Montgomery whereby the office-premises shall be conveyed to me, as an equivalent for the £400—from my Aunt Margaret—"for a house which I can always call my own".

19th Thermometer 80°. Mr McCrae presented me with a new bridle and new whip, the latter in lieu of my dear old silver-mounted one which he lost on the Brighton Road.

20th Rode into town with Mr McCrae. Lucia on the saddle before him; left her at Dr Howitt's, and went on to Dr Thomas's. Said goodbye to Lizzie Cobham and Mark, as their marriage is to take place in her mother's house. Called at Sheriff Mackenzie's and Mr Shadforth's. Dined at Dr Howitt's. Agnes La Trobe came in the evening, and Mr G. L. Gilbert. Little Edward Howitt was brought in from Mr Brickwood's picnic in the Government Paddock, pale, cold, sick, and distracted; to his mother's great alarm. He had been knocked down by a pony and had fallen backwards on his head. His brother Willie had carried him home.

[*In 1841 William Brickwood ran a school for young gentlemen at "St Ninian's", Big Brighton, but within the space of three years left it, to become headmaster of "The Port Phillip Academical Institution".*]

21st News of Miss Patterson's marriage to Mr Foot.

22nd Mr McLure took the boys to the Kirk.

23rd Mr Crawley to dinner, with all the Sydney news.

24th Neil Black, Mr Le Souef, and Flora McLachlan to see us. Hear that Dr Barker's mother and Miss Elvidge are coming to reside at Richmond.

25th A blistering hot wind tearing through the house. Jane ironing in defiance of the elements, while I nurse Margaret Martha all the forenoon.

26th Mr Crawley and Mr McCrae rode to the Darebin, and to Mr Wills's at Chelsworth. Then home, by 6 p.m.

27th Three of us on horseback: Mr McCrae, Mr Crawley, and myself. I called at Dr Howitt's, left a card for Mrs Moor, the mayoress, and called at the Sheriff's to see Mrs Mackenzie, then, on my way home said goodbye to Mrs Lonsdale and Mrs Smythe. During our absence, Mrs and Miss Curr had called to invite us to their house-warming on January 2, 1845.

28th Cold, rainy, and boisterous.

29th Lucia three years old.

30th A hot wind. Dr Thomas, Captain McLachlan, and Wm. Mackenzie (Kinlochewe) to dinner.

31st "Kinlochewe" left early, and Mr Crawley bade us good-bye as he returns to the bush tomorrow (next year!)

SUPPLEMENT

LETTER FROM ARTHUR'S SEAT

October 26th, 1844

MY DEAR GEORGE,—

You can have no idea of what a fine place this is, with its lofty hills and deep glens, white sandy beach and rippling waves; but, above all, the mountain towering so high over the rest, that you see to an immense distance; on one side of the peninsula, Bass's Straits, on the other, the whole extent of Port Phillip Bay, over the way of Geelong and up to Melbourne. The ascent gets very steep as you approach the summit, and the sides of the mountain are, here and there, hollowed out into deep and abrupt chasms or gullies, as if dragons had been through them. If a good snowstorm, or whirlwind, could be got up, I've no doubt the ascent would be rendered as famous as that of the Brocken, if we had a Goethe, or a Howitt, to celebrate it. To be sure, we want the Witch Basin, and the Grand Spectre; but then we have the kangaroo, oppossum, and laughing jackasses, which they have not. I am very often on the top, enjoying the free air, and looking at everything far and near. I have likewise seen the little girl that was lost, who is a very fine child; she is, however, too young to be able to tell much about her sufferings during the five nights and four days she was missing. Her parents say the weather for some of the nights was very severe, with heavy rain. Her living under such circumstances for so long a time is truly wonderful. J. McLure

Note. Sarah Anne Cain, a child of Cain, the lime-burner, was at the time when she was lost, only turned of four years old. She had heard the men cooeeing and calling, but was afraid they were blacks, so did not answer. When found, she was keeping the crows off her face with her hand, and all but exhausted. Mrs Smith put her in a warm bath, and fed her only a teaspoonful of food at a time till she was quite recovered. She afterwards grew up a fine young woman.

La Trobe Described by Washington Irving

Washington Irving, in his journal (October, 1832), mentions among his fellow-travellers through the Far West, "Mr La Trobe, an Englishman, by birth; but descended of foreign stock; and who had all the buoyancy and accommodating spirit of a native of the Continent. Having rambled over many countries, he had become, to a certain degree, a citizen of the world, and easily adapted himself to any change. He was a man of a thousand occupations: a botanist, a geologist, a hunter of beetles and butterflies, a musical composer, a sketcher of no mean pretensions; in short, a complete virtuoso, added to which he was a very indefatigable, if not always a very successful, sportsman. Never had a man more irons on the fire, and, consequently, never was a man more busy or more cheerful. My third companion was one who had accompanied the former from Europe, and travelled with him as his Telemachus, being apt, like his prototype, to give occasional perplexity and disquiet to his mentor. He was a young Swiss Count (Portales), twenty-one years of age, full of talents and spirit, but galliard in the extreme, and prone to every kind of wild adventure." [*News of the "young Count's" death arrived at Melbourne in 1868.*]

THE LA TROBE—MONT MOLLIN ALLIANCE

Jean de Blaquière, descended of a family of that name in Languedoc, married Mary Elizabeth, daughter of Peter de Varennes (who died, 1780, aged eighty-one) and left issue: Lewis, who died unmarried, 1754; Matthew, John, Elias, Catharine, Jane, and Susanne, born 1730, who married Samuel de Meuron, Councillor of State in Switzerland.

Their son, Adolphe, married Susanne de Mt Mollin, sister of Sophie de Mt Mollin, who married C. J. La Trobe. In 1850 Adolphe de Meuron came to Australia on a visit to his aunt and uncle, but, not liking the colony, returned to his native land a year or two later.

Mrs La Trobe died at her mother's house in Neuchâtel, April 1854; subsequently C. J. La Trobe married Adolphe de Meuron's widow, Susanne (i.e. his deceased wife's sister). Susanne survived Mr La Trobe till 1883, when she died leaving three daughters.

By his first wife Sophie, C. J. La Trobe had issue: Agnes, born 1836, married Count de Salis; Nellie, Cecile, and Charles Joseph (born 1844, and married in America).

LETTER FROM LITTLE GEORGE GORDON MCCRAE

Arthur's Seat,
March 1845

I hope you are well and will be soon coming to Arthur's Seat. We were surprised to hear of Mrs Green's death; for we saw her at Captain Bunbury's in apparently high spirits. We learnt lately that Mr Barker's house was burnt which I suppose you have heard of already. Tuck was ill with quinsy, but is now better. The black-wood logs for the partitions are all sawn; and the house is nearly shingled. The chimneys, on the Rumford plan, are finished, the kitchen one begun, but the copper is not yet set. Tell Lucia that two of her rabbits are dead. The *Delaware* arrived here on Sunday and set sail on Monday after having discharged all our goods. As we were at the saw-pit, the dogs startled a kangaroo which leapt very near us, and Perry declared that he felt its tail touch his back. The "Bishop's" unfortunate goose, upon which you intended to dine so sumptuously, perished during Perry's perilous voyage, and with the fowls was consigned to the deep. Perry is much puzzled to know what bag of apples you mean to be kept under lock and key; and I would like to know what that particular and familiar case is that you sent for our discussion. Tuck and Neale killed a large guano 4 ft. 8 ins. in length and forked tongue four or five inches long . . . its feet and claws are as large as those of an eagle.

The blacks set fire to the top of the mountain for the purpose of driving out the wallabies from the bushes and killing them. The fire gradually encircled the brow of the Mount like a diadem on the head of a monarch. In the dark night its appearance was magnificent and imposing in the extreme; the smoke curling up among the trees in the morning made it appear as if Arthur's Seat was covered with cottages in whose chimneys fires were burning. Tuck has made a new saw-pit by the side of his hut to save the trouble of transporting the logs of blackwood to the saw-pit on the side of the mountain. The men have made a new water-hole in the horse-paddock for the benefit of the cattle. We have the piebald and brown pony but not the colt. Captain Reid has been here several times and was so kind as to send us one pound of candles and two melons. Dunn killed a large black snake by the side of the new house; had it not been killed it might have proved a very troublesome neighbour. Since Ellen has been here we have had bread, instead of damper made with sour milk in place of yeast: and, sometimes, butter. ["*How to make a damper: take a mass of dough, shaped like a thin cheese, cover it over with hot embers, let it remain till the crust is hard, and then scrape away the ashes, and you have a damper before you. With your knife cut off a wedge, and hand the loaf to your next neighbour.*"—*The Hon. Robert Dundas Murray.*] Our hens are beginning to lay, and Ellen thinks that the ducks will begin soon. We have been reading a very amusing book called: *A New Home ... Who'll Follow?*; or a sketch of country life in Michigan, by Mrs Mary Cleavers. It contains an account of the first settlers there, and how they acted. It says that instead of settling quietly to work and making houses for themselves, they began all at once to build a grand city and to talk of the bank, the mill, and the church, which were to be. She mentions that her servant came to her one morning and asked her "if she hollered? for she thought she heard a yell."

As the two rabbits are dead, please to send up a young buck as a companion to the remaining one. I find in Chambers's that a pair of wild rabbits will produce no less than 1,250,000 in the space of four years.—I remain, etc.,

GEORGE GORDON McCRAE

*   *   *

1845

JANUARY

January 1st The *jour de l'an*: Captain McCrae, Maggie, and Sally came to tea.

2nd Went to dine at "St Helier's" with Mr and Mrs Curr, Mr and Mrs Westby, and Mr Simpson. [*Edmund Westby, with Henry Moor, A. F. A. Greeves, and J. R. Murphy, elected to the Council, November 1843.*] We were invited for half-past six, but, owing to some unforseen hitch, the dinner was not served till half-past seven. Mr Simpson escorted us home, by a blink of the moon, across the stony creek.

3rd Missed the ruby out of the head of one of the serpents of my double-serpent ring. I cannot find the stone in my glove, yet I saw it in the ring at dinner-time last night. Mr McCrae tells me he has made a bargain with a boatman of the lime-craft to convey our baggage to Arthur's Seat for £4.

[*Lime-burning, carried on between Point Nepean and White Cliff, was a profitable business in the forties, inasmuch as fifty vessels were employed to bring the stuff to town. On return voyages they accepted light freight and sometimes a passenger or two.*]

4th Captain McCrae brought some seeds of African wheat, of a pale colour, soft, and the *akis*, black. Gave Nancy Laidlaw notice that I shall not require her services after this day month.

5th Archibald Cunninghame to dinner, and Mr McCrae made him a present of our Van Goyen landscape!

6th Captain McLachlan, knowing I should not be able to take much furniture to Arthur's Seat at present, offered to buy our dining-table at my own price; I told him I preferred to lend it (and the piano) to him, until we could give them room in our house at the bush.

7th Mr Cunninghame sent his servant for the picture. Mr McLure and the boys, with as much baggage as can be got ready, are to go by the *Jemima* on Monday.

["*The 'Jemima'—an old-fashioned smack of the cod's-head and mackerel-tail pattern; a good carrier, with roomy decks, pretty heavily sparred for her size, yet as stiff as a church. I don't suppose she could have been more than two-and-thirty feet over all, with, say, about eight feet in the beam. The cabin afforded space for three bunks, and one deal table, this latter being covered with scrawls by the jack-knives of the eaters. The prevalent odour: ship rum and Irish stew. The skipper, Walter Maclaren, was a stout, freckle-faced, grey-eyed Highlander, with short crisply-curling fair hair, turned red at the ends through constant association with lime.*"—George Gordon McCrae.]

This evening Mr McCrae left on "Don" for Captain Cole's, whence he will start, with the cool of the morning, for Arthur's Seat.

8th Rose early, and packed all day. At night, too tired to sleep; hot wind racing round the house.

9th Dr Thomas came. Heard that Mary Anne Thomas is going to be married to J. H. Campbell of Kilbarry, partner with Mr Murdoch.

10th Mr La Trobe came to ask whether Nancy Laidlaw would go to them as housemaid while they stay at the Heads; but Nancy was unwilling to leave town.

11th Packed china and glass in a barrel. By Mr McCrae's advice, I sent my set of finger-glasses and six antique ale-glasses to Mr Simpson. Mr McLure told me the thermometer, in the shade, today registered 100°.

12th A dry, hot day. George, Willie, and Alexander went to St James's. Dr Thomas called in on his way to Bourke Street, with little Maggie still very ill. Thermometer, 100°.

13th A blistering wind . . . packed six cases of books, but had to neglect my other packages, because the big needle had been mislaid.

THE McCRAES' HOUSE AT ARTHUR'S SEAT: A VIEW FROM THE EAST
From a sketch by Georgiana

THE HOUSE SEEN FROM THE WEST
From a sketch by Georgiana

THE HOUSE AT ARTHUR'S SEAT SEEN FROM THE SOUTH
From a sketch by Georgiana

THE HOUSE FROM THE NORTH
From a sketch by Georgiana

14th Clouds of sand darkening the sky, and penetrating the house; then rain at night, but very little coolness.

[*These dust-storms were of frequent occurrence. Ludwig Becker, government meteorologist, in his report dated 9th November 1856 says: "Ships out at sea, far from the coast, felt the dust; and one vessel in the Bay, twelve miles from land, had quantities of gravel and sand blown on board."*]

15th Thomas nailed down the packing-cases; helped to put them in the dray. Mr McLure returned from town at 2 p.m. with news that "the men are ready to sail, as the wind is fair". Soon after Mr McLure's arrival, Mr Westgarth came, bringing letters for Mr Mc-Crae from Dr Nicholson, Mr Highett, and Mr Richardson. Mr McLure and the boys left without their dinner. When Archie returned with the dray, he was pleased to be facetious, and said the men were still waiting for some cases of wine at Cape Schanck. Ellen carried Lucia across to see Mrs Henri Bell. A fine clear night, but not a breath of air stirring.

16th A welcome breeze till 10 a.m., when rain began, and never ceased till late at night. Perry and Lucia packing their little books in boxes all day.

17th Packed, and stacked, all the picture-frames.

18th A brilliant morning. Thankful for a whole day of rest.

19th Mr McCrae arrived home suddenly, and, before he had got out of the saddle, exclaimed that the boat hadn't reached Arthur's Seat on Saturday; also, that a dray, hired at the cost of £3, was still waiting to receive the packages; then, for a climax, when he had come inside, "Tuck's fine horse is dead of a snake-bite!"

20th Frank and Neale came from town to tell us the *Jemima* lay becalmed off William's Town all Saturday evening. . . . Amazed to learn that three of Captain Reid's "roughs" were on board. Mr Kersopp informed Mr McCrae that the *Midge* will be ready to take us to Arthur's Seat on Wednesday next; also, he said the *Jemima* had at last sailed and should, by this time, have made port.

21st Neale, Tuck, and Kelly branding cattle. One cow broke the fence and is now probably in Portland Bay district, the place whence she came.

22nd Mr McCrae made Tuck a present of his fowling-piece. Mr Westgarth remained for the night.

23rd Tuck went for his bullocks and started at 11 a.m. with all our stock (excepting the lame cow) for "No-Good-Damper".

LETTER FROM MR McLURE TO MR McCRAE

Arthur's Seat,
January 20, 1845

WE landed here, on Saturday, at about half-past 9 a.m. All well except for a little seasickness which soon wore off. The wind proved very unfavourable on the evening we left Melbourne; we got no further than the Junction of the Saltwater River; next morning, we came to William's Town, proceeded down the bay five or six miles, but were obliged to put back to Hobson's Bay, where we lay till about 2 p.m. on Friday. We passed the greater part of Friday night off Indented Head; towards daybreak a fresh breeze, springing up from north-west brought us here, as I have said, on Saturday morning. To our great surprise and disappointment we found you had left two hours before our arrival; you had, of course, given up all hope of our coming, from the unusual length of our passage. The boys stood it pretty well ... poor Sandy suffered most. The voyage was rendered still more uncomfortable through our being crowded with people, there being no less than seventeen altogether (five servants of Mr Barker's and four of Captain Reid's).

The wind continued to blow fresh till yesterday afternoon. When they began to bring the furniture ashore, the greater part had to be left on the beach till morning. Lanty watched it; and Dunn came pretty early with his dray and brought it to the house. One or two articles are a little damaged; the rest, so far as I can see, remain in good order. I have stowed as much as I could in the hut; the rest is put up in a corner of the house where it will be covered to protect it from the weather. The craft has run down this morning to take in a cargo of lime for Melbourne, so I take the opportunity of sending you this scrawl." [*Here follows the description of a similar trip, remembered by George McCrae: "It took us three days to creep down from Queen's Wharf to William's Town ... but, in reckoning this, we must take into account hours on the mud near the melting-down establishment; also, a long beguilement in that aptly named bend of the Yarra-Yarra, 'Humbug Reach.'" At last the boys, with their tutor, arrived at "the town of King Billy," and they stopped at a comfortable hotel, having "clean white beds . . . with the liquid tones of a Swiss musical-box to lull them to sleep." George speaks of a time when neither gas nor kerosene was available, and mentions "the odour of train-oil in a big lamp by the front door, associated with the rich aroma of square-ended manilas."*]

23rd Neale started, on my Timor pony, and Tuck, on the new black horse Mr McCrae bought for £9 10s. yesterday. At noon Mr McCrae took part in the presentation of a piece of plate to Mr Simpson (subscribed for nearly two years ago) "In recognition of his services as the first magistrate of this colony."

24th The *Midge* ready to start on Wednesday, but, unless the *Jemima* arrives tomorrow to take our bedding I cannot possibly leave. My feet very swollen.

25th Mr McCrae went to town whence Frank Cobham drove him to Captain Cole's.

26th Quite a cool morning; and the wind south. This may bring up the *Jemima* and delay the *Midge*. The sudden change of temperature seems to have robbed me of my strength.

27th Thomas took down the bedsteads, and headed-up the casks of crockery and hardware.

28th Visited, in my disordered house, by Mrs Howitt and Mrs Hobson.

29th Sarah Thomas came to help me.

30th Had the carpets taken up, beaten, and packed, ready for the boat.

31st Sent Jane in to Mrs Howitt with all my miniatures and portfolios in Thomas's cart. In the evening, a tremendous squall from the south with distant thunder.

FEBRUARY

February 1st Left "Mayfield", *en masse*, to spend the day with Mrs Howitt, and we all slept at Dr Thomas's.

2nd   Quite unable to go to church.

3rd   Shopped early, then said good-bye to Mrs Howitt and gave her the key of my tin box so that she can take out the paintings.

4th   Captain Bunbury gave me a certificate to enable me to draw my half-year's pay. Jane took the children to Mrs Craig's.

5th   Perry and Lucia spent the day at Captain McLachlan's, and Jane walked out to "Mayfield" to stay the night.

6th   Mr McCrae attended the farewell dinner party given to Judge Jeffcott prior to his departure to England. [*One hundred and fifty people present. Mayor Henry Moor, chairman. La Trobe there also. Everything went well until, somebody proposing the toast of "The Press", three editors stood up to respond, with an effect best described in M. le Duchat's phrase, "of more than hellish hurly-burly". During the uproar, the Superintendent, and ex-judge, walked downstairs into the street.*] Judge Therry arrived from Sydney. [*Roger Therry: in 1841, Attorney General of New South Wales. On dissolution of the old Council, he was elected from Camden to the new, defeating "Slippery Charlie" Cowper by a mere hatful of votes.*]

7th   Captain McCrae and Mr C. H. Ebden spent the evening with us. Mrs Cobham "urged me sair" to make out on paper her pedigree from the Uncle of Alexander Forbes, the (?) Baron Pitsligo, her grandmother being in direct line from the Rev. John Forbes of Kincardine. It was arranged, yesterday, that Mr George Barber is to continue to carry on Mr McCrae's office business as usual.

7th   Just before late dinner at the Thomases, Mr McCrae told me that "the boatmen must have all our luggage a-board early tomorrow morning, and as much as can be sent this evening!" This is impossible. After dinner, Nancy started with our *sacs de nuit*; Jane took up Lucia; and I carried my baby every foot of the way to "Mayfield". The night so dark we could scarcely keep on the foot-track.

SUPPLEMENT

List of Portraits Painted for Fame (and Money)

At Gordon Castle 1827:

   Mrs Macpherson, wife of James Macpherson of Belleville, son of the translator of *Ossian*.

At Gordon Castle 1828-9:

Mlle Sophie Pillet, of Geneva.

Margery, Countess of Saltoun, *née* Fraser, mother of Lord Saltoun (two portraits), one for her son-in-law, Wm Macdowall Grant, the other for her second son, the Hon. William Fraser.

The Hon. Wm Fraser (two portraits).

The Duchess Dowager of Leeds, *née* Anguish (two portraits): one for the Duchess of Gordon, the other for her daughter, Lady Katherine Whyte-Melville.

Ladies Louisa and Elizabeth Cornwallis, in one picture.

The Marchioness Cornwallis; a full length; sitting at her drawing.

Lady Georgiana Elizabeth Russell.

Copy on vellum of the oil painting of Lady Cornwallis when a child; playing with a Skye-terrier . . . for Lady Cornwallis.

Copy of W. Smith's portrait of Jane, Duchess of Gordon; considered by Lady Cornwallis to be the best portrait of her mother. . . . for Lady C.

Mr James Hoy, forty-six years librarian at Gordon Castle. This portrait to hang in the library.

One miniature of the Duchess of Gordon, for a bracelet. This was painted in two days (the longest in July).

At Edinburgh 1829:

The Marquis Carmarthen, afterwards Duke of Leeds. He married the widow of Sir Felton Harvey, *née* Caton, sister of the Marchioness of Wellesley, but had no issue.

Cluny Macpherson; for his mother, "Lady Cluny".

William Campbell of —— for Charles Kirkpatrick Sharpe.

Miss Dempster, of Skibo, Miss E. Dempster, and their brother.

Mr Dempster of Skibo, a small oval for a bracelet for his wife.

Miss Mary Dundas, of Armiston.

Hon. Miss Murray, daughter of the Earl of Mansfield . . . a half length.

Lieut. James Dalrymple, R.N. (afterwards Sir James Dalrymple, of Logie, Elphinstone) of the *Orwell*, East Indiaman; for his mother, Lady Dalrymple. (The portrait of the "Bride of Beldoon", a small oil picture, and the sword worn by the bride's brother at the wedding are at Logie, Elphinstone.)

Miss Cecilia Mackenzie, of Coull, a full length portrait (niece of "The Man of Feeling".)

Mrs James Skene, of Rubislaw, daughter of Sir W. Forbes, a friend of Beattie. (Mrs Skene's brother married Miss Stuart, Sir Walter Scott's first love; now Lady Forbes.)

Mr James Skene, of Rubislaw: Sir W. Scott's most intimate friend.

Lieut. James Skene in uniform, for Mrs Skene. He afterwards married a Greek lady, and had, in her right, "the liberty to pasture his bees on the sunny side of Hymettus".

Miss Eliza Skene, Miss Felicia Skene (named after Mrs Hemans).

Mrs James Duff of Innes House (two portraits).

Mrs George Harley Drummond, of Drumtochtie (two portraits), *née* Monro.

Miss Harley Drummond.

Master Ascot Molesworth.

Miss Christie, of Baberton; a child of seven.

Mr Monro, son of the late General Sir Thomas Monro and nephew of Mrs G. H. Drummond. Group of four little girls, for Mr Wm Paul, Edinburgh.

A second portrait of Master Ascot Molesworth, for his mother.

At Cullen House:

Mrs Colonel Grant, of Grant, *née* Dunn, afterwards Countess of Seafield. Her son, the Hon. George Grant, a child seven years of age.

At Edinburgh 1830:

Lady David Wedderburn, *née* Brown (sister of Lady Hampden, and first cousin and friend of Felicia Dorothea Hemans), the most beautiful features and expression.

Miss Hope Johnstone, adopted daughter of Lady ——

Miss Sarah Riddell; she married Col. Young of Aberdeen.

Miss Elizabeth Monro, niece of Mrs Drummond.

Miss Macdowall Grant, of Rothiemurchus.

Miss Mary Dalrymple, of Logie, Elphinstone, on the eve of her marriage with Patrick, son of Lord Boyle.

Miss Jane Ogilvie of Airlie, on the eve of her marriage with Captain Cheepe.

Miss Ker, daughter of Lord Robert Ker, on the eve of her marriage with Sir William Gomm.

Mrs Captain Wauchope (two portraits), both painted at her house, Duddington.

Mr and Mrs Boothwick, of Cruikston; copies from drawings by the

celebrated Stavely; for Mr Strange, son of the famous engraver.
Miss Agnes Morison, of Anchorfield.

At Gordon Castle, August 1830:
Mr William Tighe, of Woodstock and Kilkenny.

September 25th, 1830 Left my easel, and changed my name. £225
in Sir William Forbes's bank; the result of my portraits.

★   ★   ★

8th We are to sail tonight. Thomas and Stribling have carted
two loads of packages to the boat; and a third load is now waiting
for the return of the dray. If I had free choice in this matter, I
should remain at "Mayfield" until the house is sold or let. There is a
living to be had here through my art of miniature-painting, for
which I have already several orders in hand, but dare not oppose the
family wishes that "money must not be made in that way"! At
Arthur's Seat we have only huts, and no house built for the reception of ourselves and furniture.

[*The Hon. Robert Dundas Murray thus describes the home of the average
pioneer-squatter. "In the centre, stands the principal hut, with two or
three others, to serve as offices. Their appearance is characteristic of a
savage existence. The walls are of 'wattle and dab,' while the roof is
covered with rolls of bark, pressed by wooden stretchers into place. Two
windows, a mud floor, and a huge misshapen chimney of turf, completes a
pretty fair specimen of a bush shack." The station-hands, rouseabouts,
shepherds, etc., were no worse off, as witness the following authentic
monologue: "We roughed it together in them days; 'n' if any cove
reckons 'e didn't get a fair go, just you arst 'im whether the Master 'n'
the Missus done any better?"*]

Decided not to attempt the journey this evening. Mr McCrae
approves, particularly as Mr Montgomery still avoids putting his
signature to certain requisite documents; also because Mr M.
remains in occupation of the office premises and thus forces Mr
McCrae to keep in town for an indefinite time. Arranged to send

Ellen and Perry, with the kitchenware and poultry, by this trip of the boat.

9th Sent Mr McLure Count Rumford's plan for building chimneys, since the bricklayers and three thousand bricks go by the *Jemima*.

10th £10 from O. Browne, in payment for crimson damask sent Home for sale . . . crimson damask being quite unsuitable for our house in the wilderness. This comes most "convanient" as Ellen would say, and enables me to pay her half a year's wages . . . long overdue and never asked for. [*Servants went without wages for months on end; and, at a single sitting, in 1843, a police magistrate decided thirty-three claims, involving £500.*]

11th Still no wind. Mr McCrae says the sails of the boat are hanging dead down over the decks. It is well for us we stayed behind.

12th Mr McCrae came out to say that the *Jemima* had fished her anchor, and sailed; also that his deed of partnership with Mr Barber is to be signed today. Moreover, there seems good reason to believe that Mr M. will set his hand-and-seal to the Dissolution of Partnership, tomorrow.

13th Called on Mrs Simpson, *née* Bowles; both of us sorry she will be left without a near neighbour. . . . She longs for a forenoon companion. Having been accustomed to the stir of Mrs Yaldwyn's family, the loneliness of "The Grange" affects her very much. Mr Powlett and Judge Jeffcott went to Cape Schanck yesterday, after promising to visit Arthur's Seat on their way back.

14th Lucia and I (with Nancy and the baby) walked to Dr Howitt's, and thence to Dr Thomas's. Mr McCrae accompanied me to Mr Highett's, on purpose to meet Miss Highett, who had come to keep house for her brother. During our stay, we were introduced to Mrs Richmond, the Belgian beauty. At our approach, I paid my first addresses to her in ceremonious French, whereupon she shook out her fan, and exclaimed "I speak English *well*, but, at home, I give orders to my *sarbents* in Dutch." . . . So, our Belgian is *not* a Belgian after all! To complete the picture; she appears handsome, and there is plenty of her, though she stands like a *poupée*; and her arms seem provincially put on.

After parting with the Highetts, we left cards at the Macarthurs', and at Judge Therry's.

15th We went to see Robin Russell's cameos. These cameos were carved by Mr Russell out of a charma (?) shell that used to stand on Dr Wilmot's mantelshelf. (Dr Wilmot, the town coroner. He was old, and gentle, like a woman. Later, he gave me a Homer which I had set in silver for a brooch.)★

[*In 1836 "Robin" Russell, under instructions from the Superintendent, made an original survey of Melbourne. Then, "about March 1837", Hoddle came along and entered into a second survey, which was finished in a couple of hours; presumably, because he couldn't keep the Governor waiting for his lunch . . . most likely chops in a frying-pan, and a glass of Cape Brandy, to each. Subsequently, Hoddle prepared a map, which Bourke endorsed, and, without recognizing anything that Russell had done, called the place Melbourne. According to Lonsdale, Russell was "none of the Hastings"; ergo, judged by the same standard, Hoddle must have seemed Harlequin, so quickly he flashed, where the other had clung. N.B. Mr J. M. Reid points out that Russell's survey of the site was merely topographical, not a design for a township.*]

Dr Thomas was overturned in his gig, somewhere near "Studley".

16th Frank Cobham brought letters from Arthur's Seat. Mr McLure and the boys pleased with their new *locale*, but the house does not advance, owing to the want of shingles, hammers, and nails, now on board the *Jemima*.

17th Frank warned me about the new horse which is restive, and hard in the mouth; he doubts my being able to manage him on the way to A.S. Just then, in came Lanty, bawling out that Mr Montgomery had "put on a wicked face to him" for trying to bring the "Mawster's" iron bedstead into the office where the clients were. Mr M. ordered Lanty away from the door, and told him: "This is not Mr McCrae's place; it's mine!" Mr McCrae went to town immediately, and stayed away all night.

18th A fine fresh morning, and a fair wind for the *Jemima*.

★ Added later by Georgiana.

Lanty arrived home, quite cowed, to say that he had watched Mr Montgomery go out of the office and, after he had locked the door with a pocket-key, nail up notice of his removal! Mr Moor advised Mr McCrae to force an entrance with a crow-bar; but Mr Eyre Williams thought it better that the lock should be picked. Lanty didn't relish Mr McCrae's idea that he should be put in possession!

19th Heavy rain. Mr Barber has taken over the office; and the new firm is to be advertised in today's newspapers.

20th Lanty delighted to leave tomorrow for Arthur's Seat. . . . Sent a drayload of furniture for Mr McCrae's office and bedroom. Visited Mrs Henri Bell and had hardly got home again when there came the loudest crack of thunder I have heard in my life. At once the rain streamed though the windows and made large pools under both doorways. Mr McCrae came home, wet, very late at night.

21st Rode to Mr McCrae's town office and there found Mr Simpson, Mr Moor, and Frank Cobham. The *Royal George* sailed with our letters for Home. [*On this day, Mr Jeffcott left Port Phillip. Four years later, he became Chief Justice of Criminal Judicature for Pulo-Penang and Singapore, winning his knighthood just before he died.*]

23rd Captain McCrae and Sally to late dinner [*afterwards Dr William Howitt's wife*].

24th All day cutting out chair-covers.

25th Sent Nancy, with Lucia, to Mrs Simpson, to borrow the pattern of the Queen's cape.

26th Mr Barber came out with Mr McCrae to dine with us. Heard of Mrs Shaw's death . . . a terrible loss to her poor dyspeptic husband!

LETTER FROM PERRY

Arthur's Seat,
February 25, 1845.

MY DEAR PAPA AND MAMA,

As I cannot write very well I am telling Mr McLure all about our voyage coming down and he is going to write it and send it to you.

We were tossed about very much in the *Jemima* and I was sick sometimes; and a number of the fowls died. I was one day at Captain Bunbury's; but Harry wasn't at home so I didn't see him. When we were coming down the river, we saw the steamer with a lady at her bows, and her head and breast all gold, and the rest blue paint. (*The Vesta*.) There was a great deal of wind one day; and the jib split, and we had to go back to William's Town. A good while after that, we sailed again; and they cast anchor one night in the middle of the sea with nothing but blue mountains all round; and early next morning we began to sail again, and came near to Coffey's place; and Ellen went ashore and bought some milk; after that, she got a lot of cockles which were very good. We set sail again and arrived near "Wango"; and as soon as we could see the grass on the mountains we dropped anchor. There was a great deal of thunder and lightning and heavy rain; but it didn't last long. Ellen and I then got into the boat, and Harry and Walter came with us; and when we were nearing the shore, we saw Mr McLure and the boys running along the beach; and I was very glad to go ashore. This is a fine place; only the house isn't finished; and we are stopping in a hut made of tea-tree sticks and grass outside. We went up the hill one day, and it is very high. A number of blacks were here this morning and they killed a kangaroo. I have a hind leg; and Willie and Sandy have all the other legs . . . and they gave the tail to Georgie.

["*The spot selected for the dwelling-house stood at the foot of the mountain, but the house was not yet, and we had to climb a few more yards of gently sloping ground covered with little blackwoods and wattles till we reached the huts of our first and earliest settlement. These huts were about 20 yards apart, facing each other, and built right up against the brush fence, and off what was known as 'The Mountain Road'. They appeared tent-shaped, with gable ends, and were thatched with* Xanthorrea *or grass-tree, piled on for nearly a foot in thickness. The floors were of lime and clay, and the chimney was constructed of hardwood boards nailed across a framework of slabs, tapering towards the top, and plastered internally with mud. The fireplace, lined with rough stones, composed quite a room in itself.*"—GEORGE GORDON MCCRAE.]

27th It has been arranged that Mr Barber and Mr McCrae shall reside together at the office, thereby saving £40 per annum, and servants' wages. The *Jemima* came up to the wharf today, bringing letters from Perry and Mr McLure with an account of Ellen's and Perry's eleven days' voyage from Melbourne to Arthur's Seat.

MARCH

March 1st Dear Willie ten years old today.

2nd The *Jemima* people are asking too much money for our transit, in consequence of which, Mr McCrae has decided to send our baggage aboard the *Delaware* next Thursday.

3rd, 4th. . . .

5th A hot wind. Mr Westgarth sent us a large supply of apples.

6th Mr Highett and Mr Wickham rode out in the afternoon to look at the house, of which they examined every hole and corner . . . our mattresses spread on the floor, and the rooms all but bare of furniture.

7th Archie, after he had delivered a drayload of packages to the *Delaware*, came back to say the ship is so full of Captain Reid's things there remains hardly room enough for two more tons.

8th Mr McCrae brought news of a fire in Collins Street at 2 a.m. The town alarum-bell rang, and bugles sounded.

9th A thunder-shower, with sunlight shining through the rain.

10th To Dr Thomas's, Great Bourke Street West, to stay a few days . . . Archie brought in two loads, leaving my piano, dining-table, and round Singapore table, at Captain McLachlan's. On his last trip, Archie was accompanied by Jane Shanks, in charge of our personal luggage, and the keys of "Mayfield". My lobby-table, six feet long, with three drawers (cost £6 6s.): was bartered for two chests of tea and a bag of sugar. [*In 1840, tea fetched so much as £20 per chest—Melbourne price.*] When Dr Nicholson sent for the rent, not having any money to pay it, Mr McCrae gave his half-acre of sea-frontage at Brighton to Dr Nicholson as an equivalent. A good bargain for the doctor. A cold night with everybody seated round the fire.

11th Captain and Mrs Bunbury asked me to stand proxy

godmother for their baby-boy, Cecil. Sent a reply to Mr McLure's letter by the Barkers' bullock-dray. Lucia and I called on Mrs Moor, and her niece Miss Ennis, who is about to be married to Mr Martin, the Cantab (Septimus's brother).

12th A hot wind and sandstorm, then a cool breeze, and afterwards rain!

13th Jane Shanks left for Geelong, to attend to her cousin in her confinement: *comme de raison!*

14th Captain Cole went to the Mechanics' Institute, *not* to support his brother-in-law, but to show his interest in Mr Montgomery's success as a candidate for the solicitorship.

15th Today, I enter my forty-first year.

16th Drowsy weather. Two visitors with nothing to say, and, all the evening, Sarah Thomas absorbed in a novel. About seven o'clock Mr McCrae arrived from the Plenty, having driven twenty-three miles in three and a half hours in the spring-cart drawn by Sir John Franklin (the new horse)!

17th Heavy thunder, then a pretty gale of wind, which soon blew itself out.

18th Lucia and I went to the office where we found Captain McLachlan, dressed in black, waiting for Mr McCrae to join him in a visit of condolence to poor Mr Shaw.

Ash Wednesday, 19th Made up my packet of letters, sketches, etc., to send to London by Captain Cain.

20th The *Delaware* has, at last, landed our bricks at Arthur's Seat; but Tuck unable to do anything on account of his being ill of quinsy. Dunn has gone off with a drayload of potatoes, as the boys complain of not having any.

Good Friday, 21st Mr McCrae and I at church in our own pew. Mr Thomson spoke on a proper observance of the day: "No buying and selling, or—picnic parties!" "*Il a beau parler!*"

22nd Miss Cunninghame saw my miniatures, and praised them very much.

23rd Easter Day. Remained to communion; and, afterwards, Mr McCrae left for Arthur's Seat, taking with him two new kangaroo-dogs in the spring-cart.

24th Mrs Burke (*née* Montgomery) came to say good-bye; not very happy at the thought of a two hundred mile journey in a spring-cart over roads only fit for a bullock-dray.

25th Visitors, and yet more visitors.

26th A very busy forenoon. . . . Too tired to continue after luncheon.

27th Met Mrs La Trobe who tells me she is sending Agnes home by the *Rajah* next week: Agnes to be under the care of the captain's wife, Mrs Fergusson, niece of my artist-friend, Charles Hayter Senr, and first cousin to Sir George of that ilk.

28th A hot wind and threatening rain. Tremendous downpour in the afternoon and through the night.

29th A lovely morning. Captain Cole took Mrs Thomas and her baby in her gig to Brighton. The proud husband *à cheval*.

30th A piercingly cold day. No milk for the children's breakfast. Mr McCrae writes to say that it will be a month before the house will be ready for occupation; and ever since we left "Mayfield" Dr Nicholson has paid a woman 5s. a week to sleep there and show applicants the premises, all of which I could have done *gratis*.

31st Mr and Mrs La Trobe have invited me to a farewell dinner to Agnes before she leaves for Neuchâtel. The *Rajah* to sail April 15. During the voyage, Mrs Fergusson to give Agnes daily lessons "to break her in for her grandmother's management".

APRIL

April 1st Bought a new dress from Donaldson and Budge. A procession of cold nights more difficult to bear, in this weather-board house, than any of those we experienced within the walls of "Mayfield".

2nd Agnes La Trobe eight years old today.

3rd James Grahame, Mrs Howarth, Mr Westgarth.

4th Mrs Thomas and her children returned from Brighton. Sarah, frilled and furbelowed for Mrs Lauchlan Mackinnon's party at Newtown.

5th After luncheon at Mrs La Trobe's, I took Lucia to see Mrs Howitt, who kept her for Edward's birthday tomorrow.

6th A dark morning . . . only Sarah Thomas to church. Lucia returned, with a note from Mrs Howitt to say she "regrets exceedingly Mr McCrae's opposition to my wish to employ my professional talent to profit".

7th A visit from Dr Barker and Archibald Jamieson. Dr Barker tells me not to expect Mr McCrae's return until the end of next week.

8th A letter from J. H. Campbell, perplexing for Mary Anne!

9th Captain Cole whisked Mr Campbell off to Brighton, where "To be, or not to be" will be decided.

10th A cold north wind. Dr Thomas in conference with Captain Cole.

11th Mr and Mrs John Barker start for Cape Schanck tomorrow; they have promised to carry letters for Arthur's Seat "if sent early in the morning".

12th William Campbell came in the afternoon, with Mr Jamieson.

13th J. H. Campbell avoided both my questions with regard to Mary Anne.

14th J. H. Campbell to dinner. He told me his sister, Mrs Foster of Wynding Hall, had written to say that Simeon Watson Taylor had taken Lady Charlotte Hay for his second wife. Went to Mr Westgarth's about batten-nails. He weighed Lucia in his scales and found her 30 lb.; then I stepped on to one scale, and he placed a bag of rice in the other; my weight proved to be only 119 lb.

15th Mr McCrae surprised me by suddenly arriving on "some business that may detain him in town for a fortnight to come". Sketched "Argyle Cottage", and the house where Lucia was born, anticipating the time when all may pass away. Met Mr La Trobe who told me everything had been arranged for appointing Captain McCrae Clerk to the Treasury, under Captain Lonsdale, with a salary of £250 a year. Overjoyed to hear this good news.

16th A humdrum day. Mr McCrae's bad pen scratching noisily while he writes to O. Browne.

17th Called at Mrs Howitt's, and met there the Rev. Mr Morrison, minister of the Independent Church. He asked to be allowed to see my miniatures.

18th   True to his appointment, Mr Morrison arrived, in spite of a dust-storm raging outside. He declared himself well pleased with my "exhibition", and stayed on until the La Trobes came in their jaunting-car. Here we separated from Mr Morrison and went on to Jolimont to dine. Met there Mr Cowper, of Sydney, and Dr and Mrs Howitt.

[*Mr Cowper, vulgarly known as "Slippery Charley": at this date, member for Cumberland in the Sydney Council. During 1852, he became president of the Anti-Transportation League, and represented it at the Hobart conference. Moreover, he was first president and manager of the Sydney Tramway and Railway Company, 1849-53; but even then, with his hands thus full, he joined Wentworth's committee appointed to formulate the new constitution, and, at the subsequent elections, topped the Sydney poll, with Sir Henry Parkes upon his heels. Cowper was, for five occasions, premier of New South Wales. In '71, he abandoned politics, and took the agent-generalship; worked hard, and died at London, 20th October 1875.—Facts taken from the "Australian Encyclopaedia".**

Georgiana little imagined, while she sat to the same table with C.C., that her own great-granddaughter, Huntly McCrae, should one day marry this man's great-grandson, Norman Lethbridge Cowper, a solicitor and young politician, prominent in our own time.]

During dinner-time the wind chopped round south-west and rain fell hard, so that coming back we had to wade across the hollow, and only reached home at half-past ten.

19th   Woke with the noise of rain on the roof and saw through the window Mr Barker set out on the first stage of his journey to Cape Schanck: twenty-two miles! . . . his horse, with his tail down, slopping through the mud.

20th   J. H. Campbell left for the station.

21st   A bleak day.

22nd   Walked to Porter's cottages, to see Mrs Reid.

23rd   The *Rajah* sailed for London.

24th   A visit from Mrs Ailsa Craig and Mr Gurner.

25th   Heard of Janet Weir's death, November 1; also, that Dr Abercrombie died on the 4th of the same month. I thought of old

* 1927 edition.

THE KITCHEN, ARTHUR'S SEAT, 1845
From a wash-drawing by Georgiana

THE HEADS FROM BELOW THE HOUSE, ARTHUR'S SEAT, 1846
From a sketch by Georgiana

THE HOUSE AT ARTHUR'S SEAT, 1849
From a watercolour by Georgiana

ARTHUR'S SEAT, SHOWING ARRANGEMENT OF HUTS,
DECEMBER 1846
From a wash-drawing by Georgiana

days, when the doctor attended Willie, and Janet came every afternoon to sit beside his bed.

26th Mrs Howitt spoke about Captain McCrae's appointment,
and mentioned Dr Howitt's offer to give in his name as one of the
sureties to Government. Left Lucia to stay a few days.

27th Mr McCrae went to Captain Cole's until Monday.

28th Little George and Maggie Cole came up from Brighton.
Maggie threatened with carroty hair and eyebrows!

29th Young Jeffery arrived from Kyneton. [*"Kyneton was so
named by La Trobe, at the request of Mrs Jeffrey (or 'Jeffery,' as Georgiana
spells it), after her native town in Warwickshire."—Thomas
O'Callaghan.*]

30th A soaking wet day. Captain Reid came to tell me the boys
are all well . . . but the house not a bit further advanced towards
completion!

MAY

May 1st Sent Jane to Dr Howitt's for Lucia.

2nd Mrs Thomas, Mary Anne, and I went to Campbell's to
buy a wedding-garment, thence to Mrs Howitt, and, with her,
to Miss Roe.

LETTER FROM WILLIE

Arthur's Seat,
May 1845.

MY DEAR MAMA,

I hope you are all well and will come up soon, for we long to see
you very much. We got a very large kangaroo which was fully
five feet high. The tail was enormous, and the foreclaws terrible.

We have got a chimney added to our hut, which is made of
stringybark slabs, and lined inside with stones. Tuck has sawn a
log of honeysuckle of which Papa proposed to make a wardrobe
for you, which will be very pretty. Ellen's fowls are thriving;
she has already three broods of chickens, and expects to have two
broods of ducks soon. We have not suffered from the nocturnal
depredations of native dogs—except one fowl which was taken.

o

I will give you a description of the different fish we catch here: first the flathead, they have a broad head and thin body, and, when first taken out of the water, are something like tortoise shell; secondly, sharks and skate, which need not be described; thirdly, a pretty little fish, that Papa thinks are sardines, and fish like trouts which we have not yet succeeded in catching . . . but we see them sporting about in the evenings.

LETTER FROM SANDY

Arthur's Seat,
May 1845.

I hope you are well. A chimney has been made to our hut.

It is made of stringybark; it is plastered outside with mud, and lined with stones.

The kitchen is finished. It is made of posts stuck upright in the ground; it is plastered with mud. The wash-house is nearly finished. We have had very wet weather for the last week or so, and the nights are cold—but it has not been so cold as it was on the Yarra.

I think it would be a fine thing to follow the course of the sun, as some birds do—to have no winter.

There was an eclipse of the moon the other night, which lasted four or five hours.

The way to build a house is, first to dig a trench and put some posts in; next to daub it, then to shingle it, or to thatch it. The chimney may be made of brick or split she-oak.

The weather is very fine today; and I hope Papa will have a good day for his journey, and that it may continue fine till you all come down.

3rd Mr McCrae drove to "La Rose" [*Dr McCrae's house.*] Edith Howitt and Emily Le Souef came to keep me company.

4th Mrs Thomas and I at church in the afternoon.

5th Mary Anne has romantic ideas of being married in her riding-habit, and going away *à cheval* on her wedding journey! Captain McCrae takes his seat at the Treasury today.

6th Mr McCrae is determined I shall travel to Arthur's Seat in his horrid spring-cart! Frank Cobham says it is *not* a good machine; and told me how he had had to stand up most of the way to avoid being thrown out. The journey by Archie's dray well worth the £2 he asks.

7th A piercingly cold morning. Saw Neale, just arrived from A.S., and ascertained from him that the kitchen-hut, which is to be my temporary abode, is still without a roof! Mr McCrae resolved to go down at once and set Tuck to work.

8th The weather bad. Rain mixed with hail, and bitterly cold. I fainted.

9th A perfect deluge. Young Mr Green of "Woodlands" swam in to dinner. At four o'clock candles had to be brought; then, after Mr G. had gone, I read aloud to Mrs Thomas from Mary Howitt's *Rural Life in Germany*, but she was unable to hear on account of the storm. The doctor away, at Mr Gurner's party.

10th Mr McCrae left for Mordialloc, *en route* for Arthur's Seat. Lucia and I took a gentle walk, so far as the Terrace, Collins Street East.

11th Still feeling faint; and, in any case, it is far too cold to venture to church.

12th Unwell.

14th Damp and drizzling. Mrs Thomas in bed with influenza. Mrs Howitt and Mrs Robin Russell came.

15th Visited Mrs Craig.

16th Lucia and I strolled to the Post Office where we met the Rev. Mr Forbes going in at the door. He appeared more tidy than he used to be in his bachelor days; his coat brushed, and his boots blackt.

17th Mrs Cole came to see her sister.

18th A letter from Mr McCrae. "Our hut will be finished next week", and he expects me to be ready to leave "*on very short notice*"!

19th The Rev. James Forbes brought his bride, *née* Clow, to visit us. They repeated Mrs Clow's invitation for Mr McCrae and myself to make "Tirrietuan" our first day's halting place.

20th Too ill to go out.

21st Almost an empty house. Dr Thomas, Mrs Thomas, and Mary Anne gone to Heidelberg for the day.

22nd Sarah in her tantrums, because David won't go to the ball tomorrow night.

23rd Sarah Thomas completes her twentieth year. A note from Miss Cotton promising to assist at Mary Anne's wedding.

24th Terrible gusts of wind. The chimney (not built on the Count Rumford plan) has filled the room so full of smoke I have had to put my needlework away.

25th Dined at Captain Cole's.

26th Dr Thomas dined with Mr J. F. Palmer.

27th Lucia and I went to Mr Westgarth's. [*A cottage at South Yarra Yarra, on the Dandenong Road.*] Met Mrs Ailsa Craig, full of happiness at the idea of returning Home by the first ship. Lucky she!

28th Rainy; with south-west wind. Four ships came in! Mr McCrae arrived, with letters from the boys; all very anxious for me to go to them.

29th George twelve years old today.

30th Still raining steadily. Captain Lewis, ex-harbour-master, to dinner. Sarah came home soaking wet, after a search for lace for a Berthe for Mary Anne's bodice. Sarah's new walking-dress ruined by the downpour, and her purchases a saturated mess. If Mrs Cole hadn't set a ban upon the riding-habit notion, all should have been well. Tuck, having arrived at four o'clock, I talked with him in the skillion-room, while he made himself a kettleful of tea. He assured me, "Marm", that the roads were "all of a muck"! This will, I hope, put an end to the spring-cart idea. Rather Archie's dray, a thousand times . . . or even the lime-boat, if it can be arranged.

31st The town-paths look like porridge; the streets like water-gruel. A letter from Ann Morison, mentioning the death of Miss Betty Gordon of Leitcheston, in her eighty-fourth year.

JUNE

June 1st Mr Sewell and Mr McCrae to dinner.

2nd William Campbell came to bid "good-bye"; also Mr and Mrs La Trobe to say "*au revoir*".

3rd In the evening Dr Thomas, Mrs Thomas, and Sarah went to "The Squatters' Ball". Jamie Campbell, Mary Anne, Mr McCrae, and I making ourselves happy at home [*quite content not to dance Mr Weinwritter's very original spirited Polka called "Kangaroo Hunt": "different to the namby-pamby imitations of modern times (1845)"*].

4th Mr Westgarth and I dined at Captain Cole's. Mr McCrae dined at Captain McCrae's and came up in the evening.

5th Invited to be present when Mrs Cole opened her box from Home. She gave me a pink muslin dress-piece, a belt to match, and a cap-flower! In the evening, wrote wedding-cards for Mary Anne. All of us up till nearly midnight.

6th Pouring rain; then a break in the weather at 9 a.m. when Jamie Campbell, Ward Cole, Dr Thomas, Mr McCrae, Mr Faulkner, Mrs Thomas, Sarah, and little Maggie Thomas went to Captain Cole's to fetch the bride. C. H. McKnight arrived after the party had gone to the church, so he remained with me till their return, when the number was augmented by the arrival of Captain Cole and Mr John Thomson, the best man who was to have been (his duties having been fulfilled by Mr Faulkner), Mr Gurner, James Grahame, and the Rev. A. C. Thomson who said grace at the head of the breakfast-table. By noon, the sun was shining prettily on the wet roofs and the trees, and the newly-wedded pair already two hours on their journey through life! I wrote the advertisement to send to the papers "MARRIED, by the Rev. A. C. Thomson, at St James's, Melbourne, 6th June, 1845: James Henry Campbell, fourth son of the late John Campbell, Esq., of Kilbarry, Argyleshire, Scotland, to Mary Anne, eldest daughter of the late William Thomas, Llanybethland, Carmarthenshire, S.W."

7th Sent two drayloads of luggage to the *Jemima*. Captain Cole, Ward Cole, James Grahame, Mr Gurner, and the Rev. A. C. Thomson to dinner. In the evening, very late, Mr McKnight, James Grahame, and Sarah went to Mrs Wickham's grand party. A letter from Octavius Browne, telling us of the birth of a son and heir, January 9 (six months since).

8th "*Much Ado —— !*" By Mr McCrae's instructions, we are to board the *Jemima* in half an hour's time. After that it doesn't much matter what happens. In any case, we are to lie all night at the Junction, where ballast will be taken in. Had everything ready; when a chain-man from Robin Russell came to say "the vessel requires an overhauling": so we must delay until Monday, at a.m.

Thank heaven for the reprieve; I'm so worn out!

Captain and Mrs Cole came to bid us good-bye.

9th After a candle-light breakfast, started at 9 a.m., with Sarah Thomas, Mr McCrae, Jane Shanks, Baby, and Lucia, as passengers on the steamer *Vesper*, which also carried Robin Russell and his men; proceeded in the *Vesper* as far as William's Town (or *Koort Boork*, as it used to be called) where we transhipped to the *Jemima*. Sailed at 10 o'clock, and, with wind and weather to serve, made good progress till an hour after dark, when I picked up a light which Mr McCrae recognized as coming from the schoolhouse-lantern, sometimes obscured by the door flinging about in the breeze. Meanwhile, a boat had been lowered, and the skipper hurried us over the side.

When we came to the landing-place, we cooeed to the boys who ran through the scrub to meet us: Willie first, then Alexander, holding on to George.

By the time we got to the hut the moon had set, and the breeze freshened into a gale which raged all night. I had no bedstead, only a mattress on the mud floor, and found it impossible to lie still. Towards dawn, I went into the servant's room, adjoining, and saw Jane and Lucia fast asleep.

10th Blowing hard all day. The *Jemima* rolling about heavily, and no chance of getting a boat off to land Mr Russell and his men.

11th After a night of storm and rain, Mr Russell came ashore, bringing my carpet-bag which I had left behind. He talked about the six thousand acres he would have to survey, and refused our offer of breakfast, saying *"Breakfast wastes time!"* Meanwhile Tuck and Walter Maclaren, assisted by Lanty, had brought up our things from the beach, and many packages had to be opened for fear of damage by rain.

12th Had the barrels and cases removed from Ellen's hut, where they have been stored for five months past; then, when the sun began to shine, we dragged outside all mattresses and blankets

and left them to be aired across Tuck's empty cart. Worked till
6 p.m. carrying books into the house which is roofed, but not yet
floored. The kitchen-hut crammed with bedsteads and two chests
of drawers.

13th A fire in the hut kept us comfortable and warm. Found the
new dress for Mrs Tuck. In the evening Mr McCrae and Mr Mc-
Lure and Tuck returned from fishing, with fifty-six flathead, and
nine ground-sharks for bait.

14th Taking advantage of a break in the weather, Sarah and I
went along the beach to look at the headland called "Anthony's
Nose".

15th After dinner, Sarah sat outside and listened to the noise
of the sea; *comme des mugissemens de taureaux* . . . when a man,
seeming to come from nowhere, asked her for accommodation
for the night. This was Mr Meyrick, who explained that his bullocks
had been prevented from getting round the "Nose", on account
of the tide coming in. He said he had observed Sarah on the cliff
yesterday, and wondered how so young a girl happened to be there
alone? (Apparently I remained unseen!) Mr Meyrick had to content
himself with a shake-down under the table in Mr McLure's hut.

16th Mr Meyrick went early to yoke up his beasts, but, either
because they had strayed, or his heart had, he returned to
breakfast. . . . By ten o'clock, he was off again.

17th Climbed a spur of the mountain to a spot chosen by Mr
McCrae for a Hermitage. Thence, home by the beach. Lanty
overtook me, bringing fresh beef from Mr Jamieson, with his
compliments to myself.

Mr Barker, passing through to Cape Schanck, told me that at
one stage of his journey he had had to drive round Mr Meyrick's
dray, which was up to the axles in mud, and that Mr Meyrick lay,
with his dog, by the road; . . . both of them fast asleep! [*Barker
remembered the feud between his brother and Meyrick, so he "let sleeping
dogs lie". See Note 17th February 1844.*]

18th Tuck and Lanty marched across the mountain slope seeking
for suitable timber to buttress the dining-room walls, also, if
need be, to help Mr Meyrick with his dray. Neither Mr McCrae
nor Mr McLure seem to have thought about hearths, each fireplace

being heartless, with great risk, in a wind, of our house burning down. . . . Rain has trickled in through the roof of my hut, and, as my boxes were becoming glued to the floor, I removed them to "The Warehouse" . . . Sarah's name for a corner of the new house where the roof is secure.

19th A fine morning. Before breakfast Mr McCrae went to fish, and returned with eighteen flathead. Lanty and the dog, "Captain", ran down a kangaroo.

20th Sarah and I strolled for an hour on the beach. In the evening sorted seeds and bulbs for the garden. I fear many of the larger bulbs have been destroyed by sea-water getting into the bag.

21st Emptied the barrel of hardware, and found the putty to glaze our windows with. Unpacked three casks of crockery and stored it all in "The Warehouse".

22nd The landscape hidden by mist. After we had said prayers, and Mr McCrae had read a sermon, walked a mile or so on the Cape Schanck Road. The boys went on towards Smith's [*George Smith, Wooloowooloobloolook, seven miles from Arthur's Seat. He married a niece of Captain Hobson, after whom Hobson's Bay was named.*] and brought home a quantity of scallops, which, when cooked, filled our *terrine*, and provided a savoury meal for all. A dense sea-fog in the evening. Enjoyed the warmth of a large fire in the school-house-hut till 9 p.m., when Sarah and I retired to the "Lodge".

23rd Tuck began to nail down the flooring-boards in the new house. Sarah and I indoors all day, and evening, too.

24th Hoar frost in the morning. Perry came to tea with Sarah and me and we took turns in reading aloud some chapters of Mrs Moody's *New Home in America*, telling of *her* troubles on first settling in the bush. At 9 p.m. Mr McCrae came for Perry to go up to bed.

25th Little Maggie completes her first year today and can jabber most unintelligibly, sings her own little songs and jumps about like a "Joey" . . . the picture of health and happiness! The weather being unsuitable, the boys cannot take their promised holiday, so they are to have the first fine day instead. Sarah unpacked a case sent on board the boat by Mr Westgarth and found the contents . . . bottles of raspberry and ginger cordial. We next emptied the barrel of hardware and discovered nothing at fault, except the spice-box which was broken on top. Went to the school-hut for dinner at three, and found Ellen had done her best in honour of little Maggie's birthday. First, a soup made of scallops, with green peas, and potatoes and milk; then roasted goose, which I found not easy to distribute satisfactorily among four hungry boys and ourselves. At four o'clock, the rain began to pour down in torrents, and Sarah and I had to run to the "Lodge", where we spent the rest of the evening. The boy was late in returning with the milkers, as the black-and-white cow had dropped a bull-calf, which the boy brought home on his shoulders. Tuck nearly completed flooring the lobby of "The Warehouse".

26th Bitterly cold, and a piercing wind. The windows in the dining-room are only open spaces at present, so, although the floor is laid, one cannot sit there in gusty weather. . . .

Mr McCrae came to tea with us, and we could hardly keep our candles alight, owing to the draughtiness of the roof. My cabin candle-shade not yet unpacked. [*In a book of directions, intending emigrants are advised that "a glass safety-lantern, to burn wax candles for the cabin, is indispensable."*]

27th This morning Tuck dropped the door among Ellen's tin dishes, and, being in bed, I sent for Ellen to ask her what the noise meant. Mr McLure ploughed the space intended for our garden. The door is now securely fixed and Tuck has set Lanty to clean off the mud. Thunder and rain. The paths between the huts have become a mass of mire and there is nothing for us to do but stay inside. . . . I am most unhappy. . . . The last six months of suspense, worry, hurry, delays, packing and unpacking, detention in town, and now this scattered way of living in huts until the completion of our house has worn me out.

28th Breakfasted in our own cabin, and I busy unpacking till dinnertime. Tuck put in frames for the dining-room windows. In the afternoon, a brilliant rainbow spanned the spur of the mountain.

Tried my hand, with George, at the cross-cut saw, and accomplished some three inches; too exhausted to do any more. All the cattle trooped out of the yard while the boy was guiding the bullocks in the plough for Mr McLure. (Mr McCrae contends that bullocks are better than horses in the plough; because they don't require rubbing down, or stabling, after their day's work.)

29th After prayers, walked on the beach. Sarah and I took tea in the school-hut; the night so dark we could scarcely keep to the track when we returned to the "Lodge".

30th As Mr Barker's Melbourne dray is expected to pass through tomorrow I have had to look out bed linen for McCrae's use at the office.

JULY

July 1st Packed the box for town; and another one, of shells, for little Maggie Thomas.

2nd After we had finished breakfast, Waddell and Mackenzie (from Barragunda), with their wives and children arrived. Waddell sold Ellen eighteen fowls at 6d. each; the women and girls warming themselves in Ellen's hut while she made them "a comfortable cup of tea". Then she killed and pluckt a goose to send as a present to Mrs Thomas. . . . A ship passed inwards at noon.

3rd Unpacked books till dinner-time (2 p.m.). Sarah and I walked to the sheep yards, just one mile hence towards Cape Schanck.

4th Prepared bulbs for the garden, and "corms" for the newly-ploughed field. In the evening, Mr McCrae came to keep us company, but soon fell asleep; so we were left *tête à tête* as usual!

5th Planted three hundred bulbs before dinner-time. In the afternoon, Lanty drove over in the spring-cart to the Survey, to stay with the Simons and his little boy till Monday.

6th A tranquil morning. After sermon we all set out to climb the mountain (a mile from its base to its top); reached the first point easily, but before I came to the next, my heart went so rapidly I had to lie down. Then on again, till we got to the summit. There, the view was beautiful: on one side of us, the sea as far as one might look, on the other, Port Phillip Bay. Returned to the school-hut for tea, where Sarah and I were storm-stayed till late in the evening.

7th Had begun to weigh out rations, when I was seized with a shivering fit and had to go to bed. [*The usual quantity was 10 lb. flour; 7 lb. meat; 2 oz. tea, and 1 lb. sugar: weekly. Samuel Butler says, without mentioning quantity: damper, mutton, or beef; green tea; and very brown sugar.*]

8th Mr Barker's cart, from Melbourne, arrived in torrents of rain. . . . When Ellen told Sarah her trunk had come she danced a Strathspey! Tuck and Lanty both taken ill, and only one stub of candle left. Prepared grease-lamps, and had six trimmed and lighted by sundown. [*A dirty job: filling up blacking-bottles with fat or grease, and twisting bits of cotton-rag round splinters of deal to make emergency wicks.*]

9th Lanty and Tuck convalescent; the former employed in making a hearth for the dining-room fireplace. George unwell. Mr Jamieson rode across and took tea with us in the school-hut. I brought George down to sleep in the "Lodge", so that Mr Jamieson may have his Chinese sofa-bed for the night.

10th A white frost, which I knew of before I got up, by hearing the crows outside. Mr McCrae and Mr Jamieson talked loudly on their way to the beach. When they returned they brought thirty flathead between them.

11th Mr Jamieson left early for the Survey. Sarah and I walked through the scrub to look at a fine banksia, 3 ft. 2 in. in diameter, which Mr McCrae and Mr McLure had sawn through, for making the doors of the new house. Mr McCrae leaves tomorrow for "Kangerong", to ride with Mr Jamieson to Melbourne.

12th Today a traveller named Currie arrived, bringing with him a note from young Wright (D. C. Macarthur's nephew), who asks our hospitality towards bearer who was for five years in the employ of Lyon Campbell, as overseer. Currie goes to offer his services to Mr Barker, and expects to be returning to Melbourne on Monday.

13th Currie started for Cape Schanck, Mr McLure, with Willie, Sandy, and Perry accompanying him as far as the first mile; while George stayed with Sarah and me. Mrs Tuck's boy taken ill.

14th A small drizzle, or "Australian Scots Mist". . . . Sarah and I with the little girls all day, and took our share of sago and milk. About 8 p.m. (Jane having come back) we said good night to

Lucia, and left the baby with all the spoons in her lap! Arrived safely at the new house, where we found a fire lit, and the chimney venting well.

15th This afternoon the geese got at the plot where I had planted the bulbs, and had eaten nearly all the crocuses in the border before they were driven off.

16th The first bulb has sent up bright green leaves. Lanty prepared a piece for potatoes.

17th The second last bit of beef boiled today. The "round" still in the cask. George chopping banksia bark to make a dye to colour his pinafore. Lanty opened both pits of potatoes and found them much more sprouted than he thought they would be. Ellen made a grand sea-pie for dinner, to save the beef for Tuck and Lanty.

"Mister Mann", "Horsfall", and two other blackfellows, with their lubras, came to *quamby* [*camp*] for the night. After sunset the men went to look for kangaroo and saw five; but their dogs "no good"; and ours too supercilious to take their commands. The poor wretches begged hard for the loan of a tumbelgumbel (gun); but I was afraid to lend them Mr McCrae's though they had no meat for supper, and I hadn't *pulgane* for them!

[*Had the diarist allowed them the use of her husband's gun, she would have broken one of the Port Phillip Association rules (1836): "That all parties protect aborigines; but never teach them the use of firearms; or allow them to possess firearms."*]

18th A quantity of brown sugar that had been covered away, behind boxes, in the kitchen hut, has been sucked white by ants. Ellen put some of the sugar on her tongue, and, finding it tasteless, threw it away. Gave Tuck half of the round of beef for his rations. Had a fire put in the dining-room for Sarah and me to fold and air the linens from the laundry. "Ben-Benjie", "Eliza", and "Sally", with her brother "George", came to *quamby* for the night.

19th Lanty found, on the beach, a cask with rope handles, so that Tuck will now have the extra bucket he was asking for last week. Mr McLure has at last granted the expected holiday, and he and the boys spent the whole morning, besides most of the afternoon, in the boat. The "catch" amounted to a hundred and two flathead, a few of which we had for our late dinner, all the rest going to Ellen to be salted down. Tuck, sulky or ill. . . . In either case, he has shut himself up in his hut without finishing the kitchen-door, which is urgently needed: as witness, yesterday, our bedroom candlestick was carried off by one of the dogs; and the candle eaten out of it. Then, today, the mug of grease for burning in the tin lamps was licked clean; this, in addition to half a pound of curd soap devoured at our very threshold! One of George Smith's blackfellows, on his way from Mr Walpole's, rested under a gum-tree near Ellen's hut, and, while he slept, Ellen rummaged in Mrs Smith's bag, intending to take a few onions (and to owe them) which supposed onions turned out to be daffodil bulbs: so Ellen took but one, to plant in her garden.

20th A freezing south wind. Sarah and I, indoors, watched Mr McLure and the boys struggle down the track towards the beach.

21st Archie arrived on "Don", and Neale, with nine head of cattle. Lanty began to make a shed for the cart.

22nd Dead calm. The bay like a mirror. Lanty and Neale went out to fish. Tuck fastened the two halves of our door to the hinges, thus excluding the dogs and the geese; also, Master Tommy (Tuck junior). Obliged to give up my last packet of sperm candles, other-wise the school-hut will have to close on account of darkness.

23rd Since the flour sacks are full of holes, I have removed my dresses from the tinned chest and filled it with flour instead.

24th At dawn Archie started for Melbourne. Waited dinner for Mr McCrae; hope Archie meets him and makes him aware of the distress we are in for want of beef, tallow, etc. [*Professor Shann quotes Bennett's "Christison of Lammermoor": "It's a hungry place Lammermoor; nothing to eat but pigweed and mutton. No flour. No stores, of any description."*] Cold north wind. Tuck completed the flooring of the bedroom and dressing-closet. Sarah and I busy at needlework.

25th Gave Tuck the piece of hung beef we had reserved for Mr McCrae. Lanty laid the hearth in the bedroom; and fenced it with Perry's bedstead, to prevent people from treading on it before it dries.

26th Sent Lanty on "Don" to ask Mrs Smith to lend us some beef. At noon, he returned with a round of beef, a ham, and a bag of greens. George and Sandy saw a man drive a bullock into our stockyard. This man proved to be Mr John Barker, who told us Mr McCrae was on the road, and might be expected to arrive in about an hour. Mr Barker went on, and Tuck mounted guard over the beast. After dinner, sent Lanty to Mr Jamieson's to borrow some salt. The moment Mr McCrae arrived, Coffey came to ask him to buy a fat cow for £4; to enable Coffey to take his wife to town by tomorrow's boat. . . . Coffey binds himself to supply 50 lb. of salt, and to assist in killing both the cow and the bullock. Mr McCrae got bushed on Sunday, and slept under a native cherry; made Horsfall's next morning; but, since their people were without tea, he had cold milk to drink, and bread to eat with it; nothing to warm him after his night in the icy wind.

27th After service, Mr McCrae told us how Captain Newby's ship had foundered at sea, and all hands and passengers lost, except himself and Mrs Newby, his three children being washed away before his eyes! Much blame is attributed to the parties who chartered the vessel: "She wasn't seaworthy when she left port." Captain Newby and his wife utterly destitute.

AUGUST

August 7th This morning I showed Mr McCrae where to find the vine-cuttings for the new bed, and had just returned to my hut, when a loud peal of thunder caused Sarah to close both door-flaps, bottom and top. Rain followed immediately, pitching down so hard on the roof it was difficult to hear each other speak, so that when Mr McCrae came and called for us to undo the wooden button that fastened the upper half of the door, we didn't at once understand what he said. But, on his calling out a second time, I crossed, with little Maggie on my arm, towards the door. Then I noticed that the button had left the flap free and exclaimed: "You can push it open." I had hardly spoken when the door burst inwards, and, striking my forehead with terrific force, threw me on to the floor. Mr McCrae did all he could for me, Sarah being too shocked at the appearance of the wound to be able to dress it. Had I carried dear little Maggie on my left arm, instead of my right, she must have been killed on the spot, for Mr McCrae had struck the heavy blackwood door a tremendous blow, as the blood upon his knuckles could attest!

8th Restless at night on account of the pain in my head; my eye swollen.

9th Mr and Mrs John Barker called in on their way to Cape Schanck, both shocked at the spectacle I made.

10th My head still painful. Had to ask Tuck to give up hammering for the day.

11th Not much better. Any noise intolerable.

★   ★   ★

20th Just as we were sitting down to our tea, a bugle sounded, and Mr Powlett arrived. He brought news of the wreck of the *Cataraqui* (Liverpool to Melbourne) August 4, with the loss of four hundred and thirteen lives . . . only nine being saved. Thick weather. The captain (seventy miles out in his reckoning), thought he was off the Otway and drove the ship on to the rocks at King's Island! This happened at four o'clock in the morning, within three hundred yards of the shore. Of these unfortunates, twenty-five families were from Ashby-de-la-Zouch in Leicestershire—seventy children, and from thirty to forty single men, besides twenty-five single women—altogether a very superior lot of labourers, and an irreparable loss to the colony.

[*A sealing party on the island buried three hundred and four bodies. Isaac Selby tells of one emigrant, Sol. Brown, who escaped the wreck, only to be drowned in a creek a few months afterwards. Mr E. P. S. Sturt, an eye-witness of the scene upon King's Island, used to say one recollection would haunt him all the days of his life . . . "the body of a woman, half buried in sand, only the head and torso free. The face, in which there was an expression of determination, was thrown back, the eyes stared, and the arms stretched upward, holding aloft the corpse of an infant child." At a public meeting held in Melbourne, with the object of raising funds for the* relief of survivors, Mr Cunninghame, "the talking automaton of the Supreme Court", moved that a lighthouse should be built above the rocks where the disaster took place, and, furthermore, that a tablet should be set up, inscribed with the following words: "Erected by the Government of New South Wales, to commemorate its neglect which caused the wreck of the ship 'Cataraqui'; occasioning, thereby, measures to be taken to meet such a calamity—when too late—by George Gipps and C. J. La Trobe." Mr Alexander Sutherland bought the wreck, lock, stock, and barrel, making between eleven and twelve thousand pounds profit.]

MR McLURE'S HUT

From a painting by Latrobe Bateman, the friend of D. G. Rossetti. The hens and chickens were added by Nicholas Chevalier.

The School Hut.

THE SCHOOL HUT OR "UNIVERSITY OF ARTHUR'S SEAT"

From a pencil sketch by Georgiana

ARTHUR'S SEAT ABORIGINALS

ELIZA
Drawn by Georgiana

BEN-BENJIE
Drawn by Georgiana

SALLY
From a photograph

GEORGE
From a photograph

Scrip-Scrap

BEING EXTRACTS FROM JOURNAL

DATED BETWEEN

JULY 1845 AND JANUARY 1852

WITH AN OCCASIONAL OVERFLOW INTO THE SIXTIES

[*This portion of the diary, called "Scrip-Scrap", was discovered separated from the rest, higgledy-piggledy, blackened through contact with papers of ink-powder, in the box of a desk. Lifting them up, two quill pens tied with red tape came into sight. Will the reader become, with the editor, a discoverer, and enjoy the excitement of reading the manuscripts, unsorted, just as they were?*]

A GOLD CUP (weight 100 oz.) was presented to Mr La Trobe by his friends in Victoria, November 28, 1853, at a ball given in the then Treasury Buildings. A stormy night: the wind burst open the doors, scattering hot grease from the composite candles over the men's, and some of the ladies', shoulders.

The elm-trees in Fitzroy Square [*now Fitzroy Gardens*] were planted on September 30, 1859. At that time, they appeared to be of about three years' growth.

Early in the year 1853, Mrs James Simpson hired a house opposite to ours in Latrobe Street West, and installed therein an honest woman whose business it was to care for three orphan children. This establishment became the nucleus of the present Orphan Asylum at Emerald Hill.

On my way back from town one night in 1855, I had to "walk the plank" across the gully in Fitzroy Square, and, because the moon had not yet risen, the boys formed a line to help me over.

October, 1847 Travelled with Willie, Lucy, and Fanny, towards Melbourne in our coach-and-six . . .! [*a dray and six bullocks.*] Willie in misery on account of the toothache, and I had a difficult time keeping the wind off his face. Two sea-chests, cushioned with mattresses, made comfortable seats for us, but the way of our going was unbearably slow.

At Davey's place we spread the same mattresses over the floor, but, finding these hard, I got up and crouched by the fire, with Fanny in my lap. Awake all night, and so *mangé de puces*, that I envied Grandmother Davey—asleep, on rags, in a box!

On our arrival in Melbourne, we found most of the population suffering from influenza, and Dr Thomas very tired for want of proper rest.

[*Sir Thomas Mitchell's opposite experience:* "*I, too, have been laid up, in London, with influenza, all which annoyances endear the recollections of Australia, where I never had a cold of any kind.*"]

Arthur's Seat, June 6th, 1849 Mr Courtney measured our heights on the wall of the dining-room, as follows:

> Fanny—Two years old, less 14 days, 2 feet 8 inches
> Poppetty—Five years, less 19 days, 3 feet 4 inches
> Lucia—Seven years and a half, 4 feet
> Perry—Ten years, seven months, 4 feet 3¾ inches
> Willie—Fourteen and a half, 4 feet 7 inches
> Sandy—Twelve and a half, 4 feet 11½ inches
> George—Sixteen years, 5 feet 2½ inches
> I, myself, me—5 feet 3½ inches
> Mr McLure—5 feet 7 inches
> Mr Courtney, and Mr McCrae—5 feet 10 inches

George was measured again in 1850, February 25, and was 5 feet 5 inches.

June 7th, 1849 Mr McCrae being asleep by the fire, Mr McLure said good night to Mr Courtney and myself, and went to bed. Soon afterwards, a loud detonation outside startled me, but, because Mr Courtney said it might be Neale firing his gun, I didn't go at once to see what had happened. However, as time went by, I became so uneasy that I went to the gun-rack, and saw that no gun was missing. This puzzled me, and I was hurrying towards the door when Perry rushed in and exclaimed, "The powder-flask has blown up in George's hand!"

Mr Courtney went out, and, after a while, returned to tell me that the top joint of George's right-hand little finger was hanging by a shred. Mr Courtney cut the skin with the scissors, then washed and dressed the wound. George pale, but braver than I thought he would be. It was eleven o'clock before I got him to my own room where I stripped him and saw his body speckled with powder, as he had only had linen trowsers on and a gingham blouse at the time of the accident. Mr McCrae shocked when I woke him up and told him.

Two days later, the finger became so painful that we decided to send George by dray, to the care of Dr Thomas, at Melbourne.

Arthur's Seat, January 23rd, 1850 Thermometer 76° at 7 a.m. While the boys were away at the beach, I heard somebody shout excitedly, five or six times, and, on going out of the house, I noticed Mr McLure ahead of me, running towards the saw-pit. I followed as fast as I could and was astonished to see our dray, tipped up, with the two shafter-bullocks hanging by the bows from the pole which had become caught in a native "cherry". It seems that, both wheels having fallen into a rut, the wool had dropped to the back of the cart, whereupon, the leader-bullocks suddenly faced about, so that the shafter-bullocks were forced against the tree and became entangled by their yoke. The wheels continuing to sink, the dray tilted to such an extent that the pole rose into the branches, and, despite their great weight, hoisted the shafters almost completely off the ground. After the near-side bullock had been extricated, Tuck climbed the tree and chopped away one of the boughs, but he had hardly come down again, when the pole began to ascend, carrying with it the other bullock which it effectually hanged. Mr McLure had his ribs squeezed and was lucky to escape with his life. On account of this accident, Mr Barker will have to delay sending his wool until next week. Thermometer 92°.

24th The vinegar-cask being half empty I gathered several pails of grapes. In the evening I walked to the saw-pit and found sufficient boards, ready cut, for the flooring of the little room, with some over to make Friedrich a bench.

25th Mr McLure, melancholy, said he dreamt "Poppetty" (Margaret) had fallen in the Yarra; he swam after her, and was just about to take her in his arms, when he woke up. On my repeating this to Mr McCrae, he remarked: "It was a pity Mr McLure hadn't slept long enough to find himself a hero!"

26th Sandy, on "Don", and Willie, on "Rory", went to look for two milch-cows which have been missing since yesterday. Came back with one cow, and a new calf at foot . . . the other cow still undiscovered. A cold night.

September 27th Tuck, just returned from Cape Schanck, says the youngest of the three children who were here with their father a few days ago has been lost in the bush for six days.

28th Lanty and Tuck have to leave the stockyard unfinished owning to shortage of nails; Lanty sowed some early Charlton peas and a few rows of "Jack the Painter".

October 12th Watched Lanty, with his horse and stone-roller, rolling the wheat.

13th The stockyard completed. Tuck hammering in posts for the new garden-fence, while Lanty carts three loads of tea-tree sticks to wattle it with. A sudden cloud-burst; water poured through many holes in the roof.

14th Mr Jamieson told us he had picked up a child's sock within half a mile of Mr Barker's house, but that Mr Barker had thought it prudent to conceal the fact from the mother, otherwise it might encourage false hope.

15th Tuck shot a cow which has broken its leg during the night.

30th Mr Robert Russell says that Mr Cobb talks to the blacks in their own language, and that the following is an account, given by them, of the formation of Port Phillip Bay: "Plenty long ago . . . *gago, gego, gugo* . . . alonga Corio, men could cross, dry-foot, from our side of the bay to Geelong." They described a hurricane— trees bending to and fro—then the earth sank, and the sea rushed in through the Heads, till the void places became broad and deep, as they are today.

Mr La Trobe adds the aboriginal tradition that the Yarra's course followed the Carrum Carrum Swamp and debouched into the sea at Western Port.

Near the junction of the Darebin with the Yarra, evident traces of earthquake are to be seen, especially northwards where the ground has dropped 50 feet below the surrounding surface.

Jolimont, Sunday, November 11th, 1850 At dinner Mr Harding was telling us about plantain leaves used for plates in India, when there came the sound of wheels grating on the carriage-way followed by the noise of at least two sticks hammering on the door. Mr La Trobe sent his servant to answer the summons, and, while he arranged his neckerchief, hinted at the possible arrival of a new governor in search of a night's lodging! Enter the mayor, Nicholson the grocer . . .

[Not a highly educated man, although active-minded, and honest as the day. A middling-good mayor, but, afterwards, a much better premier of Victoria. Father of the ballot. When he had had enough of politics, he retired to the Upper Yarra Yarra, where he died, 1870. Professor Scott quotes a contemporary newspaper description of Nicholson in the Council Chamber: "He has a solid cares-of-the-State sort of look."]

. . . also, the ex-mayor Augustus Frederick Adolphus Greeves . . . *[See Note, 4th March 1841]*. Nicholson, with one of his fingers tied in a rag, holding an Adelaide newspaper.

"Your Honour, allow me to draw your attention to the fact that the Separation Bill has passed through both Houses. The news is spreading quickly, and I shall be unable to restrain the people——" Here Augustus Frederick coughed, as though *he* would like to add something, when Mr La Trobe quizzically remarked "The Bill is incomplete until it has the Royal Sign Manual." Nevertheless, he gave the required permission to celebrate that night, and the mayor scuttled off to light his private bonfire which is to be the signal for general jubilation. *[The bell of the "prison-ship" "Lysander" bruited abroad the "freedom" of the Colony. Whole trees were burnt where they stood, and the town went mad.]*

12th The Prince's Bridge to be opened on Friday; the ball to take place on this day fortnight.

13th Another sitting from Charlie, but not a good likeness. Indeed, I fear the excitement of the Separation doings has had an unsettling effect upon me. Also, Master Charlie himself has grown restive since he heard that a royal salute is to be fired at one o'clock, and jumped about like a mad thing when his papa invited him to come and "see the smoke!" Arrangements for the illuminations are well in hand, stands are being built, and a hundredweight of candles has been ordered from Jackson and Rae's, and now it is whispered abroad that one of the Bishop's men-servants has composed an ode—or is it only a congratulatory address?—to be read to "The First Governor of Victoria".

14th A sitting from Charlie, who has assumed the airs of a man-about-town since he was allowed to eat the mustard Mr Bell had put upon his plate!

16th A day full of surprises and excitement. At 6 a.m. the saxhorn band began to play a reveillée outside "The Châlet": a performance which had been kept secret even from Mr La Trobe himself, who now appeared in a flowered dressing-gown, straining his eyes at the window. He held my sleeve while some of the gentlemen put down their horns to sing "Hark, Hark the Lark!" in a key that was too high for them; yet it sounded better than the French *aubade* which immediately followed. After this they re-covered their instruments and gave us stirring polka tunes, although poor Madame, who had one of her neuralgic headaches, would gladly have forgone that part of the programme. Mr La Trobe then walked out on to the veranda to put an end to the music, but with the opposite effect, for, no sooner did the performers behold him, than they joined, some with voices, some with saxhorns, in a tremendous rendition of the national anthem. His Honour bowed, and they would have gone through it again had I not led him into the house. . . . So they marched away, still playing polkas.

Upset by the saxhorn band, and fearful of any cannonading, Mrs La Trobe appointed me her deputy at the opening of the bridge, an arrangement hardly completed, when Mr Edward Bell blew a bugle to announce his arrival in a carriage and pair.

[*We should note the use of bugles during the forties and the fifties. On 20th August 1845, Mr Powlett announced his approach towards Arthur's Seat station by bugles blown from the beach; here, again, Mr Edward Bell winds "Ta-ran-ta-ra!" Also, on 13th February 1844, Mr Horsfall heralded his advent with "sundry flourishes on his cornopean"; while Aleck Hunter, writing to his mother in Scotland (1839), asks her to send him "one brace hooked pistols, and a small plain bugle". Finally, these instruments emulated the municipal geese of Rome, and, by their brazen cackling, often saved the town. See entry of 8th March 1845: "A fire, in Collins Street, at 2 a.m. The alarum-bell rang; and bugles sounded."*]

Behold me now, equipped in Madame's black satin polonaise jacket, trimmed with Australian swansdown (a present from Mr Cowper, of Sydney), and my own grey silk bonnet! The Superintendent, having first of all handed me into the carriage, entered it himself followed by Agnes, Nellie, Cecile, Charlie, and Mademoiselle Beguine. Adolphe de Meuron sat on the box, beside Mr Bell, and thus snugly packed together, we came to the Treasury, where Mr Bell changed places with His Honour who drove us, more slowly than his predecessor, to the corner of Swanston and Collins streets, and thence, after a view of the procession, to our proper stand—beside the Bishop's barouche—in front of the Prince of Wales Hotel. [*In those days, Melbourne's swagger residential, catering almost exclusively for the Major St Johns and the Edbens of Port Phillip, that is to say, for military officers and the oxocracy. Captain Bunbury, who was an* habitué, *said, ambiguously, "The Prince of Wales orchestra plays nothing so well as the national anthem."* . . . *A stranger, for the first time about town, became aware of the Union Jack purifying the democratic atmosphere for chauvinists underneath.*] From this point of vantage, we had a clear sight of the hill, with its tent and a few field-pieces, opposite, while constantly moving banners, very small in the distance, glittered and went out again, according as the phalanxes changed places in the sun. Horsemen had hard work to keep onlookers from trespassing on the field, and we witnessed many rushes, but none which broke the line. For want of control, the cheering was ragged, and, no doubt, if the two lots of instrumentalists that followed the saxhorn band had been more *d'accord*, the music would have been better.

At 12 a.m. Mademoiselle Beguine, who had been observing the hill through her *lunette d'approche*, exclaimed that she saw smoke, and, on the instant, there arose a prodigious noise of guns, the signal for us to set out for the bridge. Mr La Trobe gathered up the reins and we proceeded at a majestic pace until we reached the middle of the arch, 75 feet from either bank; here His Honour stopped, and merely saying "I declare Prince's Bridge open", drove to the opposite side. [*This part of Georgiana's history is at variance with other contemporary accounts.*] During our progress thither, we were passed by a procession of Freemasons, and each man, as he went forward, ducked his head to "Madame", whose double in the black satin jacket replied with the most gracious salaams. At the summit of the hill, Mr La Trobe alighted, and, standing by the flap of the tent, spoke a few words suitable to the occasion. Mayor Nicholson said something supplementary, after which the Superintendent proposed the Queen's health, this being drunk off in small ale drawn from a barrel under a cart where it had been placed to keep cool.

His Honour then returned to us, and we accompanied him (walking) to the Botanic Gardens, where two thousand buns were distributed to children of all denominations; deduct from these, two begged by Mr Eyre Williams for his little boy, and one each to Charlie, Cecile, and Nellie La Trobe.

Mademoiselle and myself were so hungry, we felt we could have eaten the whole two thousand between us!

The Superintendent drove us back to Jolimont, Charlie beside him, carrying the ceremonial sword. On the journey, a few spots of rain made me anxious on account of Madame's best jacket which had already been stickied by Nellie's saved-up bun. Then, when we arrived at "The Châlet", the wind blew through the house, throwing the doors open, and the children made so much noise shutting them again that poor Mrs La Trobe retired to her bed. The servants were still absent, but the gardener's old helping-man, who had stayed at home, brought in a round of beef with vegetables, and on these we dined *en famille*, most heartily.

17th Yesterday's procession is said to have been three miles long, and Mr La Trobe estimates the number of people assembled on the hill at twenty thousand. (Mr J. B. Were informs me that a ship was to sail from London on August 10, by which time the Act of Separation would probably have received the royal signature.) The *Senate* reached port, yesterday, with letters to July 27. Alfred Cummins arrived to join the staff at the Union Bank. The Lonsdales went to meet their English governess (passage paid) at £80 per annum.

Mrs Perry brought in her needlework this forenoon, and, during the course of our conversation, she said to me, *à propos* of nothing at all, "Pray, forgive me, Mrs McCrae, but I have often wondered whether you are a *Britisher*, or not? Your accentuation of certain words has given me reason for doubt. . . ." The term "Britisher" rang disagreeably in my ears, and I insisted upon my claim to English birth; at the same time, I conceded that foreign tricks may have crept into my mode of speech, through years of association with French *emigrés* at my most impressionable age.

18th *Tête à tête* with Madame, I told her of Mrs Perry's remarkable interrogation, and thus unconsciously began to dwell on my early days among the French ladies of the *ancien régime*. Madame, on her part, remarked that she, herself, was a great granddaughter of the Rev. John d'Osterwald, translator of the Swiss Bible, and that her aunt, Madame d'Osterwald, was, for two years, finishing governess to the celebrated Duchess of Gordon's daughter, with a salary of £200 per annum. I had often heard Lady Cornwallis speak of Mlle d'Osterwald, and knew that the young Duke (with his tutor) had spent five years at Geneva, having the freedom of that city presented to him. While there, he formed friendships with d'Osterwald, de Saussure, Agassiz, Piltet, and Dr Des Roches. These friendships have been continued by descendants of both sides. Mlle Sophie Piltet stayed some time at Gordon Castle with the Brodie Duchess; it was here that she sat to me for her portrait, said to be the best I have painted. She was never a handsome woman, but her face was mobile and expressive.

Although Mrs La Trobe likes to converse with me in French, she speaks in English to Mrs Perry, *always*. [*Mrs Perry, wife of Bishop Perry, whose strength of mind and body made her suited to the times.*] Mrs La Trobe's family belongs to Neuchâtel—"de Mont Mollin"——

28th   Passed Dr Thomas, on the machiner, going to the ball. He was in his Welshwoman clothes, and asked me for a lucifer—"to lal-light his segar!"

[*The "machiner" was his gig-horse, and he said "lal-light," because he stammered. The ball was a fancy-dress one, given to celebrate Separation, at St Patrick's Hall. A large company, a good band, plenty to eat and drink—especially to drink—Geelong champagne, Harper's brandy, "aromatic planchadoes", Condel's beer, and Amiet's wines. Most of the women seem to have gone as Italians, or Persians, or, as nothing at all, while the men (except for Henry Creswick, who represented a brigand) were more original. "The awe-inspiring presence of Mr Montefiore, with a donkey's head before, and an alligator's tail behind": "Dr Thomas in the dress of a Cambrian maid." Mr W. H. Campbell ("Dusty Billy") went "in a new suit of clothes". Amiet's wines, mentioned above, were the product of Monsieur Amiet, a Swiss vigneron, who married Rose Pelet, the daughter of La Trobe's housekeeper, Charlotte.*]

EXTRACT OF A LETTER FROM WILLIE

Melbourne,
June 7, 1851.

When you get the newspapers, you will be surprised at the wonderful accounts of the gold region of Ballarat. It is said that a man found a solid lump of gold, weighing *eleven pounds*. It is also said that gold is to be found at the Plenty, and there is a report that some has been discovered within four miles of Melbourne.

California is going into the shade entirely. It is feared that the discovery of gold will do a great deal of harm to the country, as the farmers were engaged in putting in their crops, and now all the labourers are "off to the diggings", and the shepherds are leaving their flocks to be devoured by wild dogs. But the Governor has passed a law that every man must show a written discharge from his latest employer before he can be granted a licence for gold-digging.

[*La Trobe's letter to Lord Grey, dated 10th October 1851, corroborates everything Willie has said: "Cottages are deserted, business is at a*

*standstill, schools are closed. In some of the suburbs, not a man is left."
On 12th December of the same year, Superintendent E. P. S. Sturt, of
the police, supplied the Governor with a list of resignations from the force.
He said the men were jealous of the success of civilians at the goldfields,
and thus it was: "James Yarra, formerly a police-constable, exhibited his
cheque for £500, the earnings of six weeks; John Hudgall, also an ex-
policeman, produced £80, the profits of three weeks; a porter of D. C.
Campbell and Coy made £1000 during the past month." Three days
later, Sturt sent again to La Trobe, stating that "Fifty out of fifty-five
of the police have resigned from the 31st inst., notwithstanding the considerable increase to their pay which I was instructed to offer."—Matter
taken from the "Victorian Historical Magazine".*

*During 1851 (the year of the gold discovery), our population figures
leapt from 15,000 to 80,000 persons, among whom were included some
very hangable scoundrels from other parts of the globe. Meanwhile, the
squatters had asked for protection against the hordes that overran their
holdings, while the diggers insisted on their right to go wherever they
pleased. Both claims wanted immediate settlement, yet La Trobe puzzled
and purred over a business which Lonsdale could have dispatched at a
glance.*]

THE FIRST VICTORIAN GOVERNMENT APPOINTMENTS

July 15th, 1851 A red letter day, on account of the publication of
a *Government Gazette*, announcing the appointments of Mr La
Trobe as Lieutenant-Governor, and Captain Lonsdale as Colonial
Secretary, also, as a member of the Executive Council.

Other appointments were:

Mr J. H. N. Cassels	..	.. Collector of Customs.
Mr Alastair McKenzie		.. Colonial Treasurer.
Mr Charles Hotson Ebden	..	Auditor-General.
Mr Robert Hoddle	..	.. Surveyor-General.
Mr Alexander McCrae		.. *Postmaster General.*
Mr Edward Bell	..	.. Private Secretary and acting *Aide-de-Camp* to the Lieutenant-Governor.
Mr Edward Grimes	..	.. Clerk of the Executive Council.
Mr Henry Ginn	..	.. Colonial Architect.
Mr John Sullivan	..	.. Colonial Surgeon.

Mr William Foster Stawell	..	Attorney-General.
Mr Redmond Barry ..	..	Solicitor-General.
Mr R. W. Pohlman ..	..	Master in Equity of the Supreme Court of New South Wales for the district of Port Phillip, and Chief Commissioner of Insolvent Estates for the Colony of Victoria.
Mr James Simpson ..	..	Sheriff.
Mr James D. Pinnock	..	Registrar of the Supreme Court of New South Wales for the district of Port Phillip.
Mr Edward E. Williams	..	Commissioner of the Court of Requests for the City of Melbourne and County of Bourke.
Mr Henry Field Gurner	..	Crown Solicitor.

The Executive Council consisted of Messrs Stawell (senior member), Lonsdale, McKenzie, and Cassels. [*Mr W. H. Hull, Georgiana's neighbour, succeeded to the Chief Clerkship of the Treasury, when Captain McCrae vacated that office to become Postmaster General.*]

March 14th, 18— Mr Chevalier came to say good-bye.

[*Nicholas Chevalier, artist, was born in Petrograd, Russia, on 9th May 1828. In his twenty-fourth year, he exhibited several pictures at the Royal Academy, and, later on, designed the setting for the Kohinoor diamond. In 1855 he came to Australia, and, making his home in Victoria, was appointed first cartoonist on Melbourne "Punch". During the sixties, he returned to England, where he remained until his death, which occurred in London, 19th March 1902.*]

LETTER FROM GEORGE DURING HIS CLERKSHIP

Savings Bank,
Collins Street West,
1853.

I got through a tedious piece of work today. A man entered the bank with a bag over his shoulders, and in the bag was ninety pounds worth of silver, which I counted out, in half-crowns, shillings, and threepenny bits. This money was deposited by an ostler from one of our hotels, and represented the amount of nine months' tips taken from gentlemen and diggers frequenting the house. Ten pounds per month in fees, over and above, and more than twice the sum total of the man's wages. Another depositor drew out of his boots soles half an inch thick, formed of layers of bank notes, on which the owner had trudged all the way from the goldfields!

[*Horne's Favourite Story. How, on the goldfields, he once fined both defendant and plaintiff. Another, which rose out of the lack of accommodation for prisoners . . . said the magistrate "Arrah, now! If there was anny lock-up in this place, Oi'd commit yez! As it is, if you don't behave yourself, Oi'll hev yes turrrned out av th' dock!"*]

October 1st, 1851 A hard frost, and I have been to visit our blacks, who are *quambied* (camped) outside the paddock fence, on the edge of Cape Schanck Road. Here I found "Bogie" in great distress, because his son, Johnnie (aged nineteen), was dying. Every few minutes the old man would spread himself over the boy's body and try to revive him by breathing into his mouth, or else he would have him in his arms to sing down his ear, or lift up the lids of his eyes, so that he might see the day.

At last, not being able to bear this sight, I returned to the house where, after I had rested an hour, I heard a loud wail from the lubras and knew that Johnnie had gone. Back at the camp, I watched the grave being dug by some, while others wrapped a possum-rug about the corpse, which they interred in a sitting position, the elbows on the knees, the chin supported by the left hand, and the opposite one laid, with the fingers open, along the angle of the jaw. Cords were drawn tightly across the shoulders and round the waist, then, a new pannikin and the last bottle of medicine I had sent him having been put into the grave, the father and (fifth) step-mother filled the hole with sand. After that "Bogie", by himself, started to fence the place with branches gathered from the scrub beside the road.

2nd "Bogie" says he is too old to kill a blackfellow—which is the usual custom.

3rd George erected a wooden slab, bearing Johnnie's name, over the burial mound.

6th At twilight, a young aboriginal came out of the bush, and, approaching the grave, thrust three gum-leaves under the sand; this done, he disappeared quietly—unrecognized—never to be seen again. Doubtless the gum-leaves were put there in token that the death had *not* gone unavenged!

This Johnnie had accompanied George Smith on a journey to California, and, on their return to Australia, he threw off the clothes of civilization and took to the bush, but the changed existence proved fatal, and he succumbed to phthisis.

Before his world-adventure, Johnnie had been a companion to my boys and they felt the loss of him more than I can tell; yet a deeper sorrow has fastened at my heart, since the time has now arrived when I must say good-bye to my mountain home, the house I have built and lived in, the trees I have planted, the garden I have formed.

[*"Bogie's" love for his son . . . Australian aboriginals have strong affections, not only for those of their own race, but also for any white man who treats them with kindness and equity, in witness whereof, read the following account of Kennedy's death, told with anguish by his native boy who stayed beside him till the end:*

"I asked him often," continued Jacky, " 'Are you well, now?' and he said 'I don't care for the spear wound in my leg; but the other two spear wounds in my side and back', and said 'I'm bad inside, Jacky.' I told him blackfellow always die when he get spear 'in there' (back): he said 'I'm out of wind, Jacky.' I asked him, 'Mr Kennedy, are you going to leave me?' and he said 'Yes, my boy; I'm going to leave you.' He said 'I'm very bad, Jacky; you take the books to the Captain, (not the big ones): the Governor will give anything for them' . . . I then tied up the papers. He said 'Jacky, give me paper, and I'll write.' I gave him paper and pencil; and he tried to write. He fell back dead. I caught him and held him; then I turned round and cried. I was crying a good while, until I got well. That was about an hour. . . . Then I buried him . . . I digged up the ground with a tomahawk and covered him over with logs; and then grass; and my shirt and trousers."—"Sydney Morning Herald", 7th March 1849.

The poor savage (?) even sacrificed his clothing; yet he belonged to a race persecuted by white people: Selby says "treated malevolently by squatters . . . convicts shot them down as food for their dogs".

Andrew Lang took an interest in Australian aborigines, and, with pauky humour, criticized their art. In a letter to George Gordon McCrae, headed "Marloes Road, Kensington W., May 16, 18——", he writes: "It is very odd that some blacks and Bushmen drew better than the Athenians did about 200 B.C., yet the Athenians later improved a good deal!"]

Friday, April 4th, 1862 Commander Norman came to see me.

[*Officer in command of the first Australian war-ship, H.M.C.S.S. "Victoria". Considered as a weapon of defence, the "Victoria" was* pour rire. *With a crew consisting of only twenty men, and with a negligible number of guns, she could do nothing. Even so, had she fired a single shot upon the high sea, she became liable, under a piracy act, worthy of Gilbert and Sullivan. This poor little sloop was paid off in '78, and the admiralty surveyor wrote her epitaph when he said in his report "She stinks villainously."*]

April 28th, 1874 Visited Mr Hoddle, who tells me he became eighty years of age, yesterday; still an active man, and busy, when I saw him, with hammer and nails, building a playhouse for his children (*sic*). His father lived to be ninety; his grandfather, a hundred and four. "The Hoddles have always been hard-working people" . . . hence their longevity! The present Mr Hoddle keeps up his interest in French by a daily task of translation from Montesquieu's *Esprit des Lois*. He told stories concerning the celebrated Bonnycastle, Master of the Military College, where he began to study for the Royal Engineers, but, leaving that school, he took to civil engineering instead, was appointed surveyor-aide to Sir Thomas Livingstone Mitchell, and had lived thirty-five years of his life in tents amid the wilds of Australia.

[*Hoddle was a good-natured, though a stubbornly-minded, man. Originally attached to an engineering corps, he accepted Brisbane's offer of the assistant-surveyorship of New South Wales; this lasted until 1840, when he quarrelled with Gipps, saying: "I am done with you!" but, because his services were valuable, he was restored into the fold. Hoddle's next step brought him to Victoria, where he was "monarch of all he surveyed". Russell had to "spring to it", and Batman found himself sacked from his job as Commissioner of Crown Lands; even La Trobe was taken to task for giving verbal orders, instead of initialled minutes, as evidence in hand. Hoddle "chained" the settlement, and the Jolimont acres, not only doing things, but doing them well. Then, to faire s'affaire he showed Bourke his map of Melbourne, and Bourke advised the Colonial Secretary how Hoddle had planned the town. Once in the Gippsland bush, Hoddle caught George Langhorn, manager of the Aborigines' Mission Station, stealing posts cut for the surveyor's exclusive use; Langhorn, nothing abashed, said he would pay for them with words, that is to say, he undertook to supply a hundred native place-names . . . an agreement which worked out at the rate of one name per post. In this way, Hoddle came by Prahran, Bulleen, Truganini, and so forth. Robert Hoddle conducted the first land sale in Melbourne, 1st June 1837, when one hundred allotments were put up, each containing half an acre, at the upset price of £25. Charles Dickens, from information given by his son (Bree and Dickens, auctioneers, at Hamilton), describes the silence that succeeded the first bid, which happened to be for the allotment where the Bank of Australasia now stands. "Who will offer an advance on the upset price of this valuable allotment? Remember, it's the principal street of the principal township in Port Phillip. Why—gentlemen!—Melbourne'll be a little city some day; with four, or five, thousand inhabitants: a mayor and a corporation . . . Joe; fill Mr Batman's glass . . . and the stocks; and a watch-house; . . . ev-er-ything to make us comfortable. . . . Any advance upon £25 for this choice half-acre allotment; corner of Collins and Queen streets; title, from the Crown; deposit, only ten per cent; and not many yards from the river. . . . Joe! . . . Open another bottle of brandy!" The appetiser had its effect, and with the restoration to a normal, healthy land-hunger, the property went for £80. However, before the time was ripe for completion of the purchase, the buyer suffered a relapse, and forfeited his deposit, losing the certainty of a fortune—a life-time chance—scarcely to happen again. The cash value resultant from this sale was £3842.*

J. H. M. Abbott's tribute ("World's News"): "No great city in the world owes quite so much to any single individual as Melbourne owes to Robert Hoddle. It still remains, a century after he planned it, the

THE SQUATTER'S REST FROM NO-GOOD-DAMPER, 1844
From a drawing by Georgiana

"UP AT SUNRISE. THROUGH THE HAZE I
COULD SEE THE *MAITLAND* HOISTING HER
SAILS."
From a drawing by Georgiana

LITTLE GEORGE McCRAE'S PICTURE OF A CORROBOREE

LUNCHEON TIME AT THE MELBOURNE CLUB, 1863
The picture includes W. Mollison, Dr W. H. Campbell, F. Almand Powlett, "Johnny" Murphy, and "Sam"

*child of his far-sighted vision and the realization of his prophetic
dreams."*]

The Balcombes. [*No date.*] Mrs Balcombe told me that when first
her parents, Doctor and Mrs Reid, came to the Sydney district,
in 1818, cattle were so valuable that settlers would not kill any, but,
for three successive years, subsisted chiefly on salt pork. Mrs Balcombe was six weeks old when they landed, and Mr Oxley, then
Surveyor-General, becoming her godfather, gave her a cow and a
calf, worth together at that time £20. [*The "Argyle" cow and calf
sold for a hundred. See entry, 3rd March 1841.*] Her father regularly
branded the increase with little Missy's own initials, always ex-
changing the bull-calves for heifer-calves, thus, when she was
twenty-three, and about to marry Mr Balcombe, she owned a
hundred and fifty cows. The sale of these enabled her to build four
houses, which now let at £70 per annum, and, for the first two
years, yielded £150 rent. It is a remarkable fact that Oxley's
original cow was living, and had a calf, on the eve of Mrs Balcombe's marriage.

On Napoleon's arrival at St Helena, before "Longwood" had been
sufficiently prepared, Balcombe *père*, ceded to him his house and
property called "The Briars", while he, himself, with his family,
found lodging among the neighbours, elsewhere. This act of
hospitality rendered him "suspect", and led to his leaving St Helena.
["*Till yesterday, Longwood had been a stable, built fifty years before,
and only at the last moment transformed into a dwelling-house. Negroes,
and the carpenters of the "Northumberland", fixed a wooden floor over
the mud of the interior, neglecting to clear away the cattle-dung. Soon
after the Emperor's entry, the planks rotted and broke, the stinking damp
soaked through the flooring, and he had to move into another room."*—
"*Napoleon*", *by Emil Ludwig.*] Napoleon liked to play with the little
Balcombe girl, and, just before she sailed for Australia, gave her a
gold watch. The Balcombes had also in their possession the Emperor's
soup-bowl, some china plates, pocket-handkerchiefs, and other
relics. These souvenirs of their Imperial guest still remain distributed
among members of the family.

From Willie Campbell's talk of yesterday evening. Night-time at the

Q

diggings: bonfires, gun-explosions, the crashing of bottles, mixed with the noise of hurdie-gurdies and dog-fights.

[*Here, below, Mr Stubbs's land-sale advertisement, taken from the "Argus", has been admitted to this book on account of its atmosphere of the sixties; also, because it proves the Stubbses of that period well able to compete with the most* babu *publicists of our time.*

To GENTLEMEN, CAPITALISTS, SETTLERS, AND SQUATTERS.
For sale by Auction

The Villa Residence, Orchards, Botanical Plants, and
grounds of
Coldblow.

Mr Stubbs is favoured with instructions from the proprietor and occupier, H. M. Wright, Esq., barrister-at-law (consequent upon his removing to Ballarat), to sell by Public Auction, on Thursday, the 7th November, 1861, at the rooms, Queen Street, at twelve o'clock precisely,
all that gentleman's well-known villa residence
Coldblow.

Note locality. It is situated on the crown of Malvern-hill, about 5½ miles from town, via High Street, Prahran, proximate to the Malvern Courthouse, school and chapel, the residences of properties of E. Charsley, Esq., solicitor, H. S. Shaw, Esq., official assignee, and many other gentlemen in the neighbourhood.

It was built by our late Solicitor-General, the Hon. Mr Sitwell, who was the first to make it the sojourn of genius, and who enriched its grounds with rare exotics and the choicest fruits, subsequently pursued by the present learned owner, with the additions of every variety of both, from India and China, etc.

The accommodation of the house is somewhat concentre, better suited perhaps to the pretensions of a small family, but the tout ensemble *will be found exceedingly comfortable, the grounds ever verdant and prolific, and embowered by illustrious trees indigenous to the productive forest lands of Port Phillip.*

The approach is from Barkly-road, down an avenue of young poplars, with the Eastern Orchard on the left. Two other orchards planted on the north and south side of the house, load the trees with burdensome profusion—apples, pears, peaches, apricots, cherries, strawberries, grapes, figs, plums, etc., the intervening spaces teem with vegetables, stomachics, and asparagus.

Mr Stubbs trusts that he may be permitted upon this occasion to move the attention of the whole body of the profession to the repute of this embryo Beacons-field. It has special recommendations and will be sold to the highest bidder.

The out-offices, fowl yard, and pheasantry, which form a small square, are ample, including coach-house, stable, piggery, etc.

Terms—One-third cash and the residue at three and six months, bearing 10 per cent.

For title, intending buyers are respectfully referred to Messrs Muttlebury, Malleson, and England, solicitors, Queen-street.]

September 3rd, 1860 Laurie Bruce came here, straight off the road.

A hundred miles out from Maitland, he had put up at J.B.'s, where he was given a shakedown in a hut, separated by only three feet of floor-space from the family tutor and his wife! Lying in the dark, the tutor told Laurie his name was Campbell, and how he had been a Captain of the Guards, in Canada, during the Papineau rebellion, 1837-8. Towards the end of '38, he and the doctor of the regiment disputed the possession of a snuff-box . . . with so much violence, that Campbell called his man out, killed him, and fled to Australia. His wife boarded the next ship, terrified by execrations of the dead man's friends watching from the shore. Arrived in a strange country, without means of livelihood, the unfortunate couple knew not what to do, until a chance acquaintance mentioned J.B. who needed a tutor. The acquaintance, also, lived at Blackwater, and, when he went back, took the Campbells in his dray with him. At the time of Laurie's arrival, the poor people had been three years with J.B. who allowed them, in return for the husband's services, barely enough rations for two, and the occupation of the hut. Their employer was a coarse illiterate creature, and we were interested in the sad lot of these gentlefolk who have to make the best of their false position, *chez* J.B.

After he had finished the story, Laurie went to bed. Next morning, we walked a mile towards Melbourne with him, and that was the last we saw of him. Seven months later, he was murdered by two aborigines; his companion, Donald McCrae, who was speared through the leg, shot both assailants, and survives to this day. Laurie's body was buried at Spring Station, Culgoa River, near Wentworth, New South Wales.

September 19th [*Year not given.*] Spent the late afternoon placing wattle-boughs over Willie's hyacinths, and my own bulbs . . . as a protection against frost. . . . Must ask Archie to be sure to remove them in the morning.

[*No date.*] Lady Mary FitzRoy killed by horses bolting with the carriage at Parramatta, December 6, 1847. Lieutenant Masters, the aide-de-camp, also killed. Sir Charles, the Jehu!

DUPLICATE OF A LETTER TO MRS W. S. BRUCE, BIGTON

> *144 La Trobe Street West,*
> *Melbourne,*
> *January 13, 1852.*

May you and yours enjoy many returns of this season, free from the harassing cares and anxieties which all here belonging to ourselves experience at this moment, owing to the present inconveniences, and dreaded future evils, consequent on, and likely to result from, the discovery of the goldfields . . . seemingly inexhaustible in wealth.

For these ten months past, about 12,000 persons of all grades have been working at Ballarat and at Mount Alexander, and several tons of gold have already been shipped for London, per the *Melbourne*, the *Hero*, and the *Brilliant*, as well as by the ship that carries this letter.

[*This was only a beginning. In 1859, Horne says: "The output has increased to such an extent, that Victoria is now exporting to the mother country seventeen or eighteen millions of gold per annum." Thereafter, he adds the last shipments of which he had a return: "Gold ships since June 17th: 'Oneida', 64,312 oz., and 49,000 1. specie; 'Agincourt', 33,410 oz.; 'Kent', 57,055 oz., and 95,000 1. specie; 'Blue Jacket', 35,907 oz., 8000 1. specie; 'Marco Polo', 54,487 oz., 77,000 1. specie."*]

In the town, trade is at a standstill. The iron foundries are closed, the mills stopped, and all the labourers and men-servants have gone to the diggings.

An inn keeper near Mount Alexander has realized £11,000, and retires on his four months' gains! Willie Campbell (son of Dr

Campbell, Edinburgh) tells me that there is a double row of tents along the banks of the main artery of the creek where the gold is washed, extending nine miles in one continuous line. Our neighbour colony, Van Diemen's Land, has turned adrift upon us a vast number of idlers, rips, and runagates . . . and, among them, every second man, an emancipist, or lag . . . no very desirable addition to our people! Certain of our townsfolk have returned from the fields, bringing gold (perhaps 7 lb. or 100 lb. avoirdupois) in scales and nuggets. Of these lucky ones, some pay their passages home by the first ship, others invest in houses and land, while not a few squander away their gains on pleasure and strong drink. Women-servants are become most saucy, since their relatives are often in better case than the house-holder himself.

For want of men to fell trees and to cart them into town, firewood is exceedingly scarce, at 35s. (or £2) for a fortnight's supply. Water costs 6s. the little barrel; bread 1s. 8d. the 2lb. loaf; flour, 4d. the lb.; washing, 5s. the dozen; groceries at double the former prices; bacon 2s. 9d. the lb.; butter, 2s. 6d. the lb.; cheese, 2s. 9d.; eggs, 3s. the doz.; milk, 1s. the pint; potatoes 2d. the lb.; vegetables and fruit hardly to be had; cherry plums, 2s. the lb.; currants, 2s. 6d. the lb. . . . Not that there is any lack, but for want of men to convey the fruit to market.

Houses, formerly "let" at £80, now bring £200 a year. A dray and horse cost £90, a gang of horse-shoes £4, hardware, exorbitantly dear; for instance, a pair of ounce scales (old value 4s. 6d.) at present, with troy weights for weighing gold, are marked £1 6s. Slop-clothing, bedding, and furniture fetch double the usual prices.

Even *dans le grande monde* every man must be his own footman, shoe-black, and knife-cleaner. The hire of a horse-dray has gone up, from 1s. 1d. per mile, to 6s. Yet, in spite of this increase in the cost of living, the Government has advanced only 50 per cent on the salaries of subs, and, in no case as yet, to heads of departments.

We arrived in Melbourne, from Arthur's Seat, four months ago, and although, for the little girls' sakes, I had hoped to remain here, the probabilities are we shall go to Alberton, in Gippsland, *par la saison d'hiver*, where firewood, at any rate, will be free of cost.

[*Having been appointed police magistrate at Alberton, Georgiana's husband went before her. From 1851 until after 1853, he controlled an area including Sale, the scene, in September '55, of a two-hundred-blackfellow-fight. A. W. Greig, in his essay entitled "The Beginning of Gippsland", says: "A Gippsland Coy, consisting of Messrs Hawdon, Orr, Rankin, McLeod, Brodribb, Kinghorne, Kirsopp, and Dr Stewart was formed within a month." Soon after, Alberton came into existence.*

"Port Albert is a little miserable place consisting of twenty habitations huddled together. It has a low marshy coast covered with mangrove; and as for tea-tree scrubs, half the country is made of them. Papa's house is in a beautiful spot, and the garden is the best I have seen, the trees being loaded with fruit. The worst is that we have to go three quarters of a mile for water in summer."—Letter from Sandy to his mother, 24th October 1851.]

Those who can do so are arranging for their immediate return to the old country: as for myself, without Aladdin's Lamp, I can never see Scotland again!

April 28th, 1847 In the forenoon, Mr McCrae being away at Bald Hill, a dumb man came up to the house and showed me something written on the margin of an old newspaper. Because the writing was small and smeared, I took out my slate, which he licked and then dried with his hand. After he had done his work, I learnt that "Sampson Lawrence, of 'Derry', was come from twenty miles on the other side of Melbourne to say good-bye to Mr Walpole who is about to leave Mount Martha for Van Diemen's Land." But Sampson Lawrence arrived too late, since Mr Walpole had already gone to Melbourne to dispose of his station and sheep. I ordered some dinner for our visitor, who took care not to stint himself at table, and away he went!

At half-past 4 p.m. we experienced a shock that made the windows rattle, and heard a sound, as if a bullock-dray had drawn up close to the house . . . but, on going outside, there was nothing to be seen. In the evening, on Mr McLure's return from his usual Saturday ramble in the woods, he told us that, on top of Arthur's Seat, he had been surprised by what he imagined to be the report of a ship's gun at sea, but accompanied with a rumbling underneath his feet.

Clearly, a shock of earthquake!

Arthur's Seat. May 4th, 1847 Up at sunrise. Through the haze, I could see the *Maitland* hoisting her sails. Four ships at the anchorage: three outward bound, one inward. Went on the beach to watch Neale put a new keel to the boat, when a man from the Heads came to tell me that Mr Barker's dray left our things at Cain's yesterday, and that he will bring them on tomorrow.

5th The lime, and our stuff from Devine's, arrived, as Bates had said they should.

6th Torrents of rain all day. At 11 p.m., after all had gone to bed, the dray reached here from Melbourne. Roused Ellen and others, and didn't go to rest again till past midnight.

7th Our new servants, Carl Schössnich and his wife Anastina came. Carl has little English, Anastina, not a word. I needed the bellows to enliven the fire, so began to agitate an imaginary pair, when the good woman, *à l'instant*, exclaimed *"Der Blasebalg!"* and tripped across the kitchen to bring it. We have our German vocabulary and grammar to help us on. This is Carl Schössnich's "Rule of Life", which he used to recite both in German and English, head erect, hand on heart:

> Live I? . . . So live I . . .
> To my Lord, heartily:
> To my King, faithfully:
> To my neighbour, honestly:
> Die I? . . . So die I.

[*No date.*] Walking round the house at 6 p.m., Mr McCrae surprised a jackass with a snake in its beak. The bird flew off, and the snake wriggled into the undergrowth where it soon disappeared. Meanwhile, I had come on to the veranda to bring in some chairs from the damp of the evening and saw Mr McLure hand Mr McCrae his stick; but, by this time, it was too dark to see, so they returned to the house. A minute later, when I went to bring in the last of the chairs, the jackass flew down and, immediately finding the snake, carried it into the scrub.

This incident provided us with enough tea-table gossip for the rest of the evening. Mr McCrae said he thought the name *Laughing* Jackass a misnomer; it should be *Hooting* Jackass . . . "There is more

Hoo-Hoo than Ha-Ha!" Mr McLure also detected something malignant in the sounds it made, and mentioned his having read in a book how the sailors of La Pérouse had used the French word *Jacasser* to describe its angry noise.

[*No date.*]   Last night I went to my room to recover a ring which I had taken off in order to wash my hands; and, without a candle, had begun to feel along the ledge when I heard a distinct rustle behind me. I waited to hear it come again, and, this time, followed the sound to the white-washed fireplace, where I perceived a young lubra in her possum-rug, her eyes beseeching pity, and her finger on her lip. I whispered to her, asking what she did there . . . but all she said was "Moonie find me! Moonie find me!" and then, in an almost inaudible cry, "Moonie kill me!" I could not bid her go out and be murdered.

At the first glimmer of dawn, Myrnong stole out of the room so softly that the distance must have been many miles between us ere I discovered she had gone.

During the day, Moonie arrived at the kitchen-hut to enquire if his lubra had been about the house, then, because nobody knew anything, he continued towards the Survey, where he came upon her and nearly waddied her to death. A week later, Myrnong once more took her place beside her brutal lord and master.

[*Here follow some not very good verses in the diarist's hand.*]

September 6th, 1848   Returning from George Smith's today, Mr McCrae came upon a fine fish, about twenty pounds weight, swimming in the shallows. It had no way of escape, since the rocks, which had been submerged on its entrance, now completely hemmed it in; the boys, informed of this, went down as soon as school was over to secure the prize—but only found the viscera!

In the night thunder and hail.

7th   At dusk, when I had put away my work to prepare for tea-time, I heard a footstep on the veranda, then a tap on the door. Taking up a candle, I undid the latch, whereupon the wind rushed into the room, and not only blew out the light, but cast the candle-stick out of my hand so that, for a moment, I was at a loss what to do. However, the visitors (of whom there were two) soon set everything right and I presently brought them in. These proved to be Mr Willbraham Frederick Evelyn Liardet and his son, Michael . . . upset from their boat last Thursday, involving a thirty mile walk to Geelong. We made both travellers welcome, and, after tea had been served, were amply repaid by Liardet *père's* conversation. Among many things, he claims to be a lineal descendant of the Sylvan Evelyn, also, that his family had a property . . . Wootton, in Surrey. . . . Item; his cousin, Captain Liardet is very intimate with the Grey family, at Kinfauns. Willbraham Frederick, himself, was a midshipman on the frigate *Pelican*, at the time of his visit to Edinburgh; after that, he became a Dragoon officer, succeeded to £30,000, took a shooting-box in the neighbourhood of Carlisle, married one of the Empress Josephine's ladies-of-the-bedchamber, and ran through his fortune. He came to Port Phillip nine years ago next November with his wife and *ten* children, invested £2000 in sheep, and set up the first inn on the "Beach", now known as *Liardet's Hotel*, Sandridge. Madame went home a few months since, with her daughters, for their education and advancement among her relatives. . . . Liardet is not only a scholar, but he has a deeper reach of understanding than many other educated men. He can sketch a horse admirably, and, in his young days, often rode to hounds, and so forth.

Later in the evening, he unconsciously amused us with his account of a large sand-mullet he had found on the beach. He said he divided it with his tomahawk, and sent one half to Mrs George Smith, reserving the head and shoulders for his own supper!

Liardet's family have a claim to the land on which Deptford dockyard stands, and, should that property be sold, Willbraham and his sons will come in for a share of the proceeds. For the present, he would be satisfied to lease portion of Jamieson's Survey, to have a boat and a seine-net, and we are all agreed that his good nature and seemingly inexhaustible store of anecdotes should make him a pleasant neighbour.

Arthur's Seat. November 1st, 1848 His Honour J. C. La Trobe, and Mr Dana called on their way to Cape Schanck. [*Henry Pulteney E. Dana: "Raw-Head and Bloody-Bones" to all bushrangers. Nothing could stop him, or his mounted black police.*] At 3 p.m. we saw them ride off in a hurricane of wind, with thunder, lightning and hail.

3rd Wakened by the swirl and roar of the deluge outside. During *déjeuner*, hailstones flew like buckshot through gaps next the "saddleboard", beating a tattoo on our cups and plates.

4th Mr La Trobe and Mr Dana, arriving at five minutes to 7 a.m., I welcomed them with my apron full of coffee-berries. His Honour begged to be allowed to grind coffee, which he did, though not well, on account of his sleeve coming too much over his hand. I managed to have breakfast served by a quarter past seven. At 8 a.m., His Honour started on "Don" and, at 3 p.m., Corporal Gellibrand (one of the black police) brought "Don" back from Carronyulk Creek, whither Mr La Trobe had arrived at 10 a.m., and expected to be at Jolimont between one and two o'clock. Gellibrand is a native of the Geelong district, and calls the largest of the three mammiloid hills opposite us, "Darooit".*
[*Now known as "The You-Yangs."*] He complained that, although he has been a long time Corporal, he "no get him pay", and hinted that the lubras of the police force might go, *en masse*, to demand "white money" from Mr La Trobe.

[*Gellibrand took his name from the attorney-general of Van Diemen's Land, who was lost in the Otway forest; but among his own people he had always been called "Berook", or "Kangaroo Rat". The real Gellibrand, Joseph Tice, was dismissed by Governor Arthur from his official position in 1824, and subsequently expelled from the magistracy by Bathurst. It was he who prepared the illegal deeds of transfer whereby Jaga Jaga, Cooloolock, Bungarie, Yan Yan, Moowhip, and Mommarala were choused of their heritage.*

Witness Horace Walpole's remark about a similar transaction, almost a hundred years earlier: "But this very morning, I found that part of the purchase of Maryland from the savage proprietors (for we do not massacre; we are such good Christians as only to cheat) was a quantity of vermilion and a parcel of Jew's-harps!"

The full strength of the native mounted police corps at this date consisted of one superintendent (white); one sergeant (white), Peter Robert

* Still persisting as "Darraweit".

Bennet. One sergeant (black); twenty-four constables. Five horses. Uniform—green jacket with opossum-skin facings; green trousers, with red stripes, green cap, with red band. Arms—short carbine and bayonet. When mounted they wore swords.

Their camp was at Merri Creek. As the years went by, the number of officers increased; while the rank and file totalled forty.—"The Victorian Historical Magazine".]

[*No date.*] Having received notification of a reserve to be made for a proposed Government village (two miles in length and one in breadth), beginning from the "Nose", and including the ground our house stands upon, as well as the best pasture, I asked Mr La Trobe about it. He said "The village is something not likely to appear in our days." I hope this will prove true, because the loss would weigh heavily with us, particularly as we had been settled here *many months before the gamboge line was made*; this, we know, was first week of this last month of October.

[*The village appeared a few years later, after the gold discovery, and became known by the Irish name of Dromana.*]*

PORTION OF A LETTER RETURNED TO THE DIARIST FROM INDIA

July 19, 1846.

It is more than a year since we squatted, or, as the aborigines say, *quambied* (camped) on Arthur's Seat—the antipodes of that ilk.

Our house is built of gum-tree slabs supported, horizontally, by grooved corner-posts, and the same artifice (used again) for windows and doors. The biggest room has been furnished with a table and chairs, but no pictures—long lines of actual landscape appearing at interstices between the planks, instead! In addition to the house proper, we have recently erected a suite of wattle-and-dab rooms, which only need plastering before we begin to flatter ourselves on the possession of as comfortable an establishment as one could reasonably wish.

Situated on a terrace of sandy soil, about two hundred yards up from the beach, we command a view of Shortlands Bluff† light-

* Dromana is some distance from the McCrae homestead. McCrae is close to it.
† Now Queenscliff.

house, the two Points . . . Nepean, and Lonsdale . . . and, in clear weather, Cape Otway, faintly sustained in the west.

Fifteen miles distant there exists the small village planted by Captain Collins, 1804, when he made the first settlement "on the Southern Coast of New South Wales to the northward of Basses Straights" (*ipsissimis verbis*: Collins's commission) . . . a settlement which he abandoned on account of the "scarcity of fresh water", yet, if he had explored very little further inland, he would have found water enough for all needs. Our own present supply of this commodity is taken from a spring welling up in a tea-tree scrub above the house, while, for other purposes, we make use of a water-hole in the front garden, yclept "St Anton's Well" . . . We are teetotalists, but only *par les circonstances*, as you may guess.

Our usual fare is salted beef, varied on occasions by wild duck, or a roasted haunch of kangaroo meat. Saturday is fishing-day, and Mr McLure and his pupils often return from the boat bending under baskets of dozens a-piece. The fish commonly caught are flathead; these, dressed on the coals, *à l'Écossaise*, seem to my taste as good as finnan haddies!

★　　★　　★

The house stands fif.y-three miles from Melbourne, the church, and—Dr Thomas! The nearest neighbour being six miles away; others are Mr Barker, at Cape Schanck, fourteen miles south; and Captain Reid, at Tichingorook, ten miles north.

Thanks to the case of drugs your Papa gave me, I have become a famous "medicine-woman", patients arriving here, even from the Heads, and, as I dispense *gratis*, my practise is likely to increase. Cuts, splinter-wounds, boils, and sand-blight, have been successfully treated. Seldom ill ourselves; the worst sickness, scarlatina, yielded to simples, and dishes of saffron tea.

Miss Peggy is two years old, lively and handsome; not yet weaned—but, since she has cut her fourth dog-tooth, the thing will have to be done.

★　　★　　★

This month of July, *here*, is like the month of January, with you . . . dark, and *glaçant*. The boys have grown beyond imagination, and George, being now as tall as I am, has literally stepped into my shoes, and boots! Sandy is stouter and taller than Willie, quite of the Harvie build and character. Willie is small-boned and wiry, fleet as a "flying-doe" (kangaroo). George, now in his thirteenth year, appears delicate and nervous, while Farquhar Peregrine is about as big as George was when you last saw him at London. He is a healthy, clever, and well-disposed child, not far behind Sandy with his lessons. George writes the Greek symbols very neatly, and shows a decided talent for drawing. The other boys are not yet beyond their Latin, but are making good progress in their studies.

On Sundays we have prayers and a sermon; then, on Mondays, the boys have to give an account of the scripture lessons of the day before. Andrew [Mr McCrae] is in better health since he has taken to horseback exercise and gardening. With the assistance of a partner, he keeps his office open, but the income is negligible. No one will invest on mortgage or in land while sheep are so profitable. [Contributing to the "Journal of Australasia", some anonymous writer gives this other reason: "The cost of conveyance trebles the value of land conveyed. Government ought to devise a clearer and cheaper method of conveyancing." Then, cynically, he adds, "There are a great number of lawyers in Melbourne; therefore, their charges must be high; or, how could they live?"] This run of ours would do for a flock . . . but, without four or five hundred pounds, one cannot purchase clean sheep.

What our own, or our children's future prospects, here—or at Home—are likely to be, remains in nubibus.

Fragment of a Diary

KEPT BY

GEORGE GORDON McCRAE

THIRTEEN YEARS OF AGE

ARTHUR'S SEAT, WANGO, AUSTRALIA
JOURNAL

DECEMBER 11th, 1846
Friday

We rose early went to the sea-side and bathed. After breakfast we went to lessons and finished Goldsmith's Roman History, read a part of Cornelius Nepos's life of Hannibal, began a list of the plants in the garden and then went out. Mr McLure was cutting the grass from before the house and I wheeled some away. After a short time we went to school again, studied the map of the world, learned some of the Latin Syntax, and heard Mr McLure read a part of the Botany book to us. It then began to rain heavily accompanied by thunder. The dinner-bell rang and we ran down to dinner. After dinner we went back to school and worked a few sums in the square root and then went out for the remainder of the day. I brought down my list of plants to make some addition to it and also the *Saturday Magazine* to read. About this time the rain ceased and the sky cleared up and everything now promises a fair tomorrow.

DECEMBER 12th, 1846

It began to rain heavily towards morning. The passage was filled with rain-water. I was obliged to go out in my night clothes to place planks across it to render it passable. Then we set to work to bale it out. We took a basin and a mug together with some clam-shells for this purpose. Mr McLure and the boys baled and I carried away the water. When it grew so shallow that we could bale no longer I ran to fetch an old sugar bag which was laid out upon the ground and soon sucked in the water. About the time we had finished baling, the rain fell heavier than ever but none of it came into the passage. Shortly after the rain abated a little. The wind blew from the north and it came on again almost as bad as ever so almost to put out the kitchen fire. The rain ceased entirely, at breakfast-time the sun shone brightly and everything promised a fine day. We went to school and went over what we had learned

MELBOURNE CLUB MEMBERS 1863
Second to fourth from left: Mr Powlett, Captain Standish, John Firebrace. Eighth to thirteenth: Edward
Bell, Hawdon Green (in uniform), Dr Ford, Dr Pugh, Captain Alexander McCrae, the Hon. W. Highett.

ANDREW MURISON McCRAE
"Mr McCrae, my grandfather, died the year before I was born; so my personal knowledge of him never got beyond family-album acquaintance. In some respects he seems to have resembled Carlyle senior, a man 'with his heart walled in', yet my mother thought otherwise and, giving me her last memory of him, she described 'an old angel', bowling apples along our veranda to my brother Cecil, who, instead of bowling them back (as he ought to have done), meanly embezzled them."— Hugh McCrae.

GEORGIANA IN HER LATER
YEARS

in the past week together with the geography of Scotland and the history of England from the time of Caesar to the Norman Conquest; we then went out for the whole day, this being Saturday. After we had gone out, Mr McLure, Sandy, Perry, and Willie, went down to the lower garden to dig potatoes and cut chardons for dinner. Before dinner we were surprised by a smart shower which hardly lasted a minute. While we were at dinner it rained again but it soon cleared up, the wind still blowing from the north. Shortly after dinner the sky became overcast and it began to rain but it soon ceased. I then went out and made a sort of a sketch of the house and sowed some Datura seeds. The boys went to the beach to gather raspberries and native currants; they soon came up and shared their fruit with Lucy and Baby. It rained until tea-time when it abated again. After tea the rain came down in torrents and the wind suddenly changed to west after having blown steadily from the north for the whole day.

DECEMBER 14th, 1846
Monday

This morning, the wind blew from the south-west. Breakfast was late this morning so we went to school later than usual. We began the history of France, our lesson in it was the reign of Clovis 1st. We then read a chapter in the Bible. After this I read a part of the fourth book of the *Æneid*. Willie and Sandy read part of Caesar's *Commentaries* and Perry was learning a Latin verb! Mr McLure made new books for us to write our lists of plants in. We then came out after having written something in them. Tom went to find the mare to take her to the Survey on his way to "Davy's"; and Jamie, the shoemaker, came up to assist him but he was away. He went out in search of Tom but could not find him. Soon afterwards we went to lessons. We studied the map of Scotland, learned some of the Syntax and began our new lists of plants but shortly after we had begun, the dinner bell rang and as usual we went to dinner. After dinner we went to lessons again, and instead of sums, we wrote part of our lists of plants, and then we came out. Mr McLure led "Duncan" down to the shed while I went to the store room to fetch the harness. We soon put the harness on him and yoked him to the plough. We ploughed one or two furrows, but then stopped as the cows were away. However we found them just below the fence. We penned up the calves. One of them is suffering severely from a swelling on the stomach, but I think it is getting better. This was a fine clear starry evening, the sea, also, was very calm. I have been watching the nest of a black hornet in the dining-room. It is ingeniously built (between two books) of clay, not like a honeycomb but more like a swallow's nest. It has a partition in it behind which I suppose its eggs are deposited. Into the open part it has dragged a large spider which I suppose it will feed upon.

Mr McLure showed me a rush-grub in a box. [*The rush-grub, of Van Diemen's Land, which takes the spores of fungus with its morning breakfast: the spores germinate, kill the grub, and, using the body as manure, come into maturity.*]

DECEMBER 15th

Tuesday

We rose rather late this morning. We walked down to the beach and bathed, I tried to swim and succeeded in swimming a few strokes. Tom and Jamie returned this morning with the bull. When he went home he took "Maggie" and her foal with him. Tom caught Archie's pony and bridled and saddled it. It was very tame considering that it had never been before handled. Tom returned it to prevent it from following Jamie. We then went to school where we learned some more of the French history and a part of the Deluge from Ovid and more of our lists of plants. We went out then and began to plant potatoes while Mr McLure ploughed. It was near dinner-time so we stopped. After dinner we went to school and worked some sums. After school I brought "Duncan" down to the field and after having watered him, yoked him to the plough. Mr McLure allowed me to try to plough but I could not. We soon finished the bag of potatoes and with it the ploughing for the night. Tom, after he had brought in the cows, went out to fetch some wood.

DECEMBER 16th
Wednesday

Very rainy morning, we rose late. Mr McLure planting lettuces. The boys making string in the kitchen. The hollyhocks are much spoiled by the rain. After breakfast lessons, French history, Cornelius Nepos and lists of plants. After lessons we went down to the lower garden and gathered peas for dinner. After that lessons, again, the map of England and questions on our Latin lesson until dinner-time. After dinner we went to school and had some more of the square root. We then went home. Tom returned from Mr Black's where he had gone to fetch beef. We went to the beach and saw shoals of sea-trout close to the shore but could not take any. We went through the bottom (gathering raspberries and currants) to the horse paddock and returned by it. Willie found a curious oblong yellow beetle streaked with black and I found a moth all black except its head and belly which were white.

DECEMBER 17th, 1846
Thursday

We rose early and awakened the servants. Tom went to the yard to milk and we took the dogs and drove away the black bull. Wind blew from south-west. Mr McLure and I went to the field and planted two furrows of potatoes. We observed a ship going out today. After breakfast we went to lessons. We learned a part of the French history. I learned a part of the third book of the *Æneid*. Willie and Sandy learned a part of Caesar. And Perry read a part of the English history. After these we wrote some more in our lists of plants. We then went out and began to plant potatoes which we continued until 12 o'clock. We then went to school and wrote a part of our *Latin Delectus* etc. until dinner-time. After dinner, Tom went for the cows so that we could not immediately begin ploughing. Accordingly we went to lessons again and worked until Tom came home. Mr McLure sent Perry down to the house to see whether Tom was ready and upon Perry's assurance that he was; we went down but found that no potatoes had been cut so we had to go up to school again. We worked some more sums in the square root. Mr McLure proved the use of the square root to us by making us find the height of his hut in this manner. Willie went up on the roof and held a line there while I measured a certain distance on the ground. Mr McLure stretched the line as far as I had measured so making a perfect triangle, the ground being the base, Willie being the top, the line being the long side and the wall of the hut being the short side. We then went down to the field to plant potatoes. Mr McLure allowed Tom and me and Willie to try to plough but none of us could manage it. We soon finished planting and went out with Tom and brought in a cart load of wood. Mr McLure had gone along Mr Smith's road to dig up orchids, a large kangaroo jumped so close to him that he struck him with the spade. Mr McLure informed us that there are plenty of cherries along the road so the boys start early tomorrow morning in quest of them.

DECEMBER 18th, 1846

Friday

Sandy and I rose early and walked along the road and found Mr McLure's cherry trees. We also found the tracks of the kangaroo that had come so near to Mr McLure. We returned by the beach. When I came home I went with Mr McLure to the barley field and brought up a dish of potatoes. After breakfast we went to school and learned French history, *Delectus*, and wrote our copies. Tom rolled the field today. Two blacks came here but did not stay above two hours. They eat the tuberous root of the spider's root. After dinner was finished we went to school to finish our lessons for the day. Instead of arithmetic, we wrote a part of our list of plants. We then went out.

DECEMBER 19th, 1846

Saturday

This morning was rather rainy; Mr Barker called on his way to town. He told us that there were some blacks at the foot of the fence. We accordingly went down and recognized several of our old friends and amongst them Ben-Benjie who readily agreed to

shoot ducks for us. We gave the gun to him after he had breakfasted and he set out. After breakfast we went to school and went
over all the French history and we came out. Mr McLure went
to dig potatoes for dinner with Willie. After dinner Ben-Benjie
returned without the ducks and gave me the charge, and three
bommerings as he was to go away tomorrow.

DECEMBER 21st
Monday

Sandy and I arose early. We walked up along the beach and
gathered some currants for a tart. After we returned we bathed and
walked up to breakfast. Having breakfasted we went to school.
We learned part of our French history, read a chapter in the Bible.
I learned a part of the *Æneid*, Willie and Sandy began a new book
in *Caesar's Commentaries* and Perry learned a part of the English
history. We all wrote part of our lists of plants and went out.
Sandy went to the lower garden to cut some lettuces for dinner
while I ran up and called Ellen from the wash-house. We soon
went to school. Mr McLure asked us a few questions on the map of
Scotland, but the bell soon rang and we ran to dinner. Lucy brought
into the house a salmon-coloured Mantis having a claret tinge and
striped with white. Tom turned out "Duncan" this day. The
school bell soon rang and we went to lessons. We read a part of
Cornelius Nepos's life of Hannibal, a part of our *Latin Delectus*.
We worked a few sums together tonight. Mr McLure and I went
to Ellen's well and thinned the lettuces. Mamma gave me a book
to sketch in but I have not as yet used it. Tom and the boys went
to the beach and caught four small fishes resembling sprats and two
or three flounders.

DECEMBER 22nd, 1846
Tuesday

We rose rather late. Sandy and Perry and I walked to the beach
where we stayed for some time. We walked up to breakfast. We
had one hour of leisure after breakfast. We went to school: learned
the reign of Charlemagne. I learned a part of Phaeton along with

Willie and Sandy. We all wrote part of our lists of plants and after a time went out, it being very hot. After a time we came in again, were examined on the northern and middle countries, read a part of our *Latin Delectus* and came down to dinner. After dinner the wind suddenly changed to south having blown from north during the whole day. We went up to school. We all read a portion of Middleton's *Life of Cicero*, worked a few sums together, and went out. We went out in search of a kangaroo which Sancho had killed but could not find it. However we had a chase of three kangaroos. When we returned the wind was still blowing violently from the south. "Flora" was run down and terribly bitten by the other dogs. Paddy one of Mr Barker's men came here, he brought with him the two puppies that we had given to Mr Barker; they were so changed that I scarcely knew them. They were twice as large as our puppy.

DECEMBER, 23rd, 1846
Wednesday

We rose pretty early and walked down to the beach and bathed. I find swimming easier than it was at first. I walked in to the sea until the water touched my throat and threw myself forward, I then floated and striking out with my arms and legs I swam for a short space. After breakfast was over, we went to school, learned a part of the French history, read a part of a chapter in the Bible, and I, Willie, and Sandy, translated an account of the Battle of Phillipi from Velleius Paterculus, wrote a part of our lists of plants. We went out it being late and also near dinner-time. After dinner we had a long play but were interrupted by the lesson bell. So we went up. We took our slates and worked a few sums together in the rule of three. Willie called out that Papa was come and that some-body was with him. Mr McLure sent Perry to see who it was and to come back and tell. But Perry not returning he despatched Sandy and as he did not return he sent me. I went, came down, searched the house, but could not find him. I went into the kitchen and inquired where he was; while I was asking, who walked in but Jamie, the shoemaker (whose horse Willie had mistaken for "Don") and Dunn from the Survey instead of Papa! Jamie informed me that Mr Campbell of the Scotch school was coming here but could not on account of the flooded state of the Mordiallock Creek. Mr McLure and I walked along Mr Smith's road where we found many native raspberries and currants of which we brought home some to Mamma. The boys brought home a blossom of the native convolvulus.

DECEMBER, 24th, 1846

Thursday

After breakfast we went to lessons and as usual learned a part of the French history. We read a chapter in the Bible and a piece from Milton's *Paradise Lost*. I almost finished the third book of the *Æneid*. Willie and Sandy translated a part of *Caesar's Commentaries* and Perry read a part of his English history. We all wrote a part of our lists of plants with their botanical descriptions. We then went out. A black boy came here with a present of veal from Mr Smith shortly after we had come out. Papa returned riding on a mare which he had lately purchased. She had been lately imported from Van Diemen's Land and was very thin. We soon came into school again. We were again examined upon the map of Scotland, learned a part of the Latin Syntax and wrote more of our lists of plants. We then went to dinner. After dinner we went to lessons again. We worked a few sums in proportion and went out. I and the boys walked to the "Nose" and back before tea. I brought some wild clematis seed home as there is much of it ripe. Willie brought home a curious hollow stone from the "Nose". It might serve the purpose of an ink-bottle.

DECEMBER 25th, 1846

Friday

Christmas! We all rose early and had a fine bathe.

After breakfast we had prayers and Papa read a sermon to us. We walked to the beach. I caught a fish which we supposed to be a young native salmon. Willie and Tom between them speared a dozen of toad fish. Papa and Mr McLure then came down and we walked to the Honeysuckles with them and collected some cockles. In the evening we managed to catch a sting ray (vulgarly termed

239

stingaree) having speared two others without being able to hold them. That which we captured was young and like the rest armed with a barbed weapon on its tail.

DECEMBER 26th, 1846
Saturday

We rose early and bathed. I stuck my spear into the back of a sting ray but he escaped. After breakfast Perry and I went to the beach in search of sting rays while Papa, Mr McLure, and Willie and Sandy went to the duck ponds to shoot ducks. We saw no rays but an enormous shark which was prowling about so close to the shore that I almost struck him with my spear. Papa, Mr McLure and the boys had better success, for they brought home two ducks, one white and one black magpie. The black magpie is of a different shape from the white. It has a curved bill and bright orange eyes inclining to scarlet and feet like those of a crow with this difference that it is pied black and white. We had the sting ray cooked for dinner today. It was very good, Tom brought back "Maggie" and her foal from the Survey having taken the new mare there in the morning. Tom saw Ben-Benjie and Eliza on this side of Dunn's they will be here tomorrow. While walking in quest of raspberries near the beach I saw a black lump on some rushes which lump proved to be a very small swarm of bees. I broke the rushes and carried the bees on them carefully to the house. I placed them in a small basket turned upside down previously smeared with honey and they are adhering to it.

DECEMBER, 28th, 1846
Monday

We rose and bathed. Ben-Benjie went out with the gun in search of ducks. We went to the scrub to look for seeds of the leafless creeper with blue pea blossoms but could not find any. After dinner Ben-Benjie returned with the hind quarters of a kangaroo, an opossum and a duck. A man came here today with a horse which he said he was bringing to Dr Hobson whom he said he expected here at night. [Dr Edmund Hobson—born at Parramatta New South Wales,

FRAGMENT OF A DIARY

August 1814. Died at Melbourne 4th March 1848—nephew of Captain Hobson, first governor of New Zealand. The doctor kept an Anatomical Museum. He sent specimens of the platypus, both in the living form and fossilized, to Professor Richard Owen in England. He helped Dr Palmer with the organization of the Melbourne Hospital movement; and was, himself, appointed Chief of Staff: "but died before entering office."— Information from Isaac Selby's book.] Ben-Benjie amused us much tonight by throwing his bommerings. We gave him some flour, tea and sugar. The man came here to reap the barley. He is to begin tomorrow morning.

DECEMBER 29th, 1846
Tuesday

We rose early as Papa and Mamma are to breakfast early. Ben-Benjie went out with the gun at break of day and returned with two ducks, one of the common kind and another of a new sort. It had a dark brown head, a blackish beak, with a broad blue band across it. It had eyes white with black pupils. Papa and Mamma started this morning for Mr Balcolmb's. Ben-Benjie, with Sandy Perry and me went to the "Nose" and speared four leather-jackets and four sting rays. We brought the fishes to Eliza and went out a second time. We saw no leather-jackets; but, as we returned Ben-Benjie struck a large Tem-Tem and brought it ashore.

After tea, late in the evening, Ben-Benjie, hearing the porpoises coming to the shore ran down to the beach and speared six large fishes each about 15 inches in length. He gave us all of these with the exception of one which he reserved for himself and Eliza.

[*According to Barron Field, the aboriginals believe that the spirits of their fathers are transformed into porpoises and drive whales and other large fish on shore for them. H. S. Russell adds that, off Amity Point, Queensland, the natives beat the water to call the porpoises, and at the conclusion of the day's sport reward their "sea-dogs" with fish.*]

DECEMBER, 30th 1846
Wednesday

Ben-Benjie gave me three bommerings one leanquil (waddy) one fishing spear, a woomera and to Sandy a mulka (shield) to keep for him, as he went to Devine's this morning. Tom went to Devine's with the horse and cart for flour. We all wrote a part of our lists of plants. We went to the "Nose" in the evening and caught some new kinds of fish which I drew.

DECEMBER 31st, 1846
Thursday

Tom returned from Devine's about one o'clock. He left the cart and flour at the bark shed because "Duncan" could draw it no farther. After dinner Tom went back with the horse. We took the boat to meet him in order to take in some of the flour to relieve the horse. We left the boat at the Honeysuckles. Mr McLure and I walked forward to meet Tom whom we found struggling onwards. With some difficulty he brought the cart near the Honeysuckles but as the tide was by this time far out we could not put any flour into the boat. We took out three bags and covered them well with bushes. We then hauled up the boat with the intention of bringing them home next morning when the tide is in. By the time we came home it was dark——

JANUARY 1st, 1846
[*Should be '47. The old habit of the old year.*]
Friday

We went this morning for the flour and brought it home safe in the boat. Afterwards we pulled to the "Nose" and using Mr Mc-Lure's coat for a sail tried to make a straight wake for the beach. But as there was little wind we returned but slowly. Tom would have taken the cart to Mr Balcolmb's this evening but he suddenly fell sick and was so prevented. This day was excessively hot. Towards night the sky darkened and a small shower fell but it soon ceased.

JANUARY 2nd, 1847
Saturday

After breakfast Tom started for Mr Balcolmb's with the dray, taking with him the plough. After dinner Mr McLure and I walked along Mr Smith's road until we came to the creek where we found an enormous bed of raspberries. Papa and Mamma returned this evening from Mr Balcolmb's.

JANUARY 4th, 1846 [1847]
Monday

This evening Papa started for Melbourne. Shortly afterwards Mr Barker's dray came up and brought for us one bag of sugar, two small boxes in one of which was Count Strzelecki's work on Van Diemen's Land etc. in the other was a letter from Jane [Shanks]. There were two tin dishes, a large tin basin and two coils of small rope.

JANUARY 5th
Tuesday

Ben-Benjie went to the "Nose" to look for fish this morning but could not see any. Tom muzzled "Dolly", the calf of "Monkey". Ben-Benjie took the gun and went for ducks. He returned bringing with him two ducks. He had also shot a kangaroo and killed a large guano . . . about eight feet long . . . Eliza told me the words of a few native songs. I noted them down. There was one which the Goulburn blacks' tribe sing when one of their number is sent to jail.

> *Malay nyar wara goma malay a a*
> *nyar wara a rindia a a malay*
> *wara goma a a a malay a a rindia*
> *a a malay a a wah wara goma etc.*

Other Native Songs (Goulburn)

> *Wittimbulbah miralbanga*
> *Thumbulbalyndia munacalebra*
> *curricullalindula wittimbulbah*
> *Miralbanga thumbulbalyndia*
> *Munacalebra curricullalindula*
> *Turee!*
> *Turee byal turil by dthon*
> *nanga turee pacoonbeen*
> *booyal pacoonbeen turee wah*

Arremootye moorunmoorun
nyinga macoonba blynturee
byrringalaca macoonba tinga
wah arremoothago ah.

Unganyanganbarra poorangalpama
Jail mine pullarwaddyn
Jail wah wah.

the last three lines composed (?) by Ningolubbel when in jail.
[*"Hark, hark, the lark at heaven's gate sings."*]

JANUARY 6th
Wednesday

Jamie came this morning from the Survey to reap our barley. He
began to mow after breakfast. Ben-Benjie went out with his dogs
and killed a large opossum for his supper this evening. I fastened a
leg on to a table which had been broken. I also glued a frame
together for Dr Leichhardt's picture.

JANUARY 7th, 1846
[*He still has the old year in his brain.*]
Thursday

This morning the sea was very stormy. Ben-Benjie amused us by
going into the sea and waiting until a large wave came up to him.
He then ducked his head and let the wave pass over him and he
jumped up on the other side. This he repeated several times. Willie
and I went into the sea to bathe but were almost laid flat by the
surge. After breakfast we went to school, our Christmas holidays,
twelve days being ended. Ben-Benjie went out in search of wild
ducks and kangaroos shortly after the school-bell rang. In a short
time we came out and soon came in again. We were examined on
the map of England until dinner time. After we went to school
again. Willie and I and Sandy worked sums in proportion and Perry
worked three sums in practice. We came out. Ben-Benjie returned
carrying part of a kangaroo. He said that he had seen no ducks
but that he had shot two kangaroos and that as he was looking in a

hollow tree for an opossum he saw eight young native dogs in it. He struck two and sent them off howling.

JANUARY 15th, 1847
Friday

I helped Mamma to put some tea-box bottoms to some bottomless chairs and made a pretty good job of it. I made a kite this morning, that is to say, I pasted paper on a frame which I had made last night. After breakfast we went to school. We learned a part of the French history read a portion of Cornelius Nepos's life of Hannibal wrote our copies and went out. Shortly afterwards we came in again and I studied the geography of England. We were then examined on the construction of our Latin lesson of the former meeting etc. until dinner-time. After the dinner was finished I fastened a latch on to our bedroom door. We went to school and having worked some sums together came out . . . tried my kite (after having attached wings to it) but it would not go as there was not enough wind. Mr Merrick and Mr De Sailey called here in a gig on their way to town.

DESCRIPTION OF A CORROBOREE

When there is a Corrobera or Native War Dance the men assemble to prepare for the dance, the fire being lighted (for they dance round a fire), the dancers tie wisps of straw or grass round their legs; they take their weapons in their hands and feet and wait till the Corrobera sticks begin to beat and the native songs begin, they then begin to dance with the utmost fury, beating the clubs and spears together, cooeing now and then. The clang of the weapons, the din of their songs and the trampling of their feet is enough to break the drums of one's ears. The men, women, and children each have a separate Corrobera. The Corrobera of the women is so like that of the men that it needs not be described. The Corrobera of the children . . . the children light a fire and dance round it, beating time with sticks till both their arms and legs get tired. As soon as they are tired they sit down and eat their repast. Each wraps himself in his opossum rug and retires to his miamia or native hut; they then huddle themselves up in their rugs and listen to the clamour of their seniors till they fall asleep. The dance ends, the men go to

their huts to sing away till day-break for the dance is kept up
nearly the whole night.

The men sleep one half of the day and send their wives or lubras
to work while they sleep because they are too lazy to do it themselves.

Every black woman that is married is her husband's slave. The
method of marrying is most brutal. The woman and her intended
husband go to meet each other. The husband knocks her down with
a stick and knocks his wife down on the spot. Sometimes the wife
jumps up laughing. The blacks have two or three, even four wives.
The wives are treated most cruelly by their husbands. While the
men sleep the women go to or are rather sent to the nearest
European Settlement to beg money. Sometimes they will take
silver in preference to copper (!), and, if copper is offered and silver
refused they will set up a great clamour.

An Essay

NEW HOLLAND is the largest island on the Globe. It is supposed to have been first discovered by a Spaniard of the name of Torres who came in sight of the northern coast but did not land probably thinking that it was only an insignificant island. Soon after, a Dutch vessel sent to explore the coasts of New Guinea came into the Gulf of Carpentaria and landed there, after that they sailed along the western coast and discovered upwards of half the circumference of the island giving names to places as they sailed along such as Endracht's Land, Arnhem Land, De Witt's Land, Lyon's Land, Nuyt's Land, and many others. Then the famous Captain Cook discovered from Cape York on the north to Cape Howe on the south-east. He gave the name New South Wales to the land he discovered, but why he called it so I cannot tell. Bass discovered that Van Diemen's Land is separated from New Holland. The straits between the two islands were called Bass's Straits after him. Flinders surveyed a great portion of the coast. When he was returned home he put in at the Mauritius or Isle of France where the French detained him prisoner for a considerable time. When he was liberated he returned home where he published his Maps and Charts. The French soon sent vessels but they made only inconsiderable discoveries. Some English vessels fell in with them in South Australia and found out that instead of sailing about and endeavouring to discover they were staying on the coast of New Holland catching Butterflies and gathering shells and what was worse [*Could anything be worse?*] were writing down extracts from the Journals of Bass and Flinders and setting them down as their own discoveries.

The length of New Holland. Its extreme length from Sandy on the east to Sharks' Bay on the west is about 2400 miles, its extreme breadth from Cape York on the north to Cape Otway on the south is about 1700 miles. The principal capes are C. York on the north, C. Howe on the south-east, Wilson's Promontory on the south and C. Leuwyn on the west. The boundaries of New Holland . . . its shores are washed on the North by the Indian Archipelago, on the west by the Indian Ocean, on the east by the Pacific, and on the south by the Southern Ocean and Bass's Straits. . . . The principal bays are the Gulf of Carpentaria on the north, Port Phillip Bay, Spencer's Gulf, St Vincent's Gulf, Western Port, Corner Inlet, and many more on the south, Port Jackson, Botany Bay, Broken Bay and Moreton Bay on the east; Sharks' Bay and a few others on the west. The principal mountains are the Pyranees, the Australian Alps, the Blue Mountains; Mount Wingen, the only known volcano in N. Holland. Station Peak, Mount Macedon, Mount Eliza, Mount Martha, and Arthur's Seat are small hills on the coast of Port Phillip Bay. The largest rivers are the Murray with its branches the Darling, the Bogan, the Murrumbidgee, and the Ovens. Swan River, the Hawkesbury, the Brisbane, the Yarra and the Glenelg. The lakes of New Holland are Lake Alexandrina and Lake George. N. Holland is divided into the colonies of New South Wales, Port Phillip, South Australia and Western Australia. There are small settlements at Port Essington, Swan River and Moreton Bay. The capital of New South Wales and likewise of the whole island is Sydney. The principal town in South Australia is Adelaide built near Lake Alexandrina, the chief town of Port Phillip is Melbourne which is next in importance to Sydney. Sir George Gipps is the Governor of New South Wales and Port Phillip. New Holland lies between 113 and 154 east longitude and between 12° and 38° south latitude. The greater part of the country lies in the Southern Temperate Zone and part within the tropics. The surface of the country is very irregular. Near the rivers are alluvial deposits, higher up is a honeycombed land (that is a sort of swamp with round clods reaching above the surface of the water)

GEORGE GORDON McCRAE IN 1922

HUGH RAYMOND McCRAE

and higher up still is loamy or sandy soil. There are some natural caverns abounding in stalactites and stalagmites. At Cape Schanck there are risings and fallings in the earth called Cups and Saucers.... Sometimes whole herds of cattle may be lost in a saucer! . . . ["*Basins: some of them of great depth and two and three miles in circumference.*" *Captain Foster Fyans. 1853*]. The wild animals are the kangaroos which the settlers hunt (for the sake of its flesh) with dogs between the Mastiff and the Greyhound . . . they are said to resemble hare in flavour. The "Old Men" as the large kangaroos are termed are dangerous to the dogs often ripping them open with their powerful claws. The opossum is another animal of the Marsupial kind; it is the principal food of the natives who prefer it to kangaroo. The Native Cat, an animal about the size of a half grown cat, it has a long pointed nose and sharp ears, it is a dangerous neighbour to the poultry-yard and it is sure to steal through very small openings: its fur is beautiful being of light brown covered with large white spots. The Native Dog is about the size of a greyhound with erect ears and a very bushy tail, it is of a light red colour and sometimes black, it is very bold and has been known to steal calves out of the yard, it does not bark but makes a very dismal howl.

[*Two Anecdotes about Dingoes:* "*In getting ready the boat we caught sight of a dog on the beach. We made for that spot and found it to be a dingo. It appeared to be quite tame and was perfectly familiar with my Sydney natives, although he would not allow them to lay hands on him. After a short time, our dogs ran him down into the water where we shot him. He proved to be a large and handsome animal of the same character as Australian dogs generally.*"—*Batman's* "*Journal*". *29th May, 1835.*

"*About a week ago we killed a native dog, and threw his body on a small bush; in returning past the same spot today, we found the body removed three or four yards from the bush, and the female in a dying state lying close beside it; she had apparently been there from the day the dog was killed, being so weakened and emaciated as to be unable to move at our approach. It was deemed mercy to despatch her.*"—*Oxley's* "*Two Expeditions into New South Wales*".]

The Emu is a large bird something like a small ostrich with hairy feathers, its eggs are very large and rough. They are of a dark green colour. The Platypus is a very extraordinary animal having a hairy body, short webbed feet and a beak like that of a duck. It lives in burrows by the side of rivers. [*"The notes peculiar to the* Ornithorhynchus paradoxus *or platypus added to the novelties which thrust themselves upon our attention."—Daniel Bunce's* coup de grâce *to the "songless birds" invention.*]

The Gurrboor, a sort of sloth inhabiting the trees; the natives sometimes catch them and say they are very good. The trees are the Eucalyptus or Gum Tree which has a very hard cross-grained wood. The She-Oak, or Beef Tree, so called from its resemblance to beef; the Banksia (named after Sir Joseph Banks) a soft easily-worked and beautiful wood, the largest I have seen grow next the sea-side. The Wattle of which there are two kinds, the one preferring a loamy soil and the other a more beautiful tree growing on the banks of rivers. The blackwood a very bushy tree with a thick stem, the wood is beautiful but very hard to work. On Mount Macedon are gigantic fern-trees having a stout stem about the thickness of a man's thigh and low long drooping branches hanging from it. The Kangaroo Apple so called from the resemblance of its leaves to the hind feet of the kangaroo has a beautiful purple blossom, and a fruit somewhat resembling a plum, but smaller. It is of a bright yellow colour and contains a multiplicity of seeds. [*"The aborigines were in the habit of eating the 'bacca' or berry part of the kangaroo-apple, first burning off the skin which in a raw state would blister the mouth. The blossoms of this shrub are produced on branches, with farina, or male powder."—Daniel Bunce.*]

The natives of New Holland are the most degraded race of human beings [*perhaps more primitive than degraded*] they are about the middle size but some of the men are very tall and well made. They are of a deep copper colour which is somewhat darkened by dirt and filth. They live in rude hovels made of branches, their only weapons being a few spears and clubs. These people lead a wandering life, scarcely occupying a hut for more than two days, their language is a harsh jargon although they have a few beautiful words in it. The different tribes have separate dialects of the same language and live in great enmity with each other. The natives make their wives (of whom they have two or even four), work for them while they lie down in their huts singing. A black principally passes his time in his hut scraping and smoothing his wooden spears or preparing opossum skins to make rugs of, but he leaves all the harder work to his wives, such as building his hut and bringing water and cutting firewood. Their amusements are but few, their greatest one however, is the Coroboree or Dance. The men dance entirely naked except a bunch of string tied round their waists and some wisps of straw round their ankles while the women, children and old men sing and beat time. The clang of their weapons, the din of their songs and the trampling of their feet is enough to deafen one. . . . They advance, or retreat, beating time with short sticks. [*The bits of wood, used for beating time with, are called "sounding-sticks", because an echoing noise can be produced by two billets clapped against each other. "When the natives hold a Corroboree, those who do not join in the dance beat time with the sounding-sticks accompanied by the continual refrain of 'Yah—Yabba! Yah—Yabba! YAH! ! !' "— "Journal of Australasia", July, 1856.*]

I will now tell you a little more about the natives. The native, in building his hut cuts some branches from a tree of which he builds his hut. As soon as it is built he lights his pipe and sends his wives to beg food of the circumjacent settlers, they return with what food they have. If they have meat and turnips he makes his favourite throw meat and turnips into the fire to cook. As soon as it is half roasted, (for he is too impatient to wait till it is roasted) he uses no knife or fork but tears it with his fingers.

A native who wants a wife goes to another tribe at night, knocks the woman who he has selected on the head so as to stupefy her and drags her away. If she does not love him he will beat her till she does (!)

The life of a black man is generally speaking lazy and indolent because he makes his wife do all the work, except making weapons and huts.

The names of the weapons are as follows:

Geenyam, a kind of oval shield.

Bommering, a weapon for throwing, is made of the root or branch of a tree.

Gerar, a kind of spear; usually made of Mitcheroo wood. [*"The little paltry playthings of spears."—Daniel Bunce.*]

Waddie, a kind of club.

Mulka, a kind of shield.

The *Wia Wight* is a kind of weapon with an oval head with a stick attached.

The natives seldom stoop to pick up anything: for instance, when getting wood for their fire they take the wood up, between their toes and lift it up to their knees, whence they lift it up with their hands and put it on the fire.

[*Notes on the resourcefulness of the aboriginals, and the adaptability of their feet.*

"In skinning the kangaroo one of the natives made his feet serve him very usefully."—"The Journal of Australasia", 1856.

"Spear in hand, the aboriginal eel-catcher ('ee-oke') walks slowly and cautiously about the shallow water until he has trodden so gently upon the object of his search as not to awaken its attention. Although half-buried in the mud, its position is judged with such accuracy that with one blow the eel is pierced. Immediately he takes it out of the water and disables it by crushing its head between his teeth."—"The Journal of Australasia", 1856.

"I found old Maggie (that Sir Thomas Mitchell gave the tomahawk to) fishing for muscles with her toes, in a waterhole up to her middle."— John Robertson of Wando Vale, 26th September 1853.]

The natives use wooden nails about 3 inches in length in stretching their opossum skins. They stretch them after this manner. One of them sits down upon the ground and stretches the skin upon a piece of bark at its full length, then he nails one side of the skin and pulls the other side with all his might so as to make it a great deal wider, then he nails the first side down well with one nail and so on until he has finished the whole. When a native has finished a great many skins, this way, he proceeds to make a rug. For this purpose he beats the sinews of the hind legs. . . .

[*the manuscript remains unfinished*]

AN ESSAY

Note. Aboriginal pegging-nails were made of dog-wood (a plant resembling the hazel); the ends pointed with a knife of broken glass, and hardened in the camp-fire. These nails were always to be found in the dilly-bags, or else in the "beenyaks" (baskets) of the lubras. After a skin had been sufficiently stretched, some artist of the tribe, using a sharpened spoon, cut, upon the soft leather, pictures of men or kangaroos. The tailor sewed material with the bone of a fish; and the thread used was manufactured from the finest tendons of the opossum itself.

THE *GOVERNOR ARTHUR* MEETS THE *ARGYLE*
From an etching by George Gordon McCrae

Index

INDEX

Abattoirs at Batman's Hill, 136
à Beckett, William, 57
Abingdon, 84
Aborigines, 91, 100, 129, 149, 196, 204, 213-14, 222, 224, 241-5, 250-1
Advertiser, Melbourne, 52
Ailsa Craig, 156
Ailsa, *Marquis* of, 155
Airey, George Sherbrook, 63, 109, 151
Airey's Inlet, 151
Alberton, 35, 221-2
Amiet, ——, 210
Anderson, William, 10-11
Anthony's Nose, naming of, 120, 191
Anti-Transportation League, 77
Aphrasia, 51
Arden, George, 31, 43
Argyle, 6, 9, 16, 17, 18; sails from Plymouth, 15; arrival at Port Phillip, 22-3; at Melbourne, 25; sails for Sydney, 28
"Argyle Cottage", Little Lonsdale Street West, 27-9; naming of, 140
Arthur's Seat, 137, 140, 147, 150; letters from, 162-3, 164-6, 170, 178-9, 185, 186, description of McCraes' house at, 179, 193, 227
Atkinson, James, purchase at Port Fairy, 66

Balcombe, *Mrs*, 217
Ballarat, 210, 220
Bank of Australasia, site of, 33, 216
Bank of Victoria, 141
Barber, George, 172, 178, 180
Bark, export of, 121
Barker, John, holder of first land order, 128, 183, 184, 191, 195, 198, 228
"Barrabang", 126-8
"Barragunda", 194
Barry, Redmond, 48, 73, 135
Batman, John, 30, 49, 61, 69, 216
Batman, Maria (Fennell), 66
Batman, *Mrs*, Mount Eliza called after, 120
Batman's Hill, 43, 136, 148
Beale, Anthony, 30
Becker, Ludwig, 62
Bedford House (hotel), 27
Bell, Edward (La Trobe's secretary), 49, 72, 151, 206
Bell, Henri, 138
Bell, William, 138

Bennet, Peter Robert, 227
Black, *Dr* Thomas, 81, 141
Boiling-down works, 136
"Boneo", 128
Boomerangs, 237, 241, 251
"Bounty" emigrants, 6-7, 15-16
Bourke, *Governor*, 24
Boyd, Benjamin, 50, 66
Boyd, Thomas Elder, 92
Boydell, C., marries Miss Broughton, 138
Brankenmoore, 52
Brickwood, William, 161
Brierly, Oswald, 68, 83
Broadfoot, A. A. (duel), 148
Broughton, *Bishop*, 46, 110-118, 138
Brown, Augusta Helen, 36
Browne, Octavius (brother of "Phiz"), 39, 40, 45, 81, 176; marriage of, 108-9, 118
Bruce, Laurie, 219
Bugles, use of, 207
Bullarook, 82
Bulleen, 216
Bunbury, *Capt.* Richard Hanmer, 11, 15, 17, 21, 73, 115, 180; career of, 19; age of, 22
Bunbury, *Mrs*, 11, 15, 21, 37
Bunbury, Harry, 11, 15, 19
Bunbury, Francis Argyle, 21, 40-2
Bushfires, 84

Cain, *Capt.* B., 157, 158
Caledonia, 61
Campbell, J. D. Lyon, of Campbellfield and Bullarook, 81, 141-3
Campbell, James Henry, 183-5, 189; marriage of, 189
Campbell, William, 10, 19
Campbellfield, 81
Cape Schanck, 128, 191
Cape Verde Island, 18
"Carron-Carronulk" (Carroncarrondall), 34, 58
Carrum Swamp, 205
Cashmore, Michael, 93
Cashmore's Corner, 93
Cattle, importation of, 39; price of, in 1818, 217
Cataraqui, wreck of, 199-200
Charsley, E., 218
Chevalier, Nicholas (artist), 212

257

Childers, Hugh Culling Eardley, 46
Cicadae (Bizzwizzes), 51
Clow, *Rev.* James, 32, 35, 139, 147
Clutterbuck, *Dr* J. B., 125
Coal, search for, 133
Cobham, Frank, 37, 44, 48, 62, 87, 145
Cole, *Hon. Capt.* George Ward, 13, 111, 137, 139, 155, 181; career of, 45-6; engagement, 53; marriage, 61; son, 82, 87; daughter, 138
Cole's Bond, 46
Cole's Wharf, 25, 28, 45-6, 154
Collingwood (Newtown), 36
Comet (Melbourne), 91
Condell, Henry (first Mayor of Melbourne), 80, 96
Convicts, 72, (called "canaries"), 123
"Cook's Voyages", folio sold for £9, 138
Corroboree, 123, 245, 251
Cost of living, 31, 32, 221
Cotter, Barry, 31
Cowper, Charles, 184, 207
Cowper, Norman Lethbridge, 184
Craig, Ailsa, 156, 184, 188
Craig Skene, vineyard of, 103, 105; duel, 148
Croke, James, 44
Crook, ——, 27
Cunninghame, Archibald, 54, 117, 135, 200
Curr, Edward, career of, 59, 80, 115, 137

Dana, H. P. E., 225-6
Dandenong (township), 63
Davidson, *Major*, 98
Davis, Peter, (Mayor of Melbourne), 111-2
Dawson, *Dr* R. N., 16
Delaware, the, 180-1
"Dibble-dibble", 52-3, 104
Dickens, Charles, 216
Dickens, Bree and, 216
Dingo, 249
Donaldson and Budge, 27
Dorcas Society initiated, 29
Dromana, village of, 227
Duchess of Sutherland, arrival of, 34
Duels, 31, 128, 148
Dust-storms, 169

Eagle, the, 24, 33
Earthquakes, 34, 222
Ebden, Charles Hotson, 62, 207; picture of, 91; career of, 97
Emigrant ships, 6-7, 15-16, 25
Emigrants, 6-7, 15-16; wages of, 25
England, the, 36
Enmore, the, 93
"Eumemmering", 63

Farebrother, *Alderman*, 5
Farie, Claude, 66, 85
Fawkner, John Pascoe, 41-3, 52; on La Trobe, 49
Fennell, Robert, married Maria Batman, 66
Fenning, William F., 132
FitzRoy, *Sir* Charles, 72, 220
FitzRoy, *Lady* Mary, 220
Fitzroy Gardens, elms in, 201
Flagstaff (Melbourne), burial place at, 29, 157
Flinders, Matthew (Arthur's Seat named), 137
Forbes, *Rev.* James, 34, 61, 159, 187
Foster, John Leslie, 63, 109; assaults Dr McCrae, 118; McCrae's lawsuit, 134-6
Franklin, *Sir* John, 121; departure, 122
Fyans, *Capt.* Foster, 26, 32, 49, 51, 73, 85; opinion of Gipps, 46-7

Gatenby, *Capt.*, 16-23, 25, 28
Geelong (Jillong), 44
Geelong champagne, 210
Gellibrand, *Corporal*, 226
Gellibrand, Joseph Tice, 119, 226
Geoghegan, *Rev.* Patrick Bonaventura, 57
Geyer, ——, American Consul, Cape Verde Island, 19-20
Gilfillan, ——, 154-5
Gipps, *Sir* George, 46-8, 98; speech of, 49
Gippsland Company, 44; members of, 222
Gisborne, Henry Fysche (will of), 155
Gold discoveries, 210, 220
Governor Arthur (ferry), 25
Grasshopper plague, 118
Greeves, Augustus Frederick Adolphus (Mayor of Melbourne), 25, 109, 205
Grey, *Earl*, 25, 77, 109
Grylls, *Rev.* J. C. (first Anglican minister in Melbourne), 26
Gunn, *Rev.* Peter, 115
Gurner, Henry Field, 93
Guy Fawkes Day, 78

Hagon, Jacob, 36
Hamilton, Thomas Ferrier, 84
Harvest Home, 23
Hawdon, John, 74-5
Hawdon, Joseph (first cattle Port Phillip), 74-5
Hawthorn Bridge, 30; formerly Palmer's Punt, 122
Heriot, Elliott, 34
Hervey, Phillip, 157
Highett, William (first manager Union Bank), 27-8, 34, 40, 63

Highlandman Hotel, 52
Higinbotham, George, 46
Hinton, Frederick, 11
Hobson, *Capt.*, 192
Hobson, Edmund, 240-1
Hoddle, Robert, 66, 215-16; survey of Melbourne, 177
Hodgson, John ("Studley"), 33, 38, 59
Hopkins River, naming of, 120
Horne, Richard Hengist, 24, 32, 33, 87
Housing, 26; imported, 139-40
Howe, Ephraim, 32-4, 38
Howitt, *Dr* Godfrey, 110, 144, 185
Howitt, William Godfrey, 144, 178
Howley (Bishop of London), 112
Hudgall, John, 211
Hull, William, exports bark, 121; clerk of Treasury, 212
Hunter, ——, partner of Marquis of Ailsa, 155-6

Independent Church (Melbourne), 183
Influenza epidemic, 1847, 202
Irvine, James, 10, 19
Isabella, wreck, 146

Jachimo Piccolo, wreck, 16-18
"Jackass" (kookaburra), 223
Jackson and Rae, 206
Jamieson, ——, 38, 125, 127, 195
Jamieson, Archibald, 183
Jamieson, Robert, 74
"Jamieson's Survey", 90, 225
Jane Cain, first ship built in Melbourne, 157
Jeffcott, *Judge*, 100, 103, 104, 135; farewell dinner, 172; departure, 178
Jemima, 168, 176, 179-80, 189
John Knox Church, 159
"Jolimont Cottage", 28
Jolimont, government residency, 70
Jones, Lloyd, 26
Juno, 44

Kangarang House, 127, 195
Kangaroo, 185, 196, 236, 238; meat, 228
Kangaroo-dogs, 181
Kemp, postmaster, 156
Kersopp, *Capt.*, 44
Kilgour, *Dr*, 117, 122, 149
Kilmore, 37
"Kinlochewe", 119
Knowles, Conrad, death of, 141
Kookaburra ("jackass"), 223
"Koort Boork" (Williamstown), 24, 190
Kyneton, naming of, 185

Lamb Inn, 27, 32
Lamb, John, 76
Landells, 53
Langhorn, George, 216
Langhorne, Alfred, 63
Langhorne, *Mrs* Alfred, 51, 63
"La Rose", Dr F. McCrae's house, 186
La Trobe, Charles Joseph, 49, 71-3, 82, 100-1, 120, 128, 131, 139, 143, 160, 201, 205, 211, 225-7; Washington Irving on, 163-4; genealogy, 164
La Trobe, *Mrs*, 19, 28, 43, 100, 117, 121, 138, 182, 209
le Souef, Charles, 57
le Souef, William, 43
Lewis, *Capt.*, harbourmaster, 188
Liardet, W. F. Evelyn, 48, 116, 225
Lonsdale, *Capt.* William, 43, 63, 69, 139, 209, 211
Lonsdale, *Mrs*, 120
Lubra, 224
Lysander, prison ship, 205

Macarthur, D. C., 61
Macartney, *Rev.* Hussey Burgh, 5
McCrae, Agnes, 27, 34
McCrae, Agnes Gordon, 13
McCrae, Alexander, Captain in the 84th Regiment, 13, 143-4, 156; arrival at Melbourne, 34; financial difficulties, 134-8, 150; clerk of the Treasury, 183, 186; Postmaster-General, 211
McCrae, Alexander Gordon, 13, 26
McCrae, Andrew Murison, 1, 32, 63, 86, 116, 122, 177, 186; sailed for Australia, 3; arrival at Sydney, 4; vice-president Port Phillip Club, 33; letter from John Richardson, 47; member Separation Association, 48; quarrel with his brother, 87-8; and with Henry Montgomery, 88; financial difficulties, 92-3; welcomes Bishop Broughton, 110; loses "Mayfield", 117; at "Kinlochewe", 119; inspects Arthur's Seat, 125; money from home, 138; height, 202; partnership with George Barber, 172, 180; income, 229
McCrae, Donald, 219
McCrae, *Dr* Farquhar, 13, 25-8, 39, 138-9, 146, 150; sails for Australia, 4; station-owner, 63; departure for Sydney, 95; assaulted by J. L. Foster, 118; financial difficulties, 134; case against Foster, 134-5
McCrae, Farquhar Peregrine, 12-13, 26, 88; birth of, 1, 3
McCrae, Frances Octavia (Mrs Moore), birth of, 13

McCrae, George Gordon, 2, 12, 23-4, 84; birth of, 13; marriage, 36; opinion of Gipps, 46; letter from John Webster, 67; letter from Arthur's Seat, 164-6; height, 202; loses finger, 203; fragment of diary, 1846, 231-46

McCrae, Georgiana, shipping contract, 6; inventory, 7-8; embarks at Tilbury, 9; sails from Plymouth, 16; arrival at Port Phillip, 22-3; at Williamstown, 24; birth of Lucia, 55; of Margaret, 145; list of portraits painted by, 172-5; weight, 183

McCrae, Huntly, 184

McCrae, Lucia Georgiana Gordon, birth of, 13

McCrae, Margaret Forbes (Mrs Thomas), 13

McCrae, Margaret Martha, birth of, 13

McCrae, Thomas Anne (Mrs Cole), 13, 51; offer of marriage, 45; son, 82; daughter, 138; purchase of "St Ninians", 139

McCrae, William Gordon, 12, 26; birth of, 13

McKinnon, Lauchlan, 35, 69, 74

McKnight, Rev. Charles Hamilton, 11, 19

McLachlan, Capt., 29

McLaren, Capt. Walter, 168

McLure, John (tutor), 38-9, 63. 66, 124. 149, 203; letters from Arthur's Seat, 162-3, 170

Malcolm, James, 70, 119

Malvern Hill, 218

Manton, Frederick, 37

Masling, Charles Hamilton, 10

Mason, ——, Mayor of Williamstown, 116

Meuron, Adolph de, 164, 207

"Mayfield", Melbourne, 37, 40, 45, 59, 60, 119, 147, 156; location of, 30; occupation of, 57; site of, 58; proposed purchase of, 90, 96; garden of, 104; sale of, 157; departure from, 171

Meek, William, first Melbourne attorney, 27, 30

Meek, Mrs, 36, 38

Melbourne, in 1840, 2; in 1841, 24; naming of, 24, 120; shops, 26-7; in 1858, 27; early houses in, 28-9; early burial place, 29; water supply, 31-2; population in 1836, 120; first land order, 128; first ship built in, 157; surveys of, 177, 215; population 1851, 211; Hoddle's map of, 215; first land sale, 216

Melbourne Advertiser, 52

Melbourne Club, 27

Menteith Place (Erwin Street), 30

Mercer, G. D., a founder of Geelong, 43-4

Merri Creek, 88

Meyrick, Maurice, 128, 191

Midlothian, sails for Australia, 3, 34, 118

Minifie, ——, early resident of Melbourne, 28, 38

Mitchell, Sir Thomas Livingston, 99, 101-2, 106, 139, 202, 215; names Hopkins River, 120

Mollison, J. P., 38, 62

Montgomery, James, 93

Montgomery, Henry, partner of Andrew Murison McCrae, 34, 35, 82, 88, 89, 92, 132, 156, 161, 175-8, 181

Montgomery and McCrae, 92, 148, 161, 176

Moorabee station, 97

Moor, Henry, 74, 156, 161

Morison, Sir Alexander, 3

Morrison, Rev. Alex., 183

Mount Eliza, naming of, 120; coal at, 133

Mount Martha, naming of, 120; coal at, 133

Murchison, ——, 46

Murphy, Sir Francis, purchases "Mayfield", 157

Myer, Dr, 37-40, 94, 117; residence, 54

Myer, Mrs, 42

Naming of places, 120, 216

Newby, Capt., 198

Newman, Dr, 11

Nicholson, William, Premier of Victoria, 205

Nicholson, Mark, 52, 136, 140, 161

Nicholson, Dr, 39, 87, 90, 91, 108, 109, 117, 119

"No Good Damper Inn", 129-30, 170

Northumberland House, Flinders Street, 29

Observatory Hill, Melbourne, 157-8; burial place at, 29

O'Cock, Richard, 78

Orphan Asylum, first in Melbourne, 201

Orr, John, 59

Owen, Dr 97-8

Oxley, John, 217

Palmer, Sir James Frederick, 48, 161

Palmer's Punt, 30, 122, 130

Pentridge, 114

Perry, Bishop Charles, 31, 57, 75, 209

Plenty River, 181, 210

Pohlmann, R. W., 90-1

Point Gellibrand (Williamstown), 24

Police, 106, 211

Port Albert Company, 35, 44, 222

Port Fairy purchase, 66

Port Phillip, 23; first cattle, 39; 1836 population, 120; account of, 204

Port Phillip Academical Institution, 161

Port Phillip Association, 61, 196
Port Phillip Bank, 30, 44
Port Phillip Club, 33, 124
Port Phillip Club Hotel, 33, 124
Port Phillip Gazette, 25, 43
Port Phillip Steam Navigation Company, 46
Prahran, how named, 216
Prince of Wales Hotel, 104, 207
Prince's Bridge, opening of, 206, 208
Punt Hotel, 30

Quarry, Jephson, 9, 11, 36, 44, 90, 151-2;
    marriage of, 80
Queen's Wharf, site of, 46

Rabbits, 166
Rajah, 182, 184
Randolph, transport, 72
Rankine, *Capt.*, 11
Raymond, James, 36
Raymond, Samuel, 36
Reeve, John, 35
Reid, *Capt.*, of Tichingorook, 35, 79, 129,
    140, 228
Reid, *Dr*, 217
Richardson, John, 47
Riddell, Thomas Carre, 84
Roach, *Capt.*, 58, 69
Ronald, *Dr*, 9, 15-16
Ross, James Hunter, 44
Royal Saxon, 1, 36; sails for Sydney, 3
Russell, Robert, first Melbourne surveyor
    and architect, 41, 75, 190, 216; original
    survey of Melbourne, 177
Ryrie, William, 74, 142

Sams, Sheriff of Launceston, 31
Schnapper Point, 126
Schossnich, Carl, 223
Sconce, Madeleine, 35, 36
Sconce, Robert Knox, 11, 15, 19; ordination,
    46, 48; portrait, 50; departure from Mel-
    bourne, 51
Sconce, *Mrs* Elizabeth, 11, 15, 19, 35, 36, 50,
    51, 154
Scots School, 60, 66
Sea Horse, Ben Boyd's steamer, 50, 61; litho
    of, 67
Shamrock, the, 115
Shaw, H. S., 218
Shanks, Jane, 1, 2, 19, 25, 26, 79, 180
"Sherwood", Alexander McCrae's house,
    139
Simpson, James, 61, 98, 120, 171, 201
Simpson's Road, 120, 157

"Singapore Cottage" ("Argyle Cottage"),
    140
Sitwell, *Hon.* Robert, 218
Smith, George, Lamb Inn, 27
Smith, George, of Wooloowoolooboolook,
    192, 197
Smith, James, Batman's catechist, 49
Smith, John Thomas, 27
Smythe, George, 30
Spence, ——, storekeeper, 41
Sprott, ——, 84-5
"Squatter", 143
Squatter's Ball, 143, 189
St Anton's Well, Arthur's Seat, 137
Stawell, Sir William Foster, 100, 135
Stephen Street, (Exhibition Street, Mel-
    bourne), 30
St Francis's Church, first Roman Catholic
    Church in Melbourne, 57
St Helier's, Melbourne, 59
St James's Church, Melbourne, 25; opened,
    75-6; Bishop Broughton at, 111; La Trobe
    presents font, 131
St John, *Major*, magistrate, 41-2
Strode, Tom, 43
Stubbs, auctioneer, 218-19
"Studley", 38
Sturt, E. P. S., 211
Sunbury, town, 84
Surveys of Melbourne, 177, 215, 216

Tanti Creek, 126
Tea, price of in 1840, 180
Therry, Roger, 172
Thomas, *Dr* David John, 13, 31, 62, 85, 92,
    161; career of, 40, 41
Thomas, *Mrs* D. J., 34
Thomas, Mary Anne, marriage of, 189
Thomson, *Rev.* Adam Compton, 26, 111,
    114, 143
Thomson, *Mrs* Adelaide Zélee, 29
Thomson, *Dr* Alexander, Batman's catechist,
    39
Tichingorook, 125, 228
Tobin, pilot, 24
Towns, Robert, of Townsville, 3
Traill, *Dr*, 15, 16
Treadwell, *Captain*, 16
Truganini, 216

Union Bank, 27
Urquhart, William Swan, 66

Vesper, the, 190
Vesta, Yarra steamer, 37, 179
Victoria, first Australian warship, 215

Vignolles, *Mr*, 40

Victoria, first government appointments, 211-12

Waddell and Mackenzie, 194
Wanderer, Ben Boyd's vessel, 67
"Wango" (Arthur's Seat), 134, 137, 179
Wattle (word), 204
Warship, first Australian, 215
Waterfield, *Rev.* William, 49
Waterlily, schooner, 45
Webb, Thomas Saunders, 57
Webster, John, artist, 67
Welsh, Patrick W., 30, 36, 155
Wentworth, William Charles, 35, 36, 40, 42, 73, 137
Were, Jonathan Binns, 38, 48, 209
Wesleyan Chapel, site of, 33
Western Port, coal at, 133
Westgarth, William, 30, 77, 110
Williams, Eyre, 61, 65, 69, 135
Williamstown, 73, 190; naming of, 24; various names of (Koort Boork, The Fish-ing Village, Point Gellibrand, William's Town), 24

Willis, *Judge* John Walpole, 30, 36, 81, 100, 101
Wilmot, *Sir* Eardley, 47, 123
Wilmot, *Dr* William Bryam, first coroner, 133, 177
Wooloowoolooboolook, 192
Wright, H. M., of Coldblow, 218

Yaldwyn, W. H., 159
Yalloak (Jamieson's station), 74
Yarra, James, 211
Yarra Hotel, 25
Yarra River, 24; Elizabeth Street a tribu-tary of, 29; punt on, 30; name of, 31; water pumps on, 32; ferry at Flinders Street, 43; flood, 70; flood 1842, 153; course of, 205
York, vessel, 24
Young and Jackson Hotel, 27
You Yangs, 226